NEAL CASSADY

NEAL CASSADY

The Fast Life of a Beat Hero

David Sandison and Graham Vickers

CHICAGO REVIEW PRESS

Library of Congress Cataloging-in-Publication Data
Sandison, David.
Neal Cassady : the fast life of a beat hero / David Sandison and Graham Vickers. — 1st ed.
p. cm.
Includes bibliographical references and index.
ISBN-13: 978-1-55652-615-2
ISBN-10: 1-55652-615-6
1. Cassady, Neal. 2. Beat generation—Biography. 3. United States—Biography. I. Vickers, Graham. II. Title.
CT275.C3458S24 2006
973.931092—dc22
[B]

2006009112

All quotes from Neal Cassady's letters used by permission of Carolyn Cassady.

Photo of Neal Cassady, 1962, used by permission of Ettore Sottsass.
All other photographs courtesy of the collection of Carolyn Cassady.
Used by permission.

Cover and interior design: Emily Brackett/Visible Logic

Cover photo (top): Getty Images

First edition
Published by Chicago Review Press, Incorporated
814 North Franklin Street
Chicago, Illinois 60610
ISBN-13: 978-1-55652-615-2
ISBN-10: 1-55652-615-6
Printed in the United States of America
5 4 3 2 1

Acknowledgments

This book could not have been written without the help, hospitality, and kindness of many people. I would like to thank especially: Carolyn Cassady; John Cassady; Jami Cassady Ratto; Cathy Cassady Sylvia; David Amram; Ken Babbs; Georgia Bergman; Tim and Chris Bloch; Steve and Sonya Bruce; Tom Christopher; Paula Douglas; Lawrence Ferlinghetti; Curt Hansen; Al Hinkle; Ken and Donna Irwin; the late Ken Kesey; Andrew Kicking Horse; Dave Moore; Anne Murphy; Lynn Rogers; Leon Tabory; Seymour Wyse; my brother, Ian Sandison, for transcribing hours of interviews; Yuval Taylor at Chicago Review Press; and (definitely not least) Yvonne, my patient, long-suffering, and loving wife.

—David Sandison, 2003

I would like to add to David Sandison's acknowledgments by re-affirming the extent of this book's debt to Carolyn Cassady. Her own celebrated book, *Off the Road,* provides a uniquely valuable and lucid insight into many intimate aspects of Neal Cassady's life that would otherwise never have come to light. Her willingness to assist first David and then myself with her comments and advice is greatly appreciated. Also worthy of special mention is Dave Moore, whose knowledge of dates, facts, and figures relating to Neal Cassady, Jack Kerouac, and their circle is truly encyclopedic—all the more astonishingly so given the complex nature of Cassady's restless life, his hyperactive imagination, and his fondness for frequent, intricate and often secretive road trips. Otherwise this book draws on various written sources as well as a number of original interviews. It was never Neal's way to leave an easy trail to follow, but one hopes that something more than legend and myth emerges from this attempt to reanimate an extraordinary man's life.

—Graham Vickers, 2005

Introduction

This biography of Neal Cassady was David Sandison's idea. David had long been intrigued by Cassady, a man who had tried to reconcile a life of spectacular hedonism with the role of father, husband, and breadwinner . . . an obscure westerner who could turn manual labor into a minor art form but whose fate was inextricably caught up in the world of a handful of East Coast intellectuals led by Jack Kerouac and Allen Ginsberg.

David was fascinated not only by the wild patterns of Cassady's life but also by the strange paradox of a uniquely creative mind that somehow managed to change the course of American literature by proxy and also influence both the beats and the hippies.

So he embarked upon his Cassady book, conducting numerous interviews across the United States, pulling together a wealth of rare or previously unknown material about his subject, and eventually writing what has become more or less the first half of the present volume. David's health began to decline, however, during the course of the project and, as deadlines unavoidably drifted by, the Sisyphean task of documenting Cassady's dizzyingly complex and paradoxical life became ever more daunting, and the book's completion kept receding into the future. This was a sad irony as from the start it had been primarily a labor of love that had genuinely absorbed and fascinated him. Then, in 2004, David died unexpectedly following surgery. He left behind not only a grieving family and friends but also, on the fringes of personal tragedy, a suddenly orphaned book.

I was one of those friends. David had occasionally chatted casually to me about the project that was consuming so much of his time. (Later I was to wish that I had paid closer attention to some of those informal confidences.) After his death it became clear that his half-completed book was too good to be abandoned, and so in 2005—and with some misgivings—I took over the project, inheriting much of the source material that he had amassed as well as the goodwill and unstinting help of Neal's former wife, Carolyn Cassady. She was to provide a valuable strand of continuity without which the completion of this biography would have been impossible.

So why then should we share David's fascination with his subject? To say that Neal Cassady was a person of many contradictions is both a cliché and an understatement. A patchily educated child of the Depression, he wrote reams of effervescent personal letters but only one book, a short and uneven memoir that took him many painstaking and painful years to write. He elevated philandering and hell-for-leather cross-country driving to almost surreal levels. He undoubtedly influenced the social fabric of post–World War II America. His working life was largely, if intermittently, spent as a brakeman (later as a conductor) on the Southern Pacific Rail Road in California, yet he was a legend in New York literary circles. His appetite for sex was quite literally insatiable. He served two years in San Quentin for a drug offense that today would merit little if any penalty in most states. He died alone in Mexico at age forty-one in the vaguest, yet somehow most memorable, of circumstances. The importance of Neal Cassady, however, surpasses both the picaresque details of his life (although that is certainly an epic story in itself) and the impact he had upon contemporary American literature by inspiring Jack Kerouac to develop a groundbreaking spontaneous writing style.

Cassady, as those who knew him long enough sometimes came to realize, was a force of nature. Seeking to change him was likely to meet with about as much success as seeking to change an iceberg. Ken Kesey, a highly successful arriviste-novelist, effectively threw in the towel after meeting him, saying that writing about life paled to insignificance once you had encountered Cassady living it.

Full-blown media coverage was never Cassady's lot; therefore, we have surprisingly little in the way of movie or television footage or press interviews to go on. If we want to appreciate the qualities of this extraordinary and influential man today, we have to look back at his life and try to reanimate it through the impressions, reactions, and recollections of his contemporaries, and, of course, through his own voluptuous correspondence.

Many of those contemporaries were professional writers, a dual blessing since they often wrote insightfully (or at least colorfully) about him, and in some instances were to enjoy levels of fame themselves that would help to ensure that much of their correspondence with Cassady would be saved for posterity. At their best Cassady's own numerous letters fizz and crackle with such vitality and brio that they would be a gift to any biographer. (They were certainly a gift to Jack Kerouac, who used parts of them almost verbatim, though uncredited, in *On the Road* and several other books. In their way the letters were often little works of art even before they were reset in a literary context.)

Finally—and also indivisibly to do with the period in which Cassady lived—there is a fascinating historical arc to his short life, touching several distinct phases of modern American history.

As Lawrence Ferlinghetti has pointed out, there seems to be an almost antique Western quality to Neal Cassady's childhood years, which were spent with his alcoholic father in "the skidrows, hobo jungles, barbershops, and backstreets of Denver." Judged by today's values, Cassady's childhood can certainly sound grotesquely neglectful, a toxic blend of irresponsible parenting, harsh deprivation, and casual child abuse that set the scene for serious psychological disturbance in later life. However, it is important to remember that the West in which Neal Cassady grew up during the 1920s and '30s was in many ways still much closer to the harsh realities of the old wagon train pioneer culture than to any kind of society we now take for granted, so, for what it is worth, Neal was far from alone in his abrasive and uncertain childhood environment. Similar treatment did not affect everyone the same way. Shocking as it may now seem to some people, that is simply how things were for many children of poor families at the time.

From this sepia-tinted, old-timey childhood, Neal Cassady would progress through a rapidly changing United States, always, it seems, magically brushing up against the key artistic figures and forces of the zeitgeist—Jerry Garcia, the Jefferson Airplane, Allen Ginsberg, John Clellon Holmes, Ken Kesey, Larry McMurtry, Jack Kerouac, Lawrence Ferlinghetti, Gregory Corso, and many more. His was not a story of rags to riches—he was usually either broke or taking steps to ensure that he soon would be—but rather that of an untiring voyage of spiritual and hedonistic exploration, a journey intermittently marked by incarceration and curbed appetites as well as reckless behavior and wild thrill-seeking adventures. Wars came and went, the beats fired the warning shots of cultural change, and then the hippies led the main charge. Forrest Gump–like, Neal Cassady always seemed to be on the periphery of the main action in some guise or other, this California railroad worker with a criminal record, a taste for marijuana, a circle of East Coast literary friends, a cozy family in the West that he cherished when it suited him, countless girlfriends dotted all over the United States, and an appetite for thrills and automobiles that to this day often defies belief. Even in his haunted final years, Cassady must surely have experienced some sense of fulfillment, however bitter, at having traveled the road he did, even if that road chose him rather than the other way round. This biography is an attempt to give him a fair hearing and a new audience. If there was one thing Neal Cassady loved, it was an audience.

Here follows an excerpt from David Sandison's original introduction. I once playfully chided him that writing the introduction before completing the book sounded like an act designed to banish worries that the book might never be finished. Sometimes, in retrospect, one would rather have been wrong about certain things.

—Graham Vickers, 2005

• • •

Neal Cassady achieved immortality and legendary status when Jack Kerouac depicted him as Dean Moriarty, the amoral, feisty, funny, and frantic hero of *On the Road.* While Neal himself did nothing to acknowledge or promote himself as the unalloyed original of that supposedly fictional character (he was, in fact, hurt that Kerouac depicted only the more hedonistic and less responsible facets of his personality), he would eventually bow to the inevitable and dedicate the last years of his life to playing the part of the holy madman to perfection. He spent those years drugged and increasingly incoherent as a key player in the lives of Ken Kesey and his Pranksters. He did so, it is clear, with an increasing sense of self-loathing and largely unvoiced desperation. He really was a lost soul at the end, and it is tempting to view his death, alone and lonely by the side of a Mexican railroad track, as a blessed release from a life that had become unbearable for him and for those who loved him.

Most of us spend our lives chasing the beguiling shadows cast by wealth, success, and what we perceive to be happiness. Neal Cassady, it seems, spent his time chasing his own shadow—the thing that inevitably proves the least attainable and most elusive of all.

—David Sandison, 2003

1

IT MAY SEEM ODD to begin a biography with a correction, but Neal Cassady's story is one that is shot through with myth and falsehood from the very start. The circumstances surrounding and preceding his birth have been repeatedly misrepresented and misunderstood over the years. A tangle of contradictory accounts and false recollections has made the task of arriving at an honest version a complex one, and for authors and readers alike, the process sometimes resembles opening a set of those nesting Russian dolls that keep revealing yet another truth inside the one that you felt sure was the last. While this has the advantage of preparing us for the recurring theme of lying and creative reinvention that was to run throughout Neal Cassady's life, unpicking these familial myths and misdirections may strike some as an unwelcome delay to the start of the action. One hopes, however, that this Cassady family history does remind us that the world into which Neal was born was one in which public records and family gossip could be equally unreliable, the former often being nothing more than a record of the latter, and the latter acquiring embellishments and alterations to suit prevailing circumstances and personalities.

Neal Cassady was certainly born in Salt Lake City, Utah, and definitely grew up in Denver, Colorado, where he lived from the age of two. However, myth and ambivalence surround not only his parents' history but even distort the circumstances of his birth. Neal Cassady was not born in the backseat of a car (or any other vehicle) stopped by the roadside on the outskirts of Salt Lake City in the early hours of February 8, 1926. That was one of the romantic inventions that Neal fed Jack Kerouac many years later, fabrications that were unquestioningly accepted by the captivated author and woven into the legend of the charismatic Dean Moriarty, Cassady's alter ego and the hero of *On the Road.* Over time people came to believe the Moriarty myth, causing this fiction to become one of many spurious Cassady "facts." Only in 1981, with the posthumous publication of the second extended and revised edition of Neal's memoir, *The First Third,* was the record (more or less) set straight. In an amended prologue, he admitted that his mother had given birth to him in "the L.D.S. Hospital," a Salt Lake City medical institution supported by the Church of Jesus Christ of Latter-day Saints. In fact he was born in a maternity ward of another hospital, Salt Lake County General. His birth certificate states that an infant named Neal Cassady Jr. (whose parents were identified as a thirty-two-year-old white man, Neal Cassady, and a thirty-three-year-old white woman, Maude Jean Scheuer), was indeed born there at 2:05 A.M. on February 8, 1926.

Neal's account of his family's history in that prologue was an altogether bewildering fiction in which were buried a few tantalizingly accurate details, a confection of half-remembered stories told to Neal by his father (who spent most of his waking hours in an alcoholic stupor) and anecdotes from far-flung relatives whom Neal contacted but whose secondhand recollections of long-gone events were understandably vague.

According to this unreliable memoir, Neal's father (whose full birth name was Neal Marshall Casady [*sic*], a spelling that would come to acquire an extra *s* and sometimes even became *Cassidy*) was born into a small rural community near Queen City, in northwest Missouri, in 1893. This much we know to be fact, but if we want the real story we should ignore Neal's embroidered account of his parents' early lives and turn instead to the diligent research of Louise Marie Casady Kiser, a distant cousin of Neal's who lived in Montana and who compiled a rather more reliable Casady family history in 1972. An excerpt from this history appeared in the first part of an excellent two-part Neal Cassady magazine published during the 1980s by Tom Christopher, a Washington State–based author. Christopher's exhaustive research further added to a more reliable picture of the senior Cassady's early life and offers a plausible explanation, beyond the effects of alcoholic befuddlement, for the man's fanciful dissembling: he had much to cover up.

Mrs. Kiser discovered that the Casadys were Irish Quakers who had immigrated to America and settled in New Jersey in the early nineteenth century. Parts of the family headed west during the next few decades, some of them settling in Missouri. Neal Sr.'s father was the ninth and youngest child of Samuel Surry Casady and his wife, Permilia Ann Mullinix. *The First Third* erroneously states that Neal's grandfather was named William, and that he married his brother's pregnant widow, Cora. (Samuel and Permilia did have a daughter named Ora and that may have led to this particular mistake in Neal Jr.'s account.)

Another of Tom Christopher's sources recalled that Permilia died when Neal Sr. was a baby and that the boy left home in his mid-teens. His father, Mrs. Kiser said, remarried "a couple of times," and so did not slump into the morose, introspective, Bible-thumping, child-beating recluse that Neal Sr. described to his son.

While some details of the elder Neal's trail have proved elusive, in 1914 he can definitely be placed in Des Moines, Iowa. At that time, far from being the virginal and naïve youngster chastely courting a German girl named Gertrude Vollmer, as *The First Third* would have it, Neal Sr. actually married a local girl named Ethel on September 10 of that year. By 1919 a "Mr. and Mrs. Neal Cassady" were listed in the Des Moines directory as residing at 931 7th Street; his occupation was given as "barber" and hers as "grocery clerk." Two years later that same directory listed Neal Sr. as living alone at 207½ 6th Avenue.

Neal Sr.'s World War I military career and other career "facts" described in *The First Third* are also thrown into doubt by the sworn testimony that Ethel gave when she divorced him in 1924. According to her petition, she and Neal had lived together until June 1921, since the time when (and indeed for some time before) he had "failed in any manner to support [her]."

Ethel also claimed that during the last six years of their marriage Neal Sr. had "pursued a course of cruel and inhuman treatment" toward her, had failed to support her financially, and had made it necessary for her to perform labor for which she was unfitted "in order to gain a livelihood." Neal Sr. had also "constantly harassed and abused" her, thereby impairing her health and endangering her life. Neal Sr. did not contest his wife's action and the divorce was granted on May 6, 1924.

Neal Marshall Casady stood five feet, eight inches tall, and weighed 160 pounds. Although long in the body he had relatively short arms and legs. His son described his face as being "usually alight with the kindness of simplicity," adding that while Neal Sr. possessed a restless mind, it was "slow, with very little in it." With regard to his fanciful memoirs, Neal Jr.'s mind might, by contrast, be described as having rather too much in it. *The First Third* prologue, colorful and imaginative as it might be, proved highly untrustworthy—not only in major fact but also in minor detail.

Neal Cassady's mother, he assured his readers, was named on her son's birth certificate as Maude Jean Scheuer. She was born in Duluth, Minnesota, in 1890. The fourth and final child of a German-born master mariner Neal Sr. referred to as Otto Scheuer, Maude came from a formerly stable, respectable, and well-off family that had begun to disintegrate in 1898 when her mother died of pneumonia shortly after Otto left on one of his yearlong voyages.

Within a few months, Neal wrote, Maude's sister Carrie had departed for Sioux City, Iowa, where she took a job as housemaid with the wealthy parents of a longtime pen pal. An older brother, Charles, secured work with the Railway Express Company in Duluth. When Otto finally returned from his voyage, he arranged for Maude's twelve-year-old sister, Lucy, to join the same household staff as Carrie in Sioux City, while Maude was sent to live with the family of a seaman friend near Duluth.

When Maude was twelve years old her sister Carrie married and moved with her husband to California. Lucy took over her duties and

Otto arranged for Maude to join Carrie's erstwhile employers in their Sioux City household as well. The sisters shared a cottage on the estate, and the family for whom they worked soon made a favorite of the pretty, gracious, and mild-mannered Maude.

As Maude became a teenager she began to receive advances from prospective suitors. Among them (Neal Sr. told his son who relayed the information to readers of *The First Third*) was James Kenneth Daly, scion of a wealthy and well-connected Sioux City family.

Daly was described by Neal as "a lawyer well-up in the local political sphere, despite his youth . . . he brought his wife into a home of financial security." An Irish immigrant, Daly was characterized by Neal as intelligent, gruff, quick to anger but kindhearted and sentimental, a hard worker, a keen duck hunter, a fine marksman, and an enthusiastic consumer of McSorrell's Ale and substantial meals. He and Maude married in the autumn of 1906, when she was just sixteen years old and Daly was twenty-four.

In 1919, Neal wrote, Jim Daly was unexpectedly elected mayor of Sioux City on an anti-graft platform that proposed widespread reform of the city's legislature. Three years later and just before a second election campaign, Neal assures us, Daly died of apoplexy when he was not yet forty years old. His pregnant widow was thirty-two at the time of his death, having already given birth to four boys and four girls. One of the boys had died at birth in 1917, and the names and birth dates of the surviving seven were given as: William (1907), Ralph (1910), John (1912), Evelyn (1915), Mae (1919), Betty (1920), and James Kenneth Jr. (1922).

Maude sold the Sioux City family house and moved to Des Moines. There, with the family in financially reduced circumstances, the eldest boys went to work. William left school and got a full-time job; Ralph began working afternoons and Saturdays as a housepainter, John became a newspaper delivery boy.

Taken into a circle of bridge-playing ladies, Maude was also drawn into a Sunday concert group that ensured her presence at some of Des

Moines' most select gatherings. It was at the annual dance held by this group that Maude met Neal Sr. After a decorous courtship (during which Neal also sought to win over Maude's suspicious children), he proposed to Maude in the spring of 1925 and married her on May 1 of that year. Maude became pregnant in the first month of the marriage with the child who would be named after his father. However, here more confusion of names further clouds an already doubtful history. Neal claimed that his father wanted him to be named plain Neal Cassady and thus be known as Neal Cassady Jr. (even though Neal Sr. was still given to spelling his own surname as *Cassidy*). Maude, however, decided that the boy would be named Neal Leon Cassady, rendering the "Jr." tag further redundant.

Even more dubious facts now appear in the younger Neal's memoir. He wrote that prior to his birth, back in Des Moines, his father had built a remarkable timber house on the back of a two-ton Ford truck on which Neal Sr., his heavily pregnant wife, and her two youngest children, five-year-old Betty and three-year-old Jimmy, were to travel west in search of a better life in California. Maude's older children would stay and fend for themselves in Des Moines until this family of pioneers either returned or made its fortune and sent for them. It was during that trek, as they neared Salt Lake City and Maude began to go into labor, that Neal Sr. headed for the county hospital where his son was born. When Maude was sufficiently rested the newly extended family hit the road once more until it reached Los Angeles, where, with the last of his savings, Neal Sr. bought a barbershop on the corner of Hollywood and Vine. Within a year he sold the business and, acting on a suggestion from Maude's brother, Charles, relocated to Denver, Colorado.

In fact the Los Angeles episode appears to be yet another of the fictions that litter the prologue to *The First Third.* Neal's half-sister Evelyn was certain that the Salt Lake City expedition and the move to Denver were not interrupted by a spell in California, and said as much to Tom Christopher.

It was again half-sister Evelyn who provided conclusive evidence to show the extent to which the two Neals had, between them, fabricated an inaccurate family history. Early in 1982 Carolyn Cassady sent a copy of the newly revised *The First Third* to Evelyn, who was by then living in the Los Angeles suburb of Garden Grove. On June 16 of that year Evelyn wrote Carolyn to set the record straight. Her letter has never before been published, and it is worth quoting here in full:

> Dear Carolyn:
>
> In reply to your request, I'll try to indicate below a few of the differences I noted:
>
> Mother's name was Maud (no *e*) Webb Scheuer. (Jean was a nickname).
>
> Dad's name was James Daly (no middle initial).
>
> Our Grandad's name was John Scheuer (not Otto). He remarried and lived in Minot until his second wife's death when he moved to Denver to live with his youngest daughter, Lucy Rieger. *No one* in the Daly or Scheuer families ever lived in Des Moines. Mother and Dad lived in Sioux City, Iowa until after Ralph was born. They then moved to Denver and spent the rest of their lives there, except for the time Mother and Neal traveled.
>
> The order of our (Daly) births was as follows:

Austin Gerald (not William)	5/19/07	Sioux City, Iowa
Ralph Denton	2/19/09	" " "
Evelyn	2/19/11	Denver, Colorado
Jack Kenneth	12/19/12	" "
Mae Eleanor	11/19/16	" "
Betty Louise	5/1919	" "
James Robert	4/1921	" "

> There was another child born (blue baby) I believe between Jack and Mae, but I'm not sure. I was very young but remember it being taken to be buried.

My Mother's family and the order of their births was as follows:

Carrie

Elizabeth

Raymond (not Charles)*

Maud

Lucy

*Charles was Lucy's husband and Ray never lived in Denver although he visited on occasion.

Dad was *never* a Mayor of any town, but rather a Claim Adjuster for the Railway Express. Neal and Mother met in Denver (I was there at the time.)

To *my* knowledge, Carrie, Mother & Lucy never worked for a wealthy family. Carrie worked for the Telephone Company as a Long Distance operator after her mother died and was married at 16 years of age. Her husband (another Charles) worked with Dad in Sioux City and that is how Dad and Mother met.

Lucy lived with her dad & stepmother until she was 18 years old when she went to Denver. She worked for a family in Fort Lupton, Colo. She married the half-brother of the lady for whom she worked.

Shortly after Mother & Neal met (about 2 years after our Dad's death) Jack & I went to Sioux City to live with Dad's eldest brother Pat Daly and his wife Laura.

Some of the above is of little consequence, but since it is fact I have shown it.

Best regards

Evelyn

Evelyn may have considered her information to be of little consequence, but it changes the legend of the senior Neal Cassady in significant fashion. His account of his wife's family, her raising, and their first genteel meetings was pure invention.

Then there is his portrait of Maud's first husband, James Daly. There was in fact no hard-won election to become an anti-graft mayor of Sioux City—and no apoplectic death on September 17, 1922, when he was still only thirty-nine years old. In fact, James Daly died at his home, 3047 California Street, Denver, on October 8, 1922, after residing in that city for thirteen years. He was forty-three years old. His physician, Dr. Galen Locke, certified that the cause of his death was pulmonary tuberculosis. James Daly was laid to rest in Denver's Mount Olivet Cemetery after a requiem mass at the Sacred Heart Church.

Given that Neal Sr.'s account of his courtship of Maud was so riddled with inaccuracies, his version of the trek from Des Moines toward the Promised Land with his heavily pregnant wife (in the middle of a mid-western winter in a truck with no heater and with two children under the age of five) seems at least open to question. Yet Neal Jr. was indisputably born in Salt Lake City—so why were Neal Sr. and Maud there?

Partial clues lie in two pieces of information Neal Sr. volunteered when he filled out his son's birth certificate. (It must have been Neal who performed that duty and not Maud because she is unlikely to have added an *e* to her first name or given her nickname, Jean, as her middle name when it was actually Webb.) In the box where he had to give his occupation, Neal wrote "Barber (Deseret Gym)." For his place of residence, he wrote the Salt Lake City address "48½ West Broadway." So we must conclude that Neal was already working and living in that city.

The gymnasium in the now much-altered Deseret district of Salt Lake City has long since vanished along with its employee records, so we cannot know how long Neal Sr. stayed there. It is also impossible to know if Betty and Jimmy were, as *The First Third* prologue claims, with Maud and Neal Sr. in Salt Lake City, but it is likely that the other children from Maud's marriage to James Daly were living in Denver, safe in the care of what was, by then, a fairly large spread of kinfolk, since by the time James Daly died, three of his brothers—Bernard, John, and Joseph—were also living in Denver with their families.

And what of the fabled house on a truck? The rutted roads of mid-1920s rural America witnessed many such contraptions, and many a newly converted Mormon family must have shipped themselves to Salt Lake City in similar style. The most probable explanation is that Neal Sr. saw at least one such extraordinary mobile home and simply borrowed the image to enhance the more prosaic truth of his travels. Such vehicles, if viewed as latter-day covered wagons, surely evoked the optimistic spirit of an earlier age in which the western trails to California and Oregon promised a better life for the courageous and the desperate. Perhaps the newlyweds did plan a move to California, which stalled for several weeks in Salt Lake City with Neal's birth.

In any case, any dreams of prosperity remained stubbornly unrealized. Neal Sr. was a simpleminded and intermittently violent alcoholic who had already abused and abandoned one wife. His own life would be a process of slow and sad decline for which, in his later years, he could only mumble vague, good-natured apologies to those he had let down. Although by no means his only victim, his young son Neal would, as part of his father's ramshackle world, have to endure a skid row childhood that taught him to use his natural quickness of mind and body to survive, adapt, and exploit every opportunity that came his way. It was a pattern of behavior that would outlive Depression-era Denver and persist throughout his entire life.

2

IN 1928 MAUD'S BROTHER, Charles, who worked for the Railway Express Company and had recently been transferred to Denver, wrote to the newly expanded Cassady family, enthused by the city's virtues (he seemed particularly impressed by its number of green lawns) and suggesting they move there to make their future. This the Cassadys decided to do, and Neal Sr. took up residence at a two-chair barbershop on Denver's 23rd Street between Welton Street and Glenarm Place, sharing workspace with a shoe-repairer and installing the Daly-Cassady family in small rooms at the rear. These crowded quarters were now occupied by Neal Sr. and Maud, twelve-year-old Mae, her nine-year-old sister Betty, seven-year-old Jimmy, and the younger Neal. Evelyn and Jack had opted to live in Sioux City with their uncle Pat, while Maud's oldest sons, Austin (whom the family for some reason called Bill) and Ralph, decided to strike out on their own.

The Denver in which Neal Cassady was to spend all of his childhood and most of his teen years had been incorporated as a city in 1902—twenty-four years before his birth—and was named for General James W. Denver, a onetime governor of Kansas. The ramshackle mass of rough huts and rowdy hostelries that formed the original Denver settlement was in fact originally situated in Kansas territory; Colorado's territorial boundaries were not absolutely fixed until 1876, when President Ulysses S. Grant declared the state's addition to the Union.

Pioneering settlers had followed the trails established by Spanish and French adventurers who began exploring the lands of indigenous Ute and Arapaho in the sixteenth century. Forts and trading stations had grown into small communities, but it was not until 1858—when a prospector named Green Russell found gold deposits near the confluence of South

Platte River and Cherry Creek—that the territory began to grow quickly. It was a growth that would increase tremendously a year later when another, larger gold strike was made at Pikes Peak. The first mail coach between Leavenworth, Kansas, and Cherry Creek opened for business, and soon the first public school was founded.

Denver was established as the territory's permanent seat of government in 1867, only three years after the last great battle between soldiers, settlers, and Colorado's natives—the infamous Sand Creek Massacre, in which hundreds of Cheyenne and Arapaho men, women, and children were killed—and three years before the Denver and Pacific Railroad was constructed to link Denver with the Union Pacific Railroad at Cheyenne, Wyoming.

Mining boosted Colorado's prosperity, and soon there was a university (with two teachers and forty-four students) at Boulder, and an opera house in Denver; 1882 saw the installation of Denver's first electric lights. Vast fortunes were made in 1900 when the annual gold production in the Cripple Creek camp alone peaked at over $20 million—about $2.5 billion in modern terms. Three years later, laborers there went on strike for better wages and work conditions; after a bloody and damaging series of confrontations they returned to work with none of their demands met. In 1908 Denver celebrated the thirty-second anniversary of Colorado's admittance to the Union by plating the State Capitol dome with gold leaf.

By 1920 the population of Colorado was close to a million. The state levied a tax of one cent per gallon on gasoline and could boast one of the country's most dynamic highway construction programs. Within a year, however, many citizens were experiencing the impact of postwar deflation. Rural banks and farms were being bankrupted; land prices were declining, and financial casualties began to drift back into a city that had no work for them or even a decent place to stay. Denver became another example of the stark social division that was seen all over the United States and the rest of the industrialized world: the already wealthy retained their hilltop mansions while the poor lived in rundown tenements and vermin-infested flophouses.

Underlying Denver's social split remained the harsh pioneering values of self-sufficiency and rough justice that today are more typically associated with points farther west. Yet in its social attitudes, 1920s Denver was driven by the aggressive spirit of a Wild West frontier town, and that could hardly fail to influence the young Neal for whom the phrase "every man for himself" must have seemed a civic motto.

Operating independently of Neal's expanded family, Bill and Ralph, Maud's two oldest sons, had involved themselves with Denver's primitive entertainment industry. According to the prologue in *The First Third*, Bill met and married a young widow who had inherited her late husband's dine-and-dance club on the outskirts of town. At the time, the United States was still in the grip of Prohibition, which had been introduced nationwide in 1920, while Colorado had brought in its own draconian anti-liquor laws four years earlier. A thriving bootleg industry supplied those who could afford its sometimes lethal concoctions, while a sophisticated smuggling network dodged the young J. Edgar Hoover's FBI agents to ensure that better-off drinkers could continue to enjoy their branded bottles of choice.

Ralph was involved with one of Denver's busiest bootleggers, "Blackie" Barlow. In 1928, when he was only twenty years old, Ralph ran liquor for one of Barlow's agents—a downtown Denver dealer called Sam who based his operation at 11th Street and Larimer, a skid row shambles of rundown hotels, flophouses, saloons, and brothels. When Ralph's sixteen-year-old brother, Jack, decided to leave Sioux City and return to Denver, Ralph put in a word with Barlow, and Jack too was taken on, acting as a lookout at one of Barlow's principal distillation centers.

On one occasion, caught up in a raid by federal agents, Jack and another ineffectual lookout were captured, handcuffed together, and left in the charge of an agent while the rest of the feds moved in on the target house. Trying to escape their captor, Jack and his companion ran on either side of a tree and were recaptured immediately, whereupon the furious agent pistol-whipped Jack's face, breaking four of his upper teeth. After a brief spell in jail, and with new gold teeth in place of his lost originals, Jack returned to bootlegging, this time in partnership with Ralph.

Now making more money than they knew how to spend wisely or well, the brothers were often called on to help their mother as she tried to make ends meet on what little their stepfather was earning. They gave as generously as they could, but with one important proviso: Neal Sr. was never to be given a penny of their money. Neal Sr.'s barbershop business first languished and then failed. There was a brief upturn in his fortunes when he found a job in a successful salon near the Denver stockyards. As his son later wrote, Neal Sr. appeared for a time to "get down to the business of being a better father—a last flurry as it were."

In the summer of 1929 the bootleg brothers put a down payment on a large house on 26th Avenue, at which time Neal Sr. was doing well enough to help pay the mortgage for a few months. For the first time the entire Daly-Cassady family was able to live under the same roof.

Then the Wall Street crash of October 24, 1929, devastated the world economy and made paupers of millionaires. Neal Sr. was laid off, Jack and Ralph's income dropped through the floor, and when the impoverished family fell behind on their monthly payments the bank foreclosed on their mortgage. Bill and his wife moved into a mobile home park in west Denver, Ralph married and set up home with a student nurse, and Jack began drifting back and forth between friends' homes.

Reduced to working a Saturday-only job, Neal Sr. found his income dropped to almost nothing. He and Maud were obliged to move to a cheap two-room apartment. Maud prevailed on local Catholic authorities to give her daughters, Mae and Betty, accommodation in the Queen of Heaven Orphanage until she and Neal Sr. were back on their feet. Maud's decision was made all the more pressing by the fact that she was pregnant again. On May 22, 1930, she gave birth to her tenth and final child, a girl they named Shirley Jean. Eight months later there was a brief moment of optimism when Neal Sr. took over a bankrupt two-chair barbershop near the corner of 26th and Champa Streets, with accommodations above.

"In this sad little shop so filled with contention" the younger Neal noted lugubriously in *The First Third*, "Neal and Maude [*sic*] shared the last year of their pitiful marriage."

Despite struggling to make ends meet (with help from Jack and Ralph, who had now begun to make a dishonest buck once more), Neal could not be prevailed upon to quit drinking. Early in 1932 the little shop—his last hope for salvation and regained dignity—was closed for the last time. With it went any chance Neal might have had to save his marriage. Around this time Jack and Ralph became unforgiving enforcers, frequently assaulting Neal Sr. physically for what they saw as his dereliction of responsibility. Supported by her boys, Maud gave Neal his marching orders. She was taking her son, Jimmy, and baby Shirley Jean to a new apartment on Stout Street; her rent there would be paid by Jack. Neal Sr. and little Neal could go where they liked. We can only speculate as to why she abandoned young Neal (and not the older and more resilient Jimmy) to the care of a man whom she obviously considered irresponsible. Perhaps it was because there was already a bond of affection evident between the two Neals, or perhaps she assumed the younger child might make a stronger appeal to Neal Sr.'s sense of paternal obligation.

In any case, Neal Sr. was not inclined to argue since Ralph and Jack, whether out of a real sense of justice or simply out of a psychopathic inclination toward violence, had already demonstrated an enthusiastic willingness to beat him. Six-year-old Neal had witnessed many such beatings on Sunday mornings when a drink-addled Neal Sr. stumbled home after a rough night. While Maud cried and begged for them to stop, they would continue to beat him until they became too tired to continue. Neal too had suffered at home—his half-brother Jimmy Daly also had an unhealthy appetite for violence and liked to force him into fistfights with much bigger boys—and so it was with little regret that he followed his father a few blocks west to their new home, the Metropolitan Hotel.

If the Metropolitan had ever enjoyed a golden age it lay in the long-forgotten past. A once-grand five-story building that stood on the corner of Market and 16th Streets, it now awaited demolition, its upper floors filled with a hundred or so washed-up and wasted winos, beggars, and bums. All of them lived in small cubicles rented for ten or fifteen cents a night. Neal Sr. and his son, however, were able to rent a slightly larger two-bit cubicle on the top floor for a dollar a week, a "bargain" they enjoyed because they shared it with a third occupant, Shorty, a man without legs, who slept on a small platform built onto the elbow of a protruding water pipe. Neal and his father shared a single bed with no sheets.

Shorty, a spectacularly ugly man, was usually the first to rise, and young Neal would watch, fascinated, as the skinny double amputee used his long arms to swing himself down the five flights of stairs, climb into the homemade cart that was his only means of transportation, and, with a block of wood in each hand, propel himself around the corner to his begging position outside the Manhattan Restaurant on Larimer, one of the few half-decent eating places left in town and therefore popular with patrons who could afford to toss coins to a beggar. "When he had received the price of a bottle or two," Neal recalled, "he would return to the room and drink himself into a stupor."

From time to time Shorty would fail to return and Neal would help his father scour darkened doorways and alleys until they found the crippled drunk. Neal Sr. would carry him back to the Metropolitan on his shoulder while his son got to ride Shorty's cart home, the clattering of its metal roller-skate wheels on the cobblestones of Market Street echoing around the neighborhood.

Shorty was also an inveterate masturbator, a habit Neal condoned with the explanation that this unfortunate man was so hideous—and smelled so bad—that it must have been years since he had been with a woman; so it was that the six-year-old boy learned the true nature of what he had first taken to be egg white soiling the floor of their top-story cell. Shorty would disappear only five months after father and son moved into the Metropolitan, and young Neal never saw him again.

The rest of the Metropolitan's clientèle were, according to Neal's book, "drunkards whose minds, weakened by liquor and an obsequious manner . . . seemed continually preoccupied with bringing up short observations of obvious trash."

Neal Sr. was referred to by his fellow dropouts as "the barber" and so his six-year-old son became known as "the barber's boy." It was a soubriquet the young Neal treasured, for it confirmed his bond with his beloved father.

If his father was lax in the matter of self-discipline, he was diligent enough when it came to Neal's education. Within days of moving into the Metropolitan, the barber marched his boy almost a mile to Ebert Grammar School, where he had begun his formal education a few months earlier and where he would stay, despite many housing moves, for the next six years. Neal loved learning, once he had mastered the basics of reading and writing. It was the structure and discipline of schooldays that vexed a boy whose life was otherwise unfettered.

On schooldays Neal would be roused by the clock on the tower of the Daniels & Fisher department store, an architectural feature pretentiously modeled on the Campanile at Piazza San Marco in Venice. As the grandly mounted belltower clock struck seven, Neal would scramble from the filthy bed he shared with his father and make his way to the communal washroom one floor down and join other early risers in their rudimentary ablutions.

After checking his father "for any signs of sobriety or interest in food," Neal invariably headed to the Citizen's Mission on Larimer, where free breakfasts and suppers were doled out to about two hundred souls each day. The only charge for meals came in the form of required attendance at weekly prayer meetings. In time a Father Divine, who operated a similar refuge also on Larimer, began to serve lunches. As Neal recalled "there was a real whoopdeedoo among the boys when his place opened, for the gap between breakfast and supper at the Mission had been felt by all."

Time was tight on school mornings and Neal would cover the distance between mission and school at a run, taking shortcuts through back alleys, bouncing and catching a treasured tennis ball as he went until he reached Glenarm Street—a more upscale residential thoroughfare—running its two-block length to reach the school gate, and sprinting across its huge graveled playground at full tilt, "even though this final spurt was not always enough to beat the school bell, for [it] was usually ringing."

The school's basement cafeteria served as a lunch counter for the twenty or so needy children whose parents had applied for the city's charity. Successful applicants like Neal were given a better-than-nothing snack of crackers and milk at noon while their more fortunate friends headed home for something more substantial.

His return to the Metropolitan after school was made at a more leisurely pace and it was during his strolls back there that Neal could explore the secret corners of the Curtis Park area, including from time to time—when he missed a catch of the tennis ball—the foul-smelling depths of the sewage system. He would also scale rickety drainpipes to recover his ball when it lodged in rooftop gutters.

After joining the Larimer Street bums for supper at the mission (alone if his father was still too drunk to make it), Neal would return to the Metropolitan and the fierce but localized heat of the pot-bellied stove that stood in the center of the large, dirty lobby. In a smaller foyer he would absorb the sights and sounds of the evening's diversions. These usually consisted of card and board games played to the accompaniment of self-pitying and long-winded monologues from alcoholics lamenting times lost and opportunities blown. Neal would spend as long as he could in the lobby's warmth, for there was no heating on the flophouse's upper stories. In any case, he enjoyed the easy companionship of these sad and broken men for whom he imagined he "presented the sole replica of their own childhood."

On Saturdays Neal Sr. would drag himself from bed and prepare himself for the one day of employment he had been able to find, working one of the three chairs at the Zaza barbershop, located on Larimer between 17th and 18th. Owned by a thin, dark-complexioned Italian called Charley, this particular barbershop was a place the younger Neal remembered with fondness throughout his life, describing with relish its luxuriant miasma of pomades, oils, and talcum powder, and recalling his fascination with the copies of *Liberty News* and the *Rocky Mountain News* that Charley laid out for waiting customers. In fact young Neal was only waiting there until the start of the morning matinee at an adjoining movie theater (also called the Zaza), where a nickel would buy him a couple of hours of cinematic magic, stimulating his fertile imagination with sounds and images from exotic worlds unconnected with life in down-and-out Denver.

Even so, Denver's real-life picture palace posed serious obstacles to escapism: by any standards the Zaza Theater was a dump, and the "indescribable stench" of this fleapit stayed with Neal all his life, as potent a sensory memory as the celluloid fantasies he enjoyed there. He wrote, "Naturally, I can call up only a fraction of this Great Smell's many component parts and cannot fully imagine whence its source, but . . . each patron's shared odor added to the building's own array to form a complicated multiplicity of rot while permeating the nostrils with such a potency that, while struggling to accustom, I breathed as little air as possible through my open mouth."

Once the house lights dimmed, the shabby velvet curtains were pulled back, and the projector began filling the screen with miraculous images, Neal would quickly forget his surroundings and immerse himself in the on-screen adventures. His favorite Hollywood cowboy hero was Tim McCoy, star of a string of low-budget adventure flicks with titles like *The Man from Guntown, Roaring Guns, Aces and Eights,* and *The Lion's Den,* potboilers churned out by the small independent Puritan and Victory studios.

Neal also retained vivid memories of the musicals produced in Hollywood as frothy escapism for a nation battered by unemployment and poverty. His favorites were the Fred Astaire and Ginger Rogers 1933 classic *Flying Down to Rio* and *Rainbow on the River*, a 1936 vehicle for boy soprano Bobby Breen. Its story line—a young Civil War orphan is sent away from the banks of his beloved Mississippi to live with uncaring relatives in New York—was one with which Neal, more or less abandoned by his own mother and forced to live in the dreadful surroundings of the Metropolitan Hotel, might have identified, although he tended to look to the movies for inspirational adventure rather than real-life self-examination.

In this spirit the Zaza delivered a particularly thrilling 1933 escape for the seven-year-old in the form of *King Kong* and its hurriedly released sequel, *Son of Kong*. Then one year later he would see a movie that would transfix and enthrall him more than any other: *The Count of Monte Cristo*. This 1934 melodrama starring Robert Donat was the sixth movie version of the Alexandre Dumas novel in which Edmond Dantes, wrongly convicted of a plot against the post-Napoleonic French government due to a perfidious friend who also steals and marries his girl, is imprisoned in the daunting Château D'If. He eventually escapes and then finds an immense treasure, which he uses to fund an elaborate revenge plan. Robbed of his humanity by this obsession with vengeance, Dantes is eventually redeemed by the love of his girl, who has always remained spiritually faithful to him, despite her pragmatic marriage to his false accuser.

We can only speculate as to how this kind of morality-play plot affected the impressionable young Neal's future view of the world, but at the time it certainly prompted him to seek out the original novel in the Ebert School's library. It was there his lifelong love affair with books took root, despite decidedly discouraging beginnings.

The school librarian, a Mrs. Udderbeck (who was described by Neal's classmate, Sheldon Emeson, as "a real shriveled up old maid") accused Neal of stealing a book. Emeson said Neal claimed it was lost when he left it on the sidewalk during a street ball game. Mrs. Udderbeck refused to believe him and thereafter this voracious young reader was denied the privilege of taking out any more books from Ebert's library.

Inevitably, Neal's own account of this episode differed from Emeson's and, in an early example of his lifelong tendency to embroider upon the truth, was considerably more complicated. The book in question was indeed *The Count of Monte Cristo*, which he had just taken out for a second time (not having finished reading it when it was due the first time), when he met a friend who invited him to take a look at some turtles he kept in a backyard pool. Neal says he stashed the book in the fork of a tree for safekeeping, and it had mysteriously disappeared when he came to reclaim it a short time later. So ended his membership in the school library. Much later he claimed to have found the book, now splattered with blood from the body of a dead cat (whose destruction he describes in long and gory detail), high in a tree where someone must have tossed it as "a careless prank."

Neal Cassady, one senses, was not capable of losing a book through simple carelessness—there had to be a plot or some dramatic irony involved. He could not even be born in a hospital—it had to happen at the roadside as part of an epic adventure with a rugged vehicle involved. This fondness for self-dramatization can only occasionally be proved, but the suspicion remains that from childhood onward, Neal preferred to imbue the most mundane aspects of his life with theatrical or spiritual detail. There is certainly every reason to suppose that he was in the thrall of dramatic art. After his Saturday morning visit to the Zaza, young Neal would return to the barbershop to regale his father, Charley, and a third barber with colorful accounts of the films he had just seen; he was clearly much impressed by the spectacle of vivid lives presented as full-blooded theater and stories replete with coincidence, retribution, and redemption.

Then he would go with his father to a place called Mac's Lunch—a diner Neal described as a "busy bum beanery"—for a midday meal. When his father returned to work, Neal would embark on a junk hunt, trolling the alleys off Larimer and Market Street with a gunnysack to gather any bits and pieces that might have resale value. After stashing his haul under the Metropolitan lobby stairway, he would return to collect his father when the shop closed at 9 P.M. The two of them would stroll to Curtis Street for a second restaurant meal (with detours to allow the barber to buy a bottle of wine and his son to buy chocolate at a candy store where he could also check his weight on a penny machine). Then the two of them would head back to the Zaza for the late show. They took balcony seats so Neal's father could smoke as he sipped on his wine, while young Neal luxuriated in the taste of chocolate melting slowly on his tongue as he again entered a make-believe world.

For the first three winter months of the Cassadys' stay at the Metropolitan, Sundays were mostly spent indoors. Neal Sr. whiled away the hours playing cards with his rummy buddies while young Neal listened to their tales of hard luck and mawkish reminiscences. Then the arrival of spring transformed the Sunday routine. No matter how hungover he might be after his Saturday night drinking session, the barber would haul himself from his bed and accompany his son to a late breakfast at the Citizens' Mission. The pair would then ramble down to the Union Station on 17th Street, walk under the great 14th Street viaduct, past coal yards and auto-wreckers' lots, and eventually down an embankment to the refuge of a gravelly beach that stretched for several hundred yards along the South Platte River's edge between 15th and 17th Streets.

There, for a few happy hours, they would enjoy a simple companionship filled with the long easy silences that only true friends can share. Sometimes Neal Sr. would snooze between taking slugs from his brown-bagged wine bottle. At other times he would watch his son searching for the flat stones that he liked to send bouncing over the sewage-filled river. Before reaching his teens, Neal claimed that he could consistently achieve twenty or more skips with every throw. This early dedication to skills perfection prefigured Neal's lifelong obsession with physical accomplishments that demanded exceptional dexterity or hand-eye coordination (tire capping, pit stop wheel-changing, car parking, jackhammer juggling, driving over the speed limit) until he was certain that he had become the best there was, or at least, the very best that he could be.

As the light faded at the end of another Sunday at the beach, father and son reluctantly headed back to the mission for the six o'clock supper before returning to the Metropolitan.

These days were obviously precious to the younger Neal, for he was to recount them in affectionate detail more than thirty years later in *The First Third.* He also spoke of their magic to Jack Kerouac both when he visited Denver in 1947 and later when he and Jack were stoned on weed and ice-cold beer during the early 1950s and started rapping into a tape recorder. Jack in turn would treasure Neal's memories, transcribing and using them, verbatim, in what would eventually become *Visions of Cody.*

The young Neal came to know Denver's hidden corners and secret byways intimately. He explored many miles of Cherry Creek ("from its upper reaches," he wrote, "well past Denver's south-eastern limits of dairy farms, chicken ranches, riding academies and cowboy style night clubs") as he searched for junk to sell or convert into saleable items—old inner tubes, for instance, could be used to make slingshots that he would sell to schoolmates for a few precious pennies.

The area around the South Platte River became his favorite playground. Most of its bridges had huge steel girders where he could clamber and climb, reenacting the exploits of Olympic swimming champion Johnny Weissmuller in his movie persona of Tarzan, another Zaza Theater favorite. Beneath the 14th Street viaduct Neal learned to swim, despite his abiding fear of deep water, his embarrassment at his own nudity, and the waste-polluted water in which he was obliged to acquire the skill.

He also explored the abandoned hobo camps, the brickyards, and the railroad sheds, and he was enthralled by the giant Intercity Electrical Plant, dynamos vibrating and whining, and the desolate splendor of the Pride of the Rockies flour mill, a disused industrial building the size of a cathedral. The flour mill in particular fired his imagination and later inspired him to write evocatively of its spacious basement floor that rose a full three stories to accommodate enormous boilers; its walls interlaced with iron catwalks; the upper floors with huge "overhanging machines gathered so close that all the pathways were mere tunnels, even to one my size"; and the industrial debris—springs, wheels, bolts, and jagged lengths of strapping. Over all this lay a dead, silencing dust that Neal would scuffle through, struck by the fact that not even this movement would cause one speck of dust to rise. "Everything was dead," he wrote, "still, no activity and no sound, save one thing: hundreds of solar-energized flies buzzed over me. I felt in a tomb, so isolated was I by the thick walls from rumbling 20th Street viaduct, only yards away."

3

THE SUMMER OF 1932 offered six-year-old Neal the most thrilling event of his life to that point. He and his father were to spend a month or two on a trip to visit Eva Jones, Neal Sr.'s sister, at her home in Unionville, Missouri. Neal needed no persuading to take part in this adventure, but he was further excited by the promise of fine home-cooked food from Eva's oven.

They left Denver in mid-June, missed the freight train that Neal Sr. had intended to hop for the first leg of their journey, and instead picked up a ride with a driver on his way to Cheyenne, Wyoming. It was the first time—but certainly not the last—that Neal Cassady would participate in a meandering road trip; in this case, the trip's indirectness was the result of the vagaries of hitchhiking.

The outward zigzag leg of their journey gave young Neal his first significant impressions of the vast American interior. Mountains, plains, ranches, rivers, and small towns rolled by, offering an endless backdrop of evocative sights, sounds, and smells that engendered a lifelong sense of wonder and exhilaration at the pleasures of driving across America's immense landscape. On that trip Neal first experienced what he later described as "the straining sensation of sitting peering over the dashboard at the bouncing headlights splaying before the tractor of a semi-rig—sweet sleep, lyric to the motor's drone, deep in the enormous bed behind the driver" and "vivid hours spent sighting a travel-changing landscape." It was the start of Neal Cassady's lifelong love affair with car trips.

The stay at Aunt Eva's place (which at the time was still bearing the scars of a tornado that had reduced a big two-story house to a single-story home with a cupola-like attic room) proved as idyllic as his father had promised, with its gatherings of elderly relatives "all porch-still and smoking the standard corncob from dawn to dusk." However, Neal's memories of the stay were also colored by the furtive prepubescent games he played with female cousins in a big barn, the start of yet another lifelong preoccupation.

They left the farm laden with samples of Aunt Eva's fresh-cooked chicken. Eva's son Kenneth later confirmed that Neal Sr. was already in the grip of alcoholism and had probably taken his young son on the trip to improve his hitchhiking chances.

"Neal, the old man? . . . He liked pretty bad to drink," said Kenneth Jones. "Pretty bad, you couldn't even have [vanilla] extract. I think he stayed with one of his . . . I suppose he'd be an uncle to him, and he stayed there and he'd drink their extracts, anything he could get hold of that had a little alcohol in it.

"He said people would pick him up much easier, much better . . . he used [Neal] for to hitchhike. They'd pick that little boy up, pick him and the little boy up."

The return journey to Denver was to prove just as exciting as those first heady impressions of barreling through Middle America had been for Neal, although this leg of the trip—from Missouri through Kansas and on to Colorado—also held its share of terrors. Taken mostly by the simple, direct, and, most important, cheap method of catching free rides on freight trains in the company of hobos and drifters, it proceeded smoothly until they boarded what Neal described as "this long-car thru-hotshot which rolled all night." It stopped once at a small town, somewhere in the middle of nowhere, to take on water. Neal's father and some of the hobos decided to hop off and find some drinking water for themselves and for "the poor kid," as little Neal was parched after feasting on Aunt Eva's salty chicken and had let everyone know about it.

The train suddenly jerked into motion and began pulling out of the station with Neal Jr. on board, picking up speed. Terrified, Neal could only stand, screaming into the night, as the lights of the town fell behind them. He saw no sign of his father. Some of the men hauled him

4

THE BUILDING INTO which Maud had been moved by her loving sons was a four-story red-brick Victorian Gothic edifice Neal would describe with his usual flair for aggrandizement as "that castle of my childhood." A notorious hangout for ex-convicts, musicians, alcohol and drug addicts, the odd pervert, and freelance prostitutes, the Snowden Apartments was a building, Neal recalled, that echoed with "assorted yelping catcalls, shouted curses, frightened screams and, topping all in my mind, feminine whoops of ribald laughter." A few of its occupants were poor, law-abiding folk just trying to get by peaceably, but it was a heaven-sent recruiting center for Jack and Ralph who, Neal said, ran a Fagin-like academy for aspiring pickpockets, sneak thieves, and burglars.

The Snowden occupied a large lot at the corner of Champa and 26th Streets so that, confusingly, your address could be either 2563 Champa or 910 26th Street, depending on which part of the complex your apartment was in and which of its two main entrances you used. Thus, during the next four years, local authorities had the Cassady-Daly families listed at different times as residing at what looked like different locations when, in fact, Maud and her brood had simply moved to another part of the same building—either a larger apartment when Jack and Ralph could afford it, or a smaller place when money was tight.

The apartment into which Neal was first taken was one of the Snowden's most humble, boasting only a small kitchenette and another large room that functioned as living room and bedroom, thanks to an arrangement by which a large bed (shared by one and all) could be stowed away into the wall. In that flat lived Maud, her twelve-year-old son, Jimmy, the now seven-year-old Neal, and the constantly whining three-year-old, Shirley Jean. In time, when the older Daly boys' fortunes improved and a bigger home was financially possible, Maud was able to retrieve her teenage daughters, Betty and Mae, from the Queen of Heaven orphanage into which they had been placed three years earlier. They returned as damaged, bedwetting adolescents, both of whom would marry young to get out from under Maud's wing.

Under his mother's care Neal was subject to a regime of solicitous scrutiny that drastically curtailed the roaming he had enjoyed during the eight months he lived with his father. He was now restricted to the block. He was only allowed trips to and from the Bakery, "a combination grocery and bake shop noted for cheap prices," which stood across the street. Maud would often send him there on errands and allow him to play on the wide sidewalk that fronted it . . . but not beyond. By coincidence, the block also contained the old barbershop where Neal's parents had last lived together.

Principal among the difficulties Neal now faced was Jimmy Daly, who was not happy to see his status challenged by the prodigal's return. He quickly made his feelings clear by resuming the hostilities that had marked Neal's life before his sojourn at the Metropolitan.

Jimmy was a vicious bully whose role models were the two older brothers who had so frequently assaulted Neal Sr. His campaign against young Neal was never waged when Maud was around, but manifested itself in fights he arranged between Neal and older, bigger boys and also through a sadistic regime of claustrophobic confinements in the fold-up bed. There he would imprison Neal in the stowaway position, leaving him for up to two hours. The experience must have been terrifying. Neal was forced to suffer this ordeal in silence, partly because he knew that if his calls for help resulted in his release by Maud he would receive a punishment beating from Jimmy, and partly because he did not want to use up the little air he had by yelling.

These torments introduced Neal to a skill he would make use of in later years: the apparent ability to suspend his mind and his body's metabolic rate, allowing time to race by. This practice, Neal said, began with the sensation of what he described as an "off-balanced wheel" whirling inside his head. As this whirling sensation picked up momentum it would "set up a loose fan-like vibration" as time gradually tripled its normal speed. While this was, Neal claimed, "strangely pleasant," it was also disturbing enough to frighten him at first, especially as this quickening of his brain's activity resisted even his most rigorous attempts to throw it off.

It has been suggested (not least by Carolyn Cassady) that this was the same heightened experience that Neal sought for the rest of his life; something she calls his "courtship of death" and which was also an unconscious re-creation of zazen—an oriental discipline in which the practitioner is able to empty his mind. It also evoked the "systematic derangement of the senses" that the French poet Arthur Rimbaud sought and the beats (and others) attempted to emulate. What Rimbaud and his friend Paul Verlaine accomplished largely through prodigious consumption of absinthe (a bitter liqueur enhanced by wormwood, a deadly poison), Neal, it seems, was apparently able to achieve by force of will, concentration, and inclination.

Despite Jimmy Daly's efforts to make his life miserable, Neal seems to have enjoyed his time at the Snowden, not least because he made two new firm friends there—Bobby Ragsdale and Art "Sonny" Barlow. Barlow was the son of "Blackie," the busted bootlegger who, after serving his time in prison, took up with a younger woman, ditched his wife and family, and founded a gas station empire. Possessed of what Neal admiringly described as an "abnormally large" penis, Sonny was also a strong swimmer. These three were inseparable, scurrying through the Snowden in search of thrills and the occasional glimpse of couples in flagrante delicto. There were ladder fire escapes to climb and alleys to explore, as well as ball games and physical contests for Neal to win, leaving the others to battle for second place. And there was Neal's first real relationship with a girl.

Vera Cummings, the daughter of a new Snowden tenant who became one of his mother's few friends, offered Neal a close and easy companionship that seems to have lasted until she reached her teens (she was two years older than Neal), when she began seeking the company of boys her own age. Before that time, Vera taught Neal that girls could be confided in and might even provide no-strings friendship. Until then, the only women he had encountered were his mother, other boys' mothers, over-painted whores, prim schoolmarms, harridan librarians, or giggling girls with whom he had shared a frisson of prurient voyeurism.

Not that his relations with Vera were without sexual overtones. According to Neal, Vera liked nothing better than to engineer situations whereby rough-and-tumble playacting became a physical tussle. These little dramas were inspired by lines from favorite songs they would sing together that gave them an excuse for Neal to play a spurned swain. These stimulating flirtations perhaps marked the last stage in Neal's sexual innocence. The summer of 1934 would see him embroiled in a much darker sexual scenario.

However, in the summer of 1933 Neal and his father set off on a trip that took them initially to Salt Lake City (where Neal Sr. was arrested for public drunkenness and young Neal spent three days in juvenile hall being terrorized by older boys until his father was released and ordered to leave town), and then south to Albuquerque, New Mexico, for a couple of weeks where they shared the tortillas and beans of hospitable Mexican field workers. Finally they headed to northern California and south again toward Los Angeles, via San Francisco and a "thrilling ferryboat ride across the bay from Oakland."

In San Jose father and son were separated again when the barber entrusted his boy into the care of a complete stranger, an Italian café owner. This episode was prompted by Neal Sr.'s desperation to find work in the Santa Clara Valley's fruit groves, something he soon discovered would be impossible with a child in tow.

The Italian man stepped forward and offered to take care of little Neal for him. Terrified, Neal watched his father clamber aboard a truck for what would be a two-month absence. Despite the man's unruly appearance and young Neal's fear of him, the man treated him with nothing but kindness and affection. He even presented Neal with a jewel-handled knife in a beautiful engraved sheath. He further offered to adopt the boy and to put him through college, but Neal Sr. declined when he eventually returned to collect his son.

Although the two Neals should have set about making their return to Denver in time for the new school year when Neal Sr.'s fruitpicking duties were finally done, they headed by bus (another first for the boy) for Los Angeles. There they spent three months in the company of a woman from Oklahoma (Neal called her "a California Okie") and her ugly but likeable son, who was about the same age as Neal. She and Neal Sr. had met in the fruit groves and begun an affair that they continued in the comparative luxury of an L.A. apartment. Christmas was fast approaching before Neal's father was able to prevail on the Travelers' Aid charity to fund their train fare back to Colorado.

The following summer the two Neals remained closer to home, staying as the live-in guests of one of Neal Sr.'s drinking buddies, a German (described by Neal as a feeble-minded drunkard with a thick mustache and heavy accent) who lived in a barn with his wife and twelve children in the Barnum district of southwest Denver. In the communal barn, during a riot of drinking, smoking, and cursing, the German's oldest sons launched themselves into the systematic gang rape of their sisters. Neal wrote in *The First Third*, "I soon followed the leader in screwing all the sisters small enough to hold down—and those bold enough to lead."

Summer breaks aside, life continued at its usual pace at the Snowden for the next year or so, until Maud, weakened by years of hardship and poverty, fell seriously ill early in May 1936. Her condition deteriorated rapidly, and on May 19 she died of bronchial pneumonia at Denver General Hospital. On May 23 the Daly family gathered at Sacred Heart Church for her funeral service, after which she was buried with her first husband, James, in Mount Olivet Cemetery. Confusingly, the mortuary record of her death named her as "Jean Cassidy," as did a terse notice published in the *Denver Post* on May 20.

Neal's reaction to his mother's death was one of studied numbness, a stance informed by what he described in an unfinished and unpublished fragment of *The First Third* as a "literary sophistication, precocious living out of how I thought boys of ten should act when told of Mother's death." With nothing but books to move or instruct him, Neal created an impassive facade that carried him through the family's grieving, leaving no one wise to the fact that he did not share their sense of loss for a parent who had never, he swore, kissed or hugged him.

A family council decided that Neal and Jimmy should live with Jack Daly and his wife, Rita, in their apartment on California Street. Jimmy got a job to help with family finances while Shirley Jean became the appointed burden of her older half sister, who was now Mrs. Betty Daly Cooper and living in the same apartment building. Neal was apparently happy with this arrangement, for he had come to worship the macho Jack, whose past beatings of his father the boy now condoned as understandable and excusable expressions of dismay at Neal Sr.'s incessant drinking.

One thing soon became clear: Jack and Rita Daly were not equipped to raise a gutsy young survivor with an adventurous spirit that would lead him into perpetual conflict with the law. In 1939 Neal was sent to live with his father again.

5

ACCORDING TO Neal's own account of his eventful adolescence, he stole his first car in 1940 when he was only fourteen years old. In 1947, at the age of twenty-one, he decided to retire from auto theft. It was, Neal claimed, usually just a case of borrowing, not stealing. He later claimed that by his own definition he had "borrowed" some five hundred vehicles in that seven-year period. Inevitably from time to time he would be caught, and while he was lucky enough to get away with a warning on many occasions, at other times he would find himself locked up.

Before embarking on his borrowing binge, Neal enjoyed more than his fair share of adrenaline rushes from other adventures, most of them the usual scrapes that teenagers find themselves in when excess energy and curiosity outstrip caution or common sense. In many ways, though, he appears to have toed the line during the first year or so of his life with Jack and Rita Daly. Credit for this must partly go to John Harley Schmitt, a young man who was at the time studying for the priesthood. Schmitt was impressed by the boy he first encountered in August 1937 when Neal, age eleven, was given the chance to spend a few weeks at Camp Santa Maria in the Rockies. This was a Roman Catholic summer camp for poor children. It was built on the site of a former hotel resort that had been donated in 1930 by a philanthropic Denver couple.

Subjected to a full-force Cassady charm offensive, Schmitt found himself corralled into becoming Neal's spiritual godfather when the boy was baptized into the Catholic Church in July 1938. Demonstrating an early enthusiasm for the rituals of the Catholic faith, Neal had mastered both the intricacies of the catechism and the Latin mass. For a time he also served as an altar boy at the Holy Ghost Church, assisting the parish priest, Father Leo Slattery. But it was the newly ordained Father Schmitt to whom he would turn later, especially when the presence of a priest might be counted on to mollify even the hardest-hearted law enforcement officer or distraught mother.

By October 1939 Jack and Rita were finding Neal tough going and returned him to the care of his father. Enrolled at Cole Junior High, Neal achieved grades that started out among the best of his class but soon began to slide—as did his attendance record. School inquiries and social workers' reports in 1940 reflected a growing concern from all parties. Neal's obsession with sex was now well underway. Some years later he informed one of his best friends, Jimmy Holmes, how he had made love to one of his father's women.

Holmes told Tom Christopher: "His father brought a woman home one night, and they slept in one bed. Neal was in the bed, you know, and they made love and all that stuff, and got up the next morning and [Neal's father] went to work . . . and Neal was there with the woman, and Neal was pretty aggressive and I guess he got the woman to . . . I'm sure it wasn't the other way around . . . well, I'm not sure . . . anyway they made love, and about two years later Neal goes to school, and he has a teacher . . . damned if that isn't the same teacher."

Neal's story may well have been true, but once again there is the suspicion of literary embellishment, the flourish of coincidence that turns a sordid story into a piece of entertainment.

Neal also periodically struck out from Denver on solo trips. In May 1940, when he was just fourteen, a Denver School District investigator who called at the house where Neal was supposed to be living with his father was told by the woman who came to the door that she believed that "the boy was in St. Louis" and that Neal Sr. would "do his best" to get him to return home. On another occasion young Neal hitchhiked to Indianapolis to watch the car races. He also later claimed to have worked as a parking attendant in Los Angeles when he was sixteen.

Neal's absence from his father's care was more generally due to the fact that he spent more time living with friends' families than he did with

Neal Sr. In late 1950 he wrote an affectionate description of that time to John Clellon Holmes, including the following reflections about his encounter with a Native American boy in the course of his first real job, as a bicycle courier for the Dime Delivery Company, carrying messages and small packages. The amount Neal earned was entirely dependent on speed, for the company paid only for each successfully completed run.

"This is where I shone; you see," Neal wrote. "I had a magnificent French racing bicycle. Whereas the other bums made from 8 to 12 dollars a week, with my beautiful machine (with the rear wheel almost directly under the seat post and the shorter chain thus needed was further added to speed by a large 32 prong front sprocket and a 7 pronged rear sprocket; a single that could do 50 MPH!) I always cleared some sum in the teens and often 20 a week. So, with ease I led the field except for one, Ben Gowen. . . . At payday I watched the sum noted on each pay envelope as it was passed out, just to see who came closest to me so I could gloat and earn more next week.

"I had been doing this for some weeks and knew no one would ever catch me or even come close to making as much dough as I did, when this Ben Gowen came to work for D.D. At the end of the week he was less than a dollar from me!"

Cassady finally questioned his rival with a mixture of awe and incredulity as to how he could do so well, especially since he rode a series of stolen bikes that were usually junk. "Just keep going," was the only reply Gowen gave.

"I really came to love the guy along about then; he was not full of loud bullshit like the others, etc., and besides, I secretly knew he was faster than I. . . . Ben and I became inseparable during waking hours, working and thieving around the clock. Ben's large capacity for larceny blended well with my own undeveloped vein and so we spent full nights touring the city for any loot that struck our eyes. Auto accessories; including seats, radios, spotlights etc., likely articles in store fronts on secluded streets—a simple matter to bash in the window and run, etc., etc.;

we'd always end the night snitching bottles of freshly delivered milk from doorsteps etc. We finally quit our jobs and took to selling auto parts we'd stolen, then, vacuum cleaners from hallways of the many apt. houses I knew my way around in. Finally we took to stealing poultry, yessir, big fat hens in the revealing light of day. We got a good price and were never quizzed (possibly because the crooked owners of the fowl houses would immediately dunk the birds in scalding water and skin their feathers in 20 seconds; who could identify their own. lousy chickens then?) so, we decided to make a steady business out of it for a while. At first we'd barge about in the henhouse, floundering in the stinking shit, lunging after the birds with squawks and fearful cackles in our ears and chicken feathers and droppings plastered to our sweating clothes. Later on, with experience, we got a fine hunk of baling wire, bent the end to fit their legs and plucked them off with ease; two or three every minute stuffed in the loot sack of burlap."

During the period that Neal was supposedly under his father's wing, the old man had become a laborer with the Works Project Administration (WPA). Initiated by President Franklin D. Roosevelt in 1935 as a successful bid to put back to work the eleven million or so people left unemployed in the Great Depression, the WPA would employ more than eight million workers on its massive road-building and other public works projects over the next eight years. As soon as payday came around, Neal Sr. would go on a drinking spree, sometimes ending up in jail. On one occasion, when an investigator from the Catholic Charities came calling, he was splendidly incoherent and spent most of the visit lurching maniacally from room to room.

His dereliction of parental duty was first apparent when Neal's sister Shirley Jean was sent by the exhausted Betty to live with Neal Sr. It was less than a year after Maud's death, and social workers and neighbors had grown increasingly alarmed for Shirley Jean's well-being. On October 13, 1939, a Denver juvenile court hearing decided that she should be taken into the care of the Denver Catholic Charities. Their first task was to arrange for the nine-year-old to be baptized. Her father undertook to pay $7.50 every two weeks as contribution to her upkeep at St. Clara's, the foster home to which she was consigned, and to provide "such clothing as was necessary." Neal Sr. would default on both commitments, and Shirley Jean was doomed to spend most of her teens out of touch with her natural family. She was also the innocent focus of resentment from her foster parents about her father's lack of inclination to meet even the most basic responsibilities. Neal Cassady would remain haunted with guilt about the injustice of his sister's raising and would try to make amends in later years, only to find that Shirley Jean had been irreparably damaged by her upbringing. She was an emotional casualty, the victim of long bouts of manic depression.

It was no more than two weeks after Shirley Jean's departure that Neal moved in with his father, and only nine months after that, in August 1940, that the same juvenile court decreed that he, too, should be taken from his father's care and placed in another Catholic establishment, the J. K. Mullen Home for Boys.

Run by the Order of Christian Brothers, a teaching order with a particularly stern approach to physical discipline, the home managed to contain Neal only until New Year's Eve, when he fled the remorseless regime, taking some gym equipment with him. He moved back to his father's place, which he used as a base for his sporadic travels.

Throughout 1940 the Denver education authorities were tested by Neal's serial absenteeism. In fact at the age of thirteen he was already on the night shift at the Gates Rubber Company, one of Denver's biggest employers, where he had secured a job recapping tires. As Sheldon Emeson told Tom Christopher, "He was working there from something like eight, nine, ten o'clock at night, until three or four in the morning, or actually six in the morning, and he'd have to clean up 'cause it's dirty, dirty work, then be ready to go to school." Neal was able, Emeson said, to recap a tire in half the time it was supposed to take, "because of his dexterity, speed, and, I suggest, questionable safety factor . . . he was really burning the candle at both ends at that time."

Some aspects of school life did appeal to Neal. He shined at both football and basketball. Appointing himself manager of Cole's basketball team, Neal once cut into an argument over what the squad would be named. The usual testosterone-fueled suggestions (Tigers, Rapiers, Stallions) were being tossed around when Neal announced that their team would be called the Weavers. Confronted by a room full of puzzled faces, he quipped, "Don't you get it? Always making baskets!"

Harboring dreams of maybe becoming a professional football player (his target was to play left end for Notre Dame), Neal discovered that he was color-blind, a condition that most probably led to his being rejected by the draft board some four years later. (Later still he successfully managed to keep this disability secret while working for the Southern Pacific Railroad; he learned to identify signal lights by position and permutation, not color.) Typically, he told some friends that the draft board rejected him because he told them he still wet the bed; others he informed that he had "admitted" to same-sex proclivities.

Neal was now almost constantly on the move, staying with various friends until his welcome wore out. So it was, in October 1941, that he found himself sitting, naked and eating breakfast, in the kitchen of a house in the 2200 block of Gilpin Street, the home of John and Lucille Walters, an amiable couple of elderly alcoholics who allowed all types of waifs and strays to share their home. If Neal was taken aback when the door opened and a complete stranger demanded to know who he was and what business he had being there, he apparently responded brazenly: "The question is, who are you?" That was how Neal Cassady met Justin Brierly, the Walters' nephew, a man who was to have a significant impact on Neal's life during the next few years.

• • •

When Brierly died, in April 1985, at age 79, the *Rocky Mountain News* obituary characterized him as "one of Denver's most distinguished educators" and noted that he had retired from the city's public schools in 1971 after thirty-six years of service. A graduate of New York's Columbia University, he had helped form a talent agency in that city before returning to Denver, where he played a major role in establishing the Central City Opera festival. An English literature teacher at East High School for fourteen years (the post he was holding when he stumbled across Neal in the Walters' home), he had then been appointed supervisor of college and scholarship guidance for the Denver Public Schools. Between 1937 and 1948 he was also executive manager of the Central City Opera Association. Also a practicing attorney, Brierly became assistant to the president of Temple Buell College (later renamed Colorado Women's College) in his retirement.

During World War II, Brierly spent some time in England at the invitation of Prime Minister Winston Churchill, acting as a consultant on the evacuation of children from urban areas at greatest risk of German bombing raids. During his fifteen years as a counselor in Denver, Brierly developed a groundbreaking guidance program that helped raise funds to send needy students to college. He also founded the Martha Faure Carson Dance Library (now part of the University of Denver) to commemorate a longtime dance teacher and friend. A trustee of Colorado Outward Bound School, a board member of the American Council of Émigrés in the Professions, and adviser to the board of the Institute of International Education, Brierly was also a member of the Denver Art Museum, the Columbia University Club of Denver, the Phi Delta Phi honorary legal society, and the American Civil Liberties Union of Colorado.

Brierly was most likely also a closet homosexual, and it was probably through him that Neal Cassady would first discover and explore gay sex and serve as a hustler in Denver's gay community. One of those convinced of this is Ed Uhl, an acquaintance of Neal's at the time. From his Nevada home near Las Vegas, Ed and his wife, Jeannie (who was briefly one of Neal's girlfriends), gave an interview to Tom Christopher in which Jeannie said that she never got the impression that there was "anything physical" between Neal and Brierly's male friends. Ed thought otherwise. "Guys don't give other people money for nothin'," he said. "If he needed twenty dollars or somethin' . . . he had two or three guys around Denver that he could go see, and in a short while he could have ten, twenty dollars. He never did elaborate on how he got the twenty dollars." Others too were convinced that Neal was a sometime homosexual hustler, although the consensus seemed to be that it was less a question of his sexual preference than of his pragmatism and need for money. Gay sex was a tradable commodity, like the junk he'd once collected from gutters and alleys.

Neal's relationship with Brierly, whatever its exact nature, certainly paid off in educational terms. Recognizing Neal's keen intelligence and seeing in him a far greater potential than had been nurtured by other teachers, Brierly began to structure Neal's voracious reading to include more important authors. For the next three years Neal would frequent libraries with almost religious fervor, indulging a love of literature and ideas that would stay with him for life. Brierly also instigated discussion sessions to ensure that Neal's questions were answered and his comprehension extended; he even ensured that Neal's finances improved, at least in the early days of their relationship, by paying him to do household chores in various Brierly family homes around Gilpin Street.

Whatever Brierly's motives were (and there is little doubt that he was sincere in his efforts to help not just Neal but many others who were not fulfilling their potential due to poverty or other circumstances), he soon discovered that this particular young protégé was not about to behave any better than he had in the past. Neal continued to roam the countryside in search of thrills, to steal cars for his adventures, and to build his reputation for the enthusiastic sexual conquest of any girls and women who crossed his path.

In June 1943 Neal's inclination for larcenous adventure led him to Los Angeles, where he was arrested for joyriding. He was given a six-month custodial sentence to be served at a forestry camp. Brierly—whose name Neal gave to the California authorities—was notified. He wrote Neal a brief note of regret on July 2, only to learn ten days later that Neal had already absconded from the camp. According to Neal's later account to Kerouac, which was used in *Visions of Cody*, he had returned to Denver, after escaping from the forestry camp, and linked up once again with his father. During the following winter, he traveled with Neal Sr. to work on the building of a steel mill in Provo, Utah. In fact, he was unable to work on the site (he was still not eighteen, the minimum age for the job), so he drifted back to California in time to attend the funeral of his twenty-four-year-old alcoholic half-sister, Mae, in January 1944. While there he was detained by the police and sent to the county jail as punishment for going AWOL from the forestry camp. On March 24 he was released and "advised" to go back to Denver. It is not known if Justin Brierly, a man of some influence, played any part in this negotiation, but there is a strong likelihood that he did.

• • •

Next came the worst scrape of Neal Cassady's young life. On Fourth of July weekend 1944 two friends of Neal—Marshall "Speed" Chrisman and John Warren—broke into a Denver house with felonious intent and were disturbed by a sleepy eight-year-old girl. They promptly tied her up to ensure her silence. While this was going on, the girl's father, who had been awakened by the scuffles and whispers in his daughter's room, called the police from his bedside phone. As Chrisman and Warren left the house they were arrested by officers Al Lohr and Eugene Ater, whose subsequent investigations led them to Neal, who had allowed Chrisman to stash items from other burglaries at his apartment. Other stolen property from previous break-ins was also found in Neal's apartment, so he had little option but to admit to receiving stolen goods. On August 18 he pleaded guilty in court and five days later was taken to the Colorado State Reformatory at Buena Vista (as prisoner number 10805) to begin an indeterminate term of incarceration that would, in fact, last until June 2, 1945, when he was granted parole.

Neal's Buena Vista admittance form makes interesting reading, not least because he informed the office that he was an orphan, stating that his mother had died in May 1936 and his father succumbed in the spring of 1938. This was apparently accepted without question and the lie became a matter of official record.

The Buena Vista form also noted that Neal's half-brothers—Bill, Jack, and Jimmy—were currently serving in the U.S. Army while Ralph was residing in Alaska. Shirley Jean was still languishing at St. Clara's. Neal's vital statistics were given as: height: 5'10", weight: 150 lbs., eyes: blue, hair: brown, religion: Roman Catholic.

According to this document, Neal was also registered as being left-handed, wearing size 10 shoes, and having two brown moles on his shoulder blades. His nose had been broken at some time, the Buena Vista doctor noted. That injury, which would restrict Neal's breathing for the rest of his life, was in fact the result of a crash he'd been in when he and a buddy had been out driving with two girls in a rented car. Neal had asked the friend to steer while he kissed his date. His companion misunderstood, thinking that Neal simply wanted him to watch his technique, and did not take the wheel. "We ran smack-blam into a telephone pole," Neal recalled. "Split the bumper in two, flattened all the tires, his girl broke a rib, and since we couldn't pay the damages, we all went to jail."

In the Buena Vista document, Neal's previous recorded brushes with the law were listed as one arrest for speeding and misuse of license in

Denver six days before Christmas 1941 (a charge that was dismissed without prejudice by a police court judge), and another, also in Denver, on August 3, 1942, for auto theft. On that occasion he was released by a Sgt. Cook into the safekeeping of Justin Brierly. Finally, there was his imprisonment for car theft in Los Angeles in 1943. He made a full statement admitting his guilt: "I accepted some stolen tires, sold them and received $9.00 commission. I knew that they were stolen. I plead guilty," he told the court.

During his stay at Buena Vista, Neal apparently played it by the book, fulfilling his work details satisfactorily and becoming part of the camp's basketball team. Initially put to work on a field gang, he was then moved to the camp dairy—a job that, he told Brierly in a letter written on October 8, 1944, had him rising at 4 A.M. to milk eight cows until 6:15, when he took them out to pasture. After a 6:45 breakfast he would clean the cow barn until 9:30, carry out miscellaneous duties until noon, eat lunch, grind corn or haul hay until 2:30 P.M., take a nap until 3:30, bring the cows back to their barn, eat supper at 5 P.M., milk the cows again between 6 and 8:30, carry the milk to the camp kitchen, and retire for the night at 9:30 P.M.

Later that month Neal told Brierly that the onset of winter and the shortening of daylight hours meant that "we get up at 5 o'clock now, instead of 4 as we had been." He added wryly, "Bankers hours, huh?"

In the same letter he noted, "They have the Harvard Classics up here, the five-foot shelf of books. I've read about 2 feet of it, very nice, I especially enjoyed Voltaire and Bacon (Francis)."

There was disturbing information in the last lines of the letter. "Please excuse the penmanship, as I can only see out of one eye, this morning I took the cows out to pasture but on the way they ran out of the road into the corn field, the jackass I was riding couldn't run fast enough to head them, so I jumped off & started to tie him to a barbed wire fence so I could chase the cows on foot, just as I tied the reins to the wire he jerked so hard it pulled a staple out of the fence post and into my left eye. It gorged [*sic*] a chunk out of my eyeball, but luckily failed to hit the cornea. I may lose that eye."

Responding with a letter of concern to James Thomas, the new warden of Buena Vista, Brierly received a prompt reply confirming the gist of Neal's account but stressing that, in the opinion of an eye specialist, Neal was in no danger of losing his sight. In fact, Thomas wrote, Neal's eye already seemed to be in good shape and he was again taking part in sports and reading just as much as he had before.

Letters continued to flow between patron and protégé during the next few months, and Neal obviously widened his reading to take up what would become an abiding interest in philosophy. In February 1945 he wrote Brierly: "I rather pride myself on how completely I have become conditioned to reformatory life, adjustments in my case began with the intellect, which after some months led to control of the passions, then 90% of the battle was over, after that my psychological pattern ebbed into an objective recognition. I only hope I can retain some degree of the mental ease I have developed up here when I again plunge into civilian life. I feel certain the only way is thru a study of Philosophy & applying all the Gems of wisdom gathered by sages from Socrates to Santayana, while concentrating on the more important (to me) ones."

In a sad coda to that letter, Neal advised Brierly: "There appears to be a slight chance I may be able to obtain my youngest sister when I get out. She will be 15 in May & will graduate from the 8th grade at St. Clara's Orphanage. The usual procedure when a girl finishes the 8th grade at the orphanage is to give her a years employment as a maid in some people's home who will accept her. I'm working on several angles now, where some close friends of my will need either need a maid or adopt her in June when Shirley (her name) gets out."

If this was a none-too-subtle hint for Brierly to help find a home for his sister, or even to provide one for her himself, it met with no response. Shirley Jean's troubled life would continue along the course that others set for her.

Paroled on June 2, Neal returned to Denver and got a job vulcanizing tires. He picked up his frenetic social life, bumming meals, drinks, and a place to stay from friends who were apparently aware that they were being exploited but seemed nonetheless happy to oblige. Life with and around Neal was never boring, and apparently providing a diner meal and a glass of beer, the loan of a car, or a bed for a couple of nights was never too high a price to pay for his company.

One of these friends was Jimmy Holmes, a keen and skilled pool player. Holmes was astonished to be approached one day at Pederson's, one of two downtown pool halls, by an eighteen-year-old kid of striking appearance (shoes but no socks and a khaki Army shirt) who made him an offer he couldn't refuse. In a torrent of persuasive words, Neal proposed that in return for Holmes teaching him everything he knew about pool, he would teach him the glories of literature and philosophy. Somewhere in that flood of largesse was an additional offer to hotwire a car and drive Holmes to watch the next Notre Dame football game. Holmes was impressed until he realized that the next Notre Dame game was being held only twenty-four hours later . . . a thousand miles away.

Confused, intrigued, and overwhelmed, Holmes decided that Neal's fifteen-minute sales pitch (Jack Kerouac, who learned about it from Neal much later, described it as "the first great conman proposition of his life") had to be inspired by starvation. Taking him home for a meal with his family, Holmes went on to teach Neal the intricacies of pool as well as how to cheat at cards. He provided Neal with his first suit (a snazzy brown tweed number) and—even more generously—a place to stay, off and on, for the next three years.

Jim Holmes's grandmother put up with Neal's presence in her house but never really lost her initial reservations about him. These were largely based, Holmes later recounted, on the extreme shortness of Neal's hair, a sure sign that he had just come out of jail. Grandma Holmes was concerned what her neighbors would make of this obvious jailbird, and she never did rest easy when Neal was around. She was convinced that he was going to lead Jimmy astray.

And there were always the girls. Neal appears to have continued cutting a path through Denver's female population. One resonant affair was with a girl named Mary Ann Freedland. She lived on Cherry Street (thus rejoicing in the nickname "Cherry Mary"). Their romance was cut short when her mother learned that Mary was skipping school to spend time with this hoodlum. When she contacted her local priest and asked him to intervene, the resulting encounter proved so memorable that it formed part of the fabric of a legendary letter Neal Cassady wrote some years later, a letter that, without any exaggeration, would change the history of American letters. Before it became fiction, though, it was humdrum fact enlivened by serendipity. The priest turned out to be Father Schmitt, Neal's godfather, who subsequently tried to keep in touch with Neal, as befitted his guiding role, although in fact this would be the last time they met. "He was too elusive for me to keep up with," Schmitt admitted to Tom Christopher.

Neal's relationship with Jeannie Stewart (later Uhl) lasted a little longer, and during the spring and summer of 1945 the couple would drive to an old mining town in the mountains near Central City where Jeannie's mother owned a nine-room holiday home. Although usually occupied during the summer months by Jeannie's grandmother, the house was vacant in 1945 because the woman had fractured her hip. After breaking into the house, Neal and Jeannie used it as a headquarters for partying, sometimes inviting up to twenty friends who were thrilled to be able to get drunk, stoned, and laid without fear of discovery. The cabin boasted a player piano and closets packed with Victorian costumes, so the house gradually came to resemble a frontier town bordello at the height of the gold rush.

Otherwise Neal appears to have divided his time between Justin Brierly and the Denver demimonde, consisting mainly of his coterie of adoring female companions and the male buddies who split their leisure hours between the YMCA, Pederson's Pool Hall, and the Mir-o Bar, all of which vanished or changed beyond recognition during the gentrification of the district during the 1980s and 1990s. It was at Pederson's that Neal was to become reacquainted with Al Hinkle early in 1946. A contemporary of Neal's at East High when they were both sixteen, Hinkle had returned to Denver after a couple of years of high adventure.

Hinkle was a tall, rangy, handsome young man who had dropped out of East High at sixteen to work on a labor crew building a military camp in the mountains near Leadville. He had then trained briefly as an aircraft instruments mechanic and moved to Utah before finding work at an aircraft factory in Los Angeles. Returning briefly to Denver when he turned eighteen, he soon enrolled in the merchant marines to avoid being drafted into the military. After a memorable voyage from Los Angeles to New York via the Panama Canal, they traveled down the west coast of South America, where Hinkle and his crewmates were left stranded and unpaid in New York. There he signed on to a ship sailing to France and back. This allowed him to raise enough money to return to Denver, where he took a job with the Gates Rubber Company. In Denver he acquired an old convertible, which made him a prime target for the always-in-need-of-a-free-ride Neal.

Neal provided Al Hinkle with much-needed companionship and excitement. "I kinda liked him," Hinkle told Tom Christopher. "He had a lotta fire and enthusiasm, and he seemed to know a lot of people. I think maybe 'cause I'd been away, and then when I got back to Denver and started on that job we were working . . . I was probably a little lonely . . . so Neal seemed pretty exciting to me."

Drawn into Neal's circle of friends, Hinkle soon joined in the cabin parties and, thanks to Jeannie Stewart, acquired a new girlfriend in the shape of another Jeannie—Jeannie Williams, Jeannie Stewart's best friend. Hinkle noted that Neal's Jeannie was also clearly the object of Ed Uhl's affection, a situation that Neal was quick to use to his advantage. Uhl, son of a rancher with a spread near Cheyenne, owned a car, so whenever Neal needed a ride somewhere with Jeannie he would get her to ask Uhl. Lovesick Uhl could never refuse Jeannie's requests and so came to act as unpaid chauffeur to the couple.

Free rides were oxygen to Neal Cassady. According to Jimmy Holmes, one Cassady trick was to rent a truck for the weekend, disconnect the odometer after a couple of miles, and then head for the hills. He was also apparently able to acquire cheap gas, so his costs were minimal. Sometimes, to offset the expenditure further he would drive to the site of Buffalo Bill Cody's grave (which lay a few miles away from the cabin resort) where someone had installed a wishing well. There he would climb down into the well to retrieve the coins tossed in by tourists.

Neal's world was full of obliging girls, pals who would bail him out when money got tight, marijuana to smoke when he wanted to get mellow, and Benzedrine when the party needed to last all night. (Like teenagers all over America, the Denver crowd had picked up on the trick of removing the Benzedrine-soaked strips from nasal inhalers and chewing them to get a delicious rush.)

The agreeable summer days of 1945 continued in this undemanding fashion until one afternoon when Neal and some friends strolled into a Walgreen's to grab a soda and he caught sight of a beautiful blonde fifteen-year-old sitting with a friend in a booth. Simultaneously awestruck and smitten, he told his companions, "I'm gonna marry that girl."

LuAnne Henderson had entered Neal Cassady's life.

6

BORN IN NORTHEASTERN COLORADO and partly raised by her father when her parents divorced, LuAnne Henderson had come to Denver in 1942 at the age of twelve. She had come with her mother, who had just remarried and found work running Thelma's Crystal Bar, a pub inside McBiddy's Restaurant on Curtis Street. Her new stepfather was a serviceman stationed at the nearby air base at Lowry Field. For a few months LuAnne's relationship with him was uneventful; then he and her mother returned home drunk from a Christmas party and LuAnne watched, horrified and helpless, as her stepfather subjected her mother to a vicious, bloody assault. Later, LuAnne would tell Tom Christopher, "I was torn between emotions. I was so crazy about my mother, but my father had raised me that women just did not drink. I never saw a woman drink. I never saw my father drink, although I found out later my father was a drinker. But I was not aware of it. . . . I'd never been exposed to [alcohol] and I was very much ashamed that my mother drank."

That night LuAnne and her mother found refuge with the stepfather's mother. LuAnne stayed awake all night staring at her mother's battered face and stroking it comfortingly. To her astonishment, when they returned home the following morning LuAnne's mother silently set about cooking breakfast for her hungover assailant. Luanne asked her mother, "How can you do that after what he did to you?" Receiving no answer, she headed for the living room and a confrontation with her stepfather.

"The more I talked, the more rage would come," said LuAnne, "and I finally ended it with . . . 'If my brothers were here you wouldn't be doin' this, and if I were big enough, if I were a man, I would beat you.' He was very quiet, and he very quietly called my mother and said, 'You better get this kid outta here or I'm gonna kill her,' which I could understand later.

I was so angry at the time, though. I was daring him to hit me. I got over it, I accepted it, but I don't think it ever truly left my heart, the resentment that he could do such a thing to my mother. My resentment got to a point where I had to get it out. I had a lot of hate and resentment in me when I was young."

The resentful LuAnne showed an almost complete lack of interest in school. While she presumably attended Morey Junior High School, East High, and West High, her attendance record was, like Neal's, sporadic at best. "I really didn't go much beyond the ninth grade," she admitted, although she did enjoy the attention she received when she became a cheerleader. Forging a firm friendship with a girl named Lois Williams, LuAnne dropped out of school and took up a working life that was no steadier than her education had been. Flitting between employers, she was apparently content to shrug and move on to the next dead-end burger joint job whenever her current boss ran out of patience.

There was, for instance, the time LuAnne and Lois—who were both under the legal age for full-time employment but lied well enough to deceive a personnel manager—secured work as telephone exchange operators. Scarcely a week into this job they were on a lunch break, bumped into some friends, and decided it was too pleasant a day to spend slaving over a hot switchboard. LuAnne persuaded Lois to call in and tell their supervisor that they had been involved in a car accident. Understandably nervous and increasingly flustered, Lois needlessly elaborated the deceit by telling the woman that LuAnne had been thrown through the windshield and that she was calling from the hospital.

"I was going crazy standing next to her at the phone booth," LuAnne recalled, laughing. "I couldn't have gone back to work if I'd wanted to, unless I walked in with bandages. I said, 'Why did you tell 'em I went through the windshield? My face would be a mass of scars!' Anyway, that was the end of our telephone operating jobs."

The arrival of Neal Cassady in LuAnne's life, besides throwing her into a whirlwind relationship full of romance, excitement, and adventure, also forestalled another more dangerous and potentially ruinous association. At fifteen LuAnne had blossomed into an exceptional beauty with bronze hair and a stunning peaches-and-cream complexion. She also had a breathless little-girl voice, which made her even more attractive to many men. There are indications—but no proof—that her stepfather's attitude toward her was becoming inappropriate. LuAnne would never go into specific details, but she did say that things had become "uncomfortable" for her at home, adding revealingly, "I automatically assumed it had to be my fault somewhere, and I was so frightened that my mother would find out and be hurt, and blame me, so I just started staying away from home. I think my mother might've had suspicions, but I really and truly don't know to this day if [she] was aware of what was going on, or she thought it was simply a clash of personalities."

Today this might be seen as the encoded language of a victim of sexual abuse, but whatever the situation, Neal Cassady, an unlikely knight in shining armor, was about to ride in to the rescue, albeit fueled more by lust and self-interest than chivalry. Neal brazenly asked Jeannie Stewart to approach LuAnne and invite her into the cabin party circle, ostensibly as a date for another boy. It was a classic Cassady maneuver, with neither of the female parties remotely aware of his real objective. So, with his customary flair, Neal set about covertly courting LuAnne while continuing to squire the unsuspecting Jeannie. He also pursued sexual prey in a series of one-night stands. These were not without complications, however, and LuAnne would be stunned one day when Neal produced a letter he had just received from a girl named Betty—attached to it was a single golden curl of infant hair. Unabashed, Neal admitted to LuAnne that he was indeed—as Betty claimed in her note—the baby's father. The unfortunate Betty was not alone in her plight. Over the years it emerged that Neal had abandoned several girls when they became pregnant.

During the winter of 1945 Neal found himself in trouble with the law again. Although the reason on this occasion remains unclear, it seems he faced the very real prospect of a return to Buena Vista for being in violation of his parole. Jeannie Stewart prevailed upon Ed Uhl to drive downtown to see if he could bail Neal out or, failing that, offer some other help. While talking to the desk sergeant, Uhl also fell into conversation with a police captain who asked where he was from. On learning that Uhl hailed from a ranching family, the captain waxed lyrical about country life and hard work, concluding that it was exactly the kind of experience young city boys like Neal should have. Before he knew what was happening, Uhl found himself agreeing to act as Neal's guarantor, and with Neal's grateful agreement the two of them were soon headed north for what would be a three-month sojourn to the Uhl ranch.

During his stay, which was frequently interrupted by trips into Cheyenne or Sterling for the odd beer and something like a good time, Neal proved that learning from experience was not one of his strong points; while fixing a fence, he again almost lost an eye to a flying staple.

"Any higher and he'd've lost his eye," Uhl told Tom Christopher. "He took it out, and he's bleeding profusely, and I said, 'Boy, you're lucky.'"

Apart from that incident and the couple of nights he spent in a local jail after a New Year's celebration got out of hand, Neal apparently enjoyed his stay at the Uhl ranch, despite the fact that it was a pretty Spartan existence. As Jeannie Stewart explained: "At that time the old house up there had no electricity, no indoor plumbing—that was put in after Ed and I married—the water froze up in the winter, so you carried it from the spring and the well. So they had nothing else to do but sit around the evening and read till you couldn't stand it anymore, and go to bed. There was just a battery radio, and you were very stingy with batteries—you only used it for news and things."

The book that Neal turned to most during those dark, cold nights at the ranch was a battered copy of *The Standard Dictionary of Facts.* It was the biography section that interested him most, Uhl recalled. Neal's apparent belief was that you didn't need to read a whole book about someone if you had a thumbnail description to work with. "Then," said Neal, "if someone mentions the name, I can just tell 'em where the guy was born and where he lived and blah blah blah."

Shorthand knowledge became a staple of Neal's concept of learning. He had a prodigious memory and collecting facts obsessed him, though his knowledge often remained superficial. This led many people to mistakenly believe he was astonishingly well educated, which was no doubt partly his intention.

On April 1, 1946, Neal returned to Denver—and to LuAnne and Jeannie Stewart. He quickly settled back into his old ways—having more fun than the law would allow, shooting pool, hanging out with his male buddies, and frequenting the public library to devour more books. Meanwhile, he went on two-timing LuAnne and Jeannie, and taking up with any other woman he could get.

Early in July 1946, LuAnne and Lois joined a party of friends who broke into a holiday cabin near the small town of Golden, now a western suburb of a much-expanded Denver. The ensuing party was in full swing when the local sheriff and some deputies raided the place and hauled everyone off to jail. Although she was terrified, LuAnne brazened it out and refused to give her name and address to officers. As outraged parents came to pick up their errant offspring, LuAnne and Lois found themselves locked up for the night with a wild, eighteen-year-old blond woman named Helen Lee Gould, who had been charged with drowning her eighteen-month-old daughter in a swamp. (Seven months later, having been found guilty at the Denver district court, she was sentenced to fifteen years in prison.)

Shaken by this brush with the harshest of realities, LuAnne did not put up any kind of argument when her mother announced that she was to spend the next three weeks in the wilderness of the Rockies, in the town of Grand Lake, where one of LuAnne's brothers had settled. While LuAnne was away, Neal turned the full force of his charm on her mother, announcing that he wanted to marry LuAnne. With her mother's blessing (prompted, perhaps, by relief that someone else was going to take care of an increasingly feisty and rebellious teenager in whom her husband was showing too much interest), LuAnne was about to find out she was to be a bride. The first she knew about it was on her return to Denver for a court appearance at which Neal, with a theatrical flourish, produced a marriage license. After being given a token thirty-five-dollar fine for trespassing and a ruling that she should be placed under better supervision, LuAnne returned home to discover that her mother had already bought a wedding suit for Neal. There was obviously no doubt in her mother's mind that LuAnne would agree to Neal's unorthodox proposal, and indeed, although understandably surprised, LuAnne was delighted to do so. The following morning when the couple went downtown for obligatory blood tests, LuAnne, who had not eaten anything during the excitement of the past thirty-six hours, fainted, leaving a trail of lipstick on Neal's T-shirt as she slid to the floor. Later that afternoon LuAnne's mother and Lois Williams helped her into her wedding outfit and the two girls caught a streetcar to meet up with Neal, Jimmy Holmes, and two other friends—Bill Tomson and Jimmy Penoff—all of whom were appropriately dressed in their Sunday best clothes. Another streetcar ride took them to the rectory of a west Denver church and the briefest of ceremonies conducted by the Reverend R. A. Kerby. Holmes and Lois signed the marriage certificate as witnesses . . . and that was it. August 1 saw Neal and LuAnne legally joined in matrimony.

LuAnne had her own theory concerning Neal's rush into marriage. "When I went to jail, that night, when I didn't turn up at eleven o'clock, from what I understood later from other people, Neal was going crazy trying to find me," she told Tom Christopher. "And [when] Neal found out I was in jail, I guess he really blew it. For me to be in jail and Neal knowing the horror of jail—Neal had a real horror of it—and I think it frightened him, and that's the catalyst."

Life with Neal Cassady was never going to be boring, but LuAnne learned soon enough that neither was it going to be easy. For a while, and against all likelihood given her previous flippant approach to work,

LuAnne became the sole breadwinner, finding work at a drive-in movie theater at around the time that Neal lost his job parking cars at a garage. That arrangement did not last long, but neither did any of Neal's subsequent jobs. Being broke was the norm for the newlyweds, a situation that further encouraged Neal to cheat, steal, and defraud. His excuse was that if he did not have money, paying what he owed was not an option; and the idea of not incurring the debt in the first place was apparently never taken into consideration. Neal and LuAnne rented two or three places in Denver during the first few months, all of them rooms in shared houses. Occasionally they took a room at a cheap hotel for a couple of nights, sometimes making predawn escapes with the bill unpaid. LuAnne claimed she hated those particular episodes. "I knew it was not right, and there was this conflict in me," she admitted. "I never let him know I disapproved. With Neal it was just a matter of survival, it was just the way things were . . . he didn't think of it as wrong or stealing. We owed the money, but we didn't have it. If Neal had the money he would pay.

"When I think back now," LuAnne added, recalling the house-sharing, "my God, it's a wonder that we were allowed to stay. I mean not just the price, but, our lovemaking was noisy to say the least. I guess I was totally unaware of it, because I can't remember that it ever occurred to me that we should be quiet. We would be awake all night laughing . . . and giggling, and making love, and fighting . . . everything we did was noisy."

As LuAnne told Tom Christopher, she had strong memories of the tutoring she received from Neal in the art of lovemaking:

> He was very patient with me and took his time. I'm sure at one point he had a kind of Pygmalion attitude about teaching me lovemaking and caring, and such as that. You know, I was raw material, so to speak. Because all this was geared to his need, his wants, his desires, the lovemaking was geared to the things that pleased him. . . . It meant a great deal to him to know that

> he was pleasing me. Actually, at that time . . . Neal was more geared toward pleasing than being pleased. As time went by that scale shifted drastically . . . when I first met him the pride was there, that he could have twenty or thirty orgasms, and believe me that's not exaggeration . . . amazing . . . and I didn't realize it at the time, it was only afterwards that I used to think, and really marvel. And it almost became . . . I don't mean a twenty-four hour a day thing, but it was kind of an obsession with him. He was very gentle, very patient. He displayed all the old fashioned attributes of a man taking his virgin bride and introducing her to sex.

However, LuAnne soon learned that Neal, however considerate a lover, was not going to limit his sexual activities to her. The first time she was confronted by the truth was an evening that she finished work early and was given a ride home by a friend, only to see Neal in a car with another girl. Following an all-night screaming argument over the incident, LuAnne fled to her mother's house. On future occasions, she generally relied on Lois Williams to provide shelter and a shoulder to cry on.

Neal was also continuing his relationship with Jeannie Stewart, a fact of which LuAnne remained ignorant until a friend tipped her off. She handled this disclosure with remarkable maturity and did not challenge Neal with an ultimatum until she awoke in the middle of the night in early September to find him getting dressed and trying to sneak out of their room at the DeWitt Hotel, which stood across the street from Pederson's Pool Hall.

"Probably for the first time, rather than screaming and hollering and accusations, I got totally like—'Neal this is not the way I'm gonna live, we're either married or we're not married . . . the decision is yours.' In other words I dumped it all in his lap and I forced him to make a decision . . . because I told him—'I cannot live like this anymore. If you want to go with Jeannie, OK. This is the end, you either tell Jeannie forget it or you go live with Jeannie for good and that'll be the end of it.' Well, he wouldn't even hear that we would separate, so he said, 'OK'—and Neal did not make any rash statements . . . that night he told me: 'We'll be together, you are my one and only wife, and I'll call Jeannie, and I'll go get my clothes and belongings'—so that was made that night, and we had a beautiful, beautiful night."

At this point the story becomes complicated because Al Hinkle remembers one version of events while LuAnne recalls things rather differently. According to Hinkle, matters came to a head at his apartment, where Neal and Jeannie Stewart had spent the previous night. They were still there when LuAnne and Lois Williams arrived and it was obvious to Hinkle that, as far as LuAnne was concerned, this was going to be a decision-making day for her marriage. After an argument, Jeannie and Lois left and Hinkle watched as LuAnne defended herself against a flood of Cassady smooth talk with an ever-growing list of demands that culminated with the statement that she and Neal could only stay together if he left Denver with her, far away from temptress Jeannie. "She had an uncle in Nebraska," Hinkle recalled her telling Neal, "and they should go there and start over again."

According to Hinkle, Neal went to Jeannie's and returned about a half-hour later with a battered cardboard typewriter carrier that acted as his only suitcase.

"I can't remember what LuAnne had . . . not much," Hinkle recalled. "They took off, took the streetcar to Aurora to start hitchhiking over . . . to Highway 3, I guess."

LuAnne's recollections differ substantially in detail from Hinkle's, although the eventual outcome—departing Denver with Neal during the first snow flurries of the year—remains the same. She always said that things came to a head the morning after she had found Neal trying to slip out to be with Jeannie. It was as they stood outside Pederson's that Hinkle (whom she said she did not recall meeting before) approached and told

Neal that he had the two Jeannies—Stewart and Williams—in the car parked in the alley behind Pederson's.

"I looked at Neal, and Neal said, 'Al, I want you to meet my wife'—and Al just . . . he was so sweet, he didn't know what to say or how to get his foot out of his mouth," LuAnne continued. "Neal and I got in the car, and we went to Jeannie Williams's apartment. I don't remember now what was said, but Jeannie Stewart wanted to talk to Neal . . . and he said, 'Anything you have to say you can say in front of my wife'—and believe me it was a shock because I knew how hard it was for him to do this. He was acknowledging a relationship that was permanent.

"And Jeannie looked at him, and there were a few words back and forth, but I stayed out of it, and he said, 'LuAnne's my wife and we're going to be together, and I want to get my clothes.' And she said, 'You'll never get your clothes.' She was very upset. Neal had made her believe that she had a place in his life, and now he was telling her she didn't."

Jeannie Stewart's refusal to let Neal retrieve his few possessions was easily circumvented, LuAnne said, by them simply leaving Jeannie Williams's apartment, Neal letting himself into his abandoned lover's place and throwing his typewriter case down to LuAnne through an open window. As the snow began falling, Neal and LuAnne (most of whose clothes were still being held by one of the hotels they had defrauded) headed out of Denver, more committed to the act of leaving than to the question of where they might be going.

7

THE FIRST RIDE they got was with an old couple. With no clear idea of where they were headed, at LuAnne's suggestion they decided to make their first port of call her grandmother's home in Peetz, Colorado, just ten miles south of the Colorado–Nebraska state line. LuAnne had been born in the kitchen of that house. They stayed for a week, still wondering where to go. At the suggestion of one of LuAnne's uncles who was also staying at the house, they elected to move twenty miles up the road to Sidney, Nebraska, where another uncle and aunt lived and where Neal and LuAnne might find work picking potatoes.

Across the state line they were saved from this backbreaking labor when LuAnne was taken on as a housemaid at the home of one Radcliffe Moore and his wife, Myrtle. Blind since birth, Radcliffe Moore had, despite his disability, gained a law degree at the University of Nebraska and had also acted as the Cheyenne county attorney for several years before establishing a private practice in Sidney. Myrtle Moore kept their white two-story house on Linden Street as spotless as a show home, and it became LuAnne's task to meet her extremely exacting standards. If that meant scrubbing out toilet bowls by hand and completely recleaning any Venetian blind that betrayed one speck of dust to Myrtle's white glove, so be it.

The one good thing about this arrangement was that the Moores reluctantly agreed to allow Neal to share LuAnne's tiny room. Neal was delighted as this was next to a large den that boasted a pool table he could use when the Moores were out. Once he had investigated upstairs and discovered a library, he was in seventh heaven. "He would go crazy with all the books," LuAnne recounted. "I would sneak up at night and get whatever book he'd picked out earlier, bring it down to our room, and make sure that I got it back."

Recalling her two and a half months in the Moore household, LuAnne was scathing: "You talk about child labor. God, I had to get up at five A.M. and clean the whole house before they got up at seven. I had to wear a maid's uniform, the whole business . . . I was having some long hours, twelve, fourteen hours a day. I made twelve dollars a month. Cash. Plus room and board for me, and room for Neal. I got one day off a week. . . . Neal was not thrilled by it."

He was also not thrilled by the Moores' embargo on him eating in their spotless house, but solved that problem by finding work washing dishes at a local restaurant where he could at least snack on leftovers and tidbits.

"Anyway, it came to a head when Neal came home from work one day," LuAnne recalled. "It was snowing like crazy and the old witch had me out on the front porch with pail and water, no rubber gloves, no nothing, scrubbing . . . I mean, my hands were purple and I was there scrubbing away." On being told that LuAnne had to finish this task before setting the dinner table for the family's evening meal, Neal exploded. "Fuck this shit," he said. "That's the end of that." And he set to finishing the porch while LuAnne cleaned the railings. By seven o'clock Neal had worked up a plan—they were going to get the hell out of Nebraska, and they were going to steal LuAnne's uncle's car to do it.

Waiting until the blind lawyer and his house-proud wife had gone to bed, LuAnne crept upstairs and relieved a cigar box of its petty cash contents. In fact the haul was close to three hundred dollars, a small fortune then and certainly more money than LuAnne had ever seen. She would have had to work for three years at the slave wages of twelve bucks a month to earn that much. She also took some books from the library for Neal.

Sneaking out of the Linden Street house near midnight, they made for her uncle's home, threw their scant belongings in the back of his car, and hightailed it out of town. They headed toward North Platte, some 120 miles east of Sidney. The trip was terrifying, initially because Neal was certain that LuAnne's uncle would have raised the alarm, the local cops were bound to be on his tail, and he was likely to wind up in jail once more, and later because the weather deteriorated badly. Wind-driven sleet reduced visibility to a few yards, and Neal was forced to change places with LuAnne so that he could see the verge of the road while driving from the passenger seat, a handkerchief tied over his face to protect him against frostbite. The car had no heater, and, as he had to keep his head halfway outside an open window to maintain his view, they were both soon chilled to the bone.

LuAnne remembered being scared, not only by the perilous nature of the situation but by the fact that Neal was obviously scared, too. It was the first time she had seen him anything but cocksure and confident, and that only served to increase her fear. Paradoxically, it also created a new and stronger bond between them. "Neal and I talked about it later," LuAnne told Tom Christopher. "What a terrifying, loving, exciting, intense night that was . . . the course of our lives changing. It was a *very* important night in our lives."

Not until they pulled up outside the bus station in North Platte did Neal unexpectedly reveal a planned destination: the next stage of their journey would take them to New York. Unquestioning, LuAnne agreed. They abandoned the stolen car and bought tickets. However, if LuAnne believed that Neal's decision to make for New York was no more than a whim, she was wrong. He had secretly harbored dreams of getting there for more than a year, ever since he had bumped into a man named Hal Chase in the Denver Public Library during the summer of 1945.

• • •

The son of relatively well-off parents, Haldon Chase had graduated from East High School in 1941 and won a place at Columbia University when Justin Brierly brought him to the attention of his alma mater's selection board. A lively, talkative, and formidably intelligent young man, Chase was something of an authority on Native American culture—a knowledge that had started from a teenage interest in the subject of Colorado's original inhabitants. Like all college students in good health, Chase had his education interrupted in 1943 when he was relocated into a wartime government program for two years, but then he returned to Columbia. Chase and Cassady had heard good things about each other from Brierly, and an easy friendship was soon established. Chase filled Neal's head with stories of Columbia and a thrilling New York circle of intellectual and bohemian friends.

The list included an aspiring writer called Jack Kerouac and a young poet, Allen Ginsberg, both of whom spent much of their time in a huge five-bedroom apartment on West 115th Street owned by one Joan Vollmer Adams. This apartment Chase depicted as a nexus of sexual intrigue and intellectual fireworks. It was frequented by the gaunt figure of William Burroughs, the wealthy, Harvard-educated grandson of the man who had invented the first commercial adding machine. Other regulars included Herbert Huncke, a bisexual thief and junkie and self-appointed authority on New York's emergent counterculture; Vicki Russell, a stunning redheaded call girl with a select group of regular clients who paid her $100 a shot; Bill Cannastra, an Ivy League dropout and prince of excess given to spectacular drunkenness and acts of self-abuse; and the elfin beauty Céline Young, former girlfriend of another Columbia student, Lucien Carr, who was then serving time in prison for murdering a homosexual he claimed was stalking him. What a cast!

Now, rolling across the Midwest in the comparative luxury of Greyhound buses, Neal obviously felt that recent events, including their sudden windfall, meant that the time was now right to introduce himself and his young wife to the thrilling company that Hal Chase had evoked so seductively back in Denver. Neal and LuAnne arrived at Manhattan's midtown Greyhound terminal at West 34th Street late in the afternoon, but it was not until the next morning that Neal called Chase to let him know that they were in town. For most of the intervening hours, Neal and LuAnne, by their own admission, wandered through the area like a pair of slack-jawed hicks, soaking up the sights and sounds of Times Square—the skyscrapers, the lights of Broadway, and the impressive department store windows on Fifth Avenue. The city was so much bigger, brasher, louder, and more colorful than even Neal, who had at least spent some time in Los Angeles, might ever have imagined. For LuAnne, whose horizons had stretched no farther than the snowcapped peaks of the Rockies, it must have been quite overwhelming.

Upon receiving Neal's call, Hal Chase raced to the bus station and took the young couple back to the suite of rooms he shared with another Denver exile, Ed White, in Livingstone Hall, one of Columbia's undergraduate dorms. Having heard so much about Neal from Chase and Brierly, White was unimpressed by his first meeting with this so-called genius who told him witheringly: "Oh yes, Justin Brierly's told me about you and said you have a great social conscience, so I expected you to be out paving the streets." White's unfavorable first impression of a man he thought was nervous, jumpy, and always trying to say something impressive would change in time, and he would come to concede that Neal was "a very interesting man." Neal's first meeting with Allen Ginsberg did not, by all accounts, go particularly well either. It took place at the West End Bar, a favored hangout of Columbia students located across the street from the main university building. Neal, LuAnne, and Chase were sitting in a booth when Chase called Ginsberg over, introduced the Denver couple, and asked the young poet if he could recommend a hotel for them. Ginsberg, apparently uninterested in the fortunes of these Colorado hillbillies, shook his head and returned to his interrupted conversation. A few minutes later his face reappeared over the back of the booth and he asked the young Mrs. Cassady, "Is your name LuAnne?" On being told it was, Ginsberg remarked snootily, "What a strange name."

Hurt and embarrassed, LuAnne asked if they could leave. Neal, resentful and angry, agreed. Chase must have been mortified by this inauspicious start to what he had hoped would be a fine relationship.

One of the ironies of Neal's initial encounters with the Columbia crowd would be that he himself had always been incapable of passing even the simplest of academic examinations. Chase may have shown Neal's racy, funny letters to Kerouac and Ginsberg, and they may have found themselves reluctantly impressed by Neal's wit and unique way with words . . . but Chase's belief that Neal might even secure a place at Columbia with Brierly's assistance was highly unrealistic in light of Neal's academic record. Like many before him, Chase simply assumed that the articulate, well-read, and formidably intelligent young man he first met at a Denver library and got to know better during trips to Neal's favorite bars was at least in possession of a high school diploma. Neal had a general education diploma, an equivalent qualification awarded to those who had passed the High School Equivalency Test (HSET), a grueling three-day examination normally taken by those who failed to graduate in the conventional manner. However, even Neal's HSET qualification was phony. Al Hinkle, returning to Denver after his merchant marine adventures, had reported to the State Capitol building, completed the HSET, and passed so impressively that an exam supervisor had advised him to pursue a course in higher education. (Hinkle would put his academic life on hold until he neared retirement from the Southern Pacific Railroad in the 1970s, when he gained a Master of Arts degree from Stanford University.) He subsequently boasted to Neal about his HSET accomplishment and Neal immediately persuaded him to take the test again, this time posing as Neal Cassady. "It was one of those things," Hinkle would say years later. "He wanted it, but he didn't want to go through it."

8

ALTHOUGH JACK KEROUAC and Allen Ginsberg were destined to become the two most powerful voices in the Beat Generation, there was little in their respective backgrounds to suggest that they would also become long-term friends. In fact, their friendship was outstanding proof of the theory that opposites attract.

Jean-Louis Lebris de Kerouac was the name given on Jack Kerouac's birth certificate. He was born in Lowell, Massachusetts, on March 12, 1922, the youngest of the three children of Leo Kerouac (originally Kérouack), a hard-drinking New Hampshire journalist, newspaper publisher, sports promoter, and sometime printer who had an unerring inability to find silver linings in the many clouds that plagued him. Leo's wife, Gabrielle, a bitter, shrewish woman of French-Canadian descent, eschewed Christian charity for the unyielding sanctimony of the Roman Catholic Church at its most unforgiving.

Raised with the given certainties that Jews and Protestants were Satan's emissaries, the young Kerouac was repeatedly told that he was worthless, sinful, and bound for eternal damnation, and that he could never hope to match the uncomplaining piety of his brother, Gerard, who had died of rheumatic fever in 1926 after nine years of a life buffeted by ever worsening illness. Jack adored his sister, Caroline (called Nin by the family), and was bereft after she married and left home when he was fifteen.

There was a morbid strangeness to Gabrielle Kerouac's relationship with her son. Having closed the bedroom door to husband Leo after Jack's birth, for some years she often shared her bed with Jack and Nin, even though they had rooms of their own. She also insisted on supervising Jack's ablutions until he reached puberty, and he was a well-developed twelve-year-old when, to his lasting shame and embarrassment, his mother's soapy hands caused him to have an erection. Throughout his life Gabrielle would be a constant dark presence, berating him for his shortcomings, his friends, his lifestyle, his lengthy absences—pretty well everything he did, in fact. Ritualistically she would summon up the pale ghost of Gerard, the angelic boy against whom Jack was measured and always found lacking.

Initially educated by nuns (who also believed Gerard to be a saint) and then by Jesuit fathers (who, like the Christian Brothers who briefly raised Neal Cassady, favored harsh discipline), Jack Kerouac found solace in sports, at which he excelled, and in the radio drama exploits of *The Shadow*, as well as magazines and books. The influence of *The Shadow* would prove an abiding one; it would eventually inform *Doctor Sax*, a dense gothic novel Kerouac published in 1959.

Jack was drawn away from such pursuits by a school friend, Sebastian Sampas, who suggested that he join in discussion groups organized by the school librarian, a woman dedicated to helping more gifted students to extend their horizons. Thanks to her lead, a debating group called the Young Prometheans was formed to provide its members with the opportunity to investigate and discuss art, literature, and politics. Jack and Sebastian became almost inseparable, and it was the precocious Sebastian who introduced Jack to the works of William Saroyan and Thomas Wolfe, the two authors who would most influence his early attempts at writing. In 1944 Jack was devastated to learn that Sebastian had died of wounds received during the Allied landing at Anzio, the German military stronghold north of the Italian city of Naples. Maintaining close contact with the Sampas family, Jack eventually married Sebastian's younger sister, Stella.

Jack was in his mid-teens before he began speaking English with any confidence or regularity (he mostly spoke *joual*, a French-Canadian dialect), and when he won a football scholarship to Columbia University in 1939 he was forced to spend a year at the Horace Mann School for Boys, one of Columbia's preparatory schools, where he was able to refine his command of the English language. At Horace Mann he rubbed shoulders with Jewish boys for the first time and discovered that they were not, as his parents had led him to believe, part of a vast communist plot to throw the world into chaos. With help from one of these boys, Seymour Wyse, he also investigated live jazz during that first year in New York, finding a special joy in the music of Lester Young, Count Basie, Roy Eldridge, and Bud Freeman.

His football career at Columbia came to an abrupt end with a broken leg sustained in the 1940–1941 season. Jack stormed out of the university at the start of the following year after an argument with Lou Little, Columbia's legendary football coach, who declined to put him in the starting lineup for the first game of the season.

America's declaration of war upon Japan after the Japanese attack on Pearl Harbor in December 1941 resulted in Jack joining the Merchant Marine and working in the galley of a ship carrying explosives and construction workers to Greenland. He began writing about his experiences at this time, including an unpublished novel *The Sea Is My Brother.* Jack would also travel to England in 1943 on a merchant ship laden with bombs, but not until a bid to join the U.S. Navy had failed af- ter eight days' training, he was hospitalized, diagnosed as schizophrenic, and given a medical discharge.

In 1942 he began an affair with Edie Parker, whose fiancé Henri Cru had been one of his best friends at Horace Mann. After an open relationship in which both parties were free to date others, Parker and Kerouac were married in August 1944 following pressure from the bride's parents. (Parker's parents had paid Jack's $250 bail when he was held as a material witness in the Lucien Carr murder trial—he had helped Carr dispose of the murder weapon.)

The newlyweds lived in Grosse Point, Michigan, where Edie's parents lived and where Kerouac briefly worked at a Detroit ball-bearing factory. Then Jack and Edie separated after mutual infidelities. Jack moved to New York, returned to Columbia as a sophomore, and moved into Joan

Vollmer Adams's West 115th Street apartment, premises she had intermittently shared with Edie. He was about to be drawn into Joan's circle of friends.

• • •

Irwin Allen Ginsberg was born at Beth Israel Hospital, Newark, New Jersey, on June 3, 1926, making him four years younger than Jack Kerouac and the same age as Neal Cassady. The younger of two sons of Louis and Naomi Ginsberg (his brother, Eugene, was five years older), he grew up surrounded by the kind of radical left-wing politics that would have horrified Leo and Gabrielle Kerouac.

Ginsberg's parents were a formidably intelligent and attractive couple. A lyric poet of some repute, Louis wrote *Roots* in 1920. The work was to establish his reputation among the New York literati. His subsequent works would appear in such publications as the *New York Times Magazine* and *The New Masses*, which, while it was the cultural voice of the Communist Party, also published up-and-coming non-communists such as Ernest Hemingway and John Dos Passos. Financial realities dictated that Louis pursue a day job as a high school teacher of English, but he and Naomi regularly attended meetings of the influential Poetry Society of America in Greenwich Village.

In 1929, when Allen was three years old, his mother underwent major pancreatic surgery, emerging from the hospital with a badly scarred abdomen and the beginnings of a second nervous breakdown that led to a lengthy absence from the family home, now on Fair Street, in Paterson, New Jersey. The family spiraled into debt as Louis took out loans to pay for private sanitarium care for his wife. Naomi's increasingly eccentric behavior manifested itself in her habit of going naked around the house, oblivious to the fact that she had two impressionable sons as company. Allen would later say that he was never upset by his mother's nudity, only the arguments that it caused between his parents.

By 1935 Naomi's mental state had deteriorated to the point that she began hearing voices and harboring the conviction that Louis and his mother were plotting to kill her. Nothing Louis said convinced her otherwise, but when she began to express her paranoid fears to the boys he was forced to have her committed to the state mental hospital. A world away from the more enlightened regime she'd experienced in the private clinic that Louis could no longer afford, Naomi was subjected to a lengthy course of insulin shock treatments that reduced her delusions but left her deeply traumatized. When Louis and the boys came to visit, they found a wretched husk living in dread of shock treatments, convinced that doctors had inserted wires inside her head and forced sharp sticks into her back. Naomi would return to various hospitals over the years, and her illness caused chaos whenever she remained at home. Allen missed a lot of school to look after her. Despite this and a crippling shyness, he was able to rise to the presidency of both his school's debating and dramatic societies.

Like Neal, Allen found some respite from reality by immersing himself in the fantasies that unfolded on the screen of his local movie house, the Fabian Theater, a far grander place than Denver's Zaza. At other times, like Jack, he let himself be transported from the daily grind by tuning his radio to the latest adventures of *The Shadow* or other drama series like *Flash Gordon* and *Mandrake the Magician.*

Religion played no part in the fervently socialist Ginsberg household, with the result that neither Eugene nor Allen went through bar mitzvah or were taught Hebrew. At home his parents spoke nothing but English, slipping into Yiddish only for the benefit of family elders who spoke nothing else.

A gawky, insular youth who wore strong reading glasses and braces during his early teens, Allen began to have homosexual fantasies at an early age, and all his teenage crushes were on older boys. It was not until 1942, however, when he came across a copy of Kraft-Ebbing's *Psycopathia Sexualis* in the Paterson Public Library (where he worked part-time, putting away and tidying bookshelves for thirteen cents an hour), that he saw his own condition formalized in the section titled "Homosexuality."

By then Allen's intelligence and natural skill with words had manifested themselves publicly through pieces he had written for school magazines. His English teacher, Frances Durbin, had also introduced him to the poetic works of Walt Whitman. He later claimed that part of the thrill he got from Whitman's words came from Durbin's enthusiastic and joyous reciting of them.

During his final year at high school, Allen found himself besotted with an older boy, Paul Roth, who had gone to study at Columbia. His undeclared, unrequited love for and admiration of Roth led Allen to apply for a place at the same university, and it was there, a few days before Christmas 1943, that he first encountered the mercurial Lucien Carr. It would be Carr who opened the naive seventeen-year-old Allen's eyes to the fact that there was a whole lot more to life than study and work. Carr first introduced him to the cheery warmth of the West End Bar (Allen had never even entered a tavern before) and then to his weird circle of friends and acquaintances, including the aloof, hawkish figure of thirty-year-old William Burroughs and, eventually, Jack Kerouac.

In his 1968 book, *Vanity of Duluoz*, Kerouac recalled his first encounter with Allen, whom he characterized as "this spindly Jewish kid with horn-rimmed glasses and tremendous ears sticking out, seventeen years old, burning black eyes, a strangely deep voice." For his part, Allen remembered being immediately awed by "a big jock who was sensitive and intelligent about poetry" and described Jack as being "extraordinarily sensitive, very intelligent, very shrewd and very compassionate most of all. Compassionate toward the awkward kid." For Allen it was love at first sight.

He had come out and declared his love for Kerouac early in their friendship, a declaration that elicited no more than a dismissive groan from the object of his adoration, but he remained dogged in his pursuit of Kerouac even when Edie Parker returned to New York and reclaimed her husband's attentions for a few months. When she left again it was for good; her departure was prompted by the constant use of Benzedrine by those who treated Joan Vollmer's apartment as home and headquarters. Attempting to match Jack's prodigious consumption of the drug, Edie found herself existing on a diet of mayonnaise sandwiches. Her teeth and gums were in bad shape, and eventually her sanity was threatened by the extreme highs and lows the drug caused. She fled back to Michigan, and played no further part in Jack Kerouac's life.

Ginsberg eventually settled on an abiding friendship with Kerouac, sending him a series of love letters and cherishing the two otherwise isolated incidents on which he managed to persuade the object of his desire to indulge in a little alfresco sexual stimulation in a truck lot beneath the elevated stretch of the West Side Parkway near Christopher Street. Kerouac seemed to experience no guilt for raising and then summarily deflating Allen's hopes with a few moments of gratification.

What did unite Jack Kerouac and Allen Ginsberg was a common awe of William Burroughs, a man whose own leanings were homosexual but who also maintained a full and satisfying heterosexual relationship with Joan Vollmer ("You're supposed to be a faggot," she once famously told him, "but you're as good as a pimp in bed") that eventually led them to become an inseparable couple. Although Joan would bear two children by Burroughs and adopt his surname, they never married. Her previous marriage to the largely absent Paul Adams had ended in 1945 when he returned from military service and, appalled by her drug use and her circle of friends at the 115th Street apartment, divorced her.

Burroughs served Jack and Allen best as a guide and mentor to the world of literature, introducing the younger men to the works of Franz Kafka, Friedrich Nietzsche, Guillaume Apollinaire, Jean Cocteau, and William Blake, the eighteenth-century English poet and artist whose mystical and prophetic works were to prove especially influential on

Ginsberg. Eager to expand their horizons, Jack and Allen had every reason to owe Burroughs a debt of gratitude for all the hours he gave them, as well as for the generous loans he made to them of key books from his own huge collection. Kerouac, especially, thrilled to the realization that he was not alone—there were kindred spirits like Burroughs and Ginsberg with whom he could communicate on the same high level. Yet despite his generosity, Burroughs was a man who could also be aloof and distant . . . or so it seemed to Kerouac, who told his sister: "Nobody can actually *like* Burroughs . . . he's a cold fish all right."

Burroughs was an unusual man, to say the least. Sustained by a private income, educated at Harvard (where he studied anthropology and literature), he then attended Columbia (where he studied psychology) and Vienna University (medicine) before dedicating his life to firsthand explorations of drug cultures and the homosexual demimonde. He had also spent some time as a patient in psychiatric hospitals, once after he cut off part of his little finger when a lover walked out on him.

Burroughs's rationale for living the way he did, for flirting with danger all the time, was both wonderfully simple and remarkably beguiling to Jack and Allen: one was entitled to express opinions on the darker aspects of life only if one had firsthand experience of them. If that meant living beyond the pale of society, so be it. Burroughs reasoned that there was even a purity to be found in living outside the rules imposed by what he deemed a corrupt and impure society. In such seductive logic lay the foundations of what would, a few years later, emerge as beat philosophy. Later still, Bob Dylan would come up with a matching slogan in a line from his song "Absolutely Sweet Marie": "To live outside the law you must be honest."

Not all members of the 115th Street circle were honest. Some of them definitely lived outside the law, and this led directly to the disintegration of the group even before the newly arrived Neal Cassady could really sample it. Herbert Huncke and a friend, Phil White, had begun stashing the proceeds of robberies in Vollmer's apartment. Sometimes even the gun they used to threaten their victims was hidden there. Meanwhile, White had talked Burroughs into forging prescriptions for narcotics in the name of his physician, Dr. Grico. When the forgery was spotted, Borroughs was arrested at the apartment and immediately fled to cheap rooming houses until his case came to court. He paid his way dealing in heroin, to which he was by then addicted. When his case was finally heard, the judge gave Burroughs a four-month suspended sentence and ordered him to return to St. Louis with his father for the summer.

Hal Chase had already left New York to spend the summer in Denver, stating his intention of heading for the relative safety of Columbia's dorms in Livingstone Hall when he returned. With news of Burroughs's arrest and conviction, Chase cut off contact with everyone except Kerouac, who had meanwhile moved out to live with his mother in Queens following his father's death from cancer. This left Jack with the unenviable duty of caring for his mother, Gabrielle, for the rest of his life. Jack already felt guilty at having failed his father both as a football star and a university student. Worse, he found out that his father's final painful months had been further clouded by the knowledge that Jack had received treatment for thrombophlebitis brought on by Benzedrine abuse while hanging out with what Leo witheringly dismissed as "a bunch of Jews, queers, and hopheads."

Joan Vollmer responded to Borroughs's conviction and enforced absence with a Benzedrine binge of her own that ended with her committal to Bellevue Hospital for ten days. She became the first female the hospital's staff had ever treated for acute amphetamine psychosis. On her release Burroughs whisked her off to east Texas, where he would eventually grow and harvest marijuana on an almost industrial scale under the cover of running a citrus farm. Huncke was arrested and convicted for possession of drugs and retired (for the time being) to Bronx Prison. Allen closed up the apartment and returned to Paterson for the summer. When he returned to his studies at Columbia in September, he rented a room with an Irish family on West 92nd Street.

So it was with these disintegrating vestiges of the bohemian community Hal Chase had so glowingly described back in Denver that Neal Cassady would be confronted in late 1946. He would never be able to witness firsthand the 115th Street cultural circus in its full glory, let alone join it.

9

HAL CHASE HAD SUMMONED a variety of people to the West End Bar to meet the newly arrived Neal Cassady and his wife. They included his fellow Denver exile, architecture student Ed White; future architectural critic Allan Temko; Jack Kerouac; Allen Ginsberg; and Herbert Huncke. If Chase had envisioned the evening as being akin to a gathering of the gods at Olympus, he was to be gravely disappointed. Not only did Ginsberg offend LuAnne with his comment about her name, Neal put on a self-consciously fast-talking show intended to make himself sound wild and interesting.

Jack was not impressed; neither were Ed White and Temko, both of whom initially wrote Neal off as a fool. In the 1970s Allan Temko would go further in his condemnation of Neal. Interviewed by Barry Gifford and Lawrence Lee for *Jack's Book*, their 1979 coproduction that invited many of Kerouac's contemporaries to have their say, he described Neal as "a terribly treacherous and untrustworthy and destructive person. There was a born hatred between me and someone like Neal Cassady, because I felt he was just a sponger and useless. I didn't see his charm."

Herbert Huncke was more impressed with Neal. Ginsberg's response to him, although positive, did not turn into infatuation until a second meeting at Vicki Russell's apartment early in 1947.

Kerouac later said he remembered his first meeting with Cassady as being at a big band jazz gig at Hartley Hall, Columbia University—an event that is fictionalized in the posthumously published *Visions of Cody*. In *On the Road*, Kerouac actually depicted his first meeting with Neal as taking place at an apartment in Spanish Harlem where Neal and LuAnne were temporarily staying with Bob Malkin, a cousin of Allan Temko's.

This time Jack was blown away by Neal's energy and enthusiasm, much as Chase had suspected he would be. In *On the Road* Jack would record that on that night Neal (whom Kerouac christened Dean Moriarty) reminded him of a young boxer taking instructions, head down, nodding in assent, "throwing in a thousand 'Yes's' and 'That's right's,'" or a slim-hipped Western movie hero like Gene Autry. Cassady was certainly in full flow, and during that marathon all-night conversation, Jack and Neal became true soul brothers, not least because each possessed the very qualities the other lacked but yearned for.

Jack envied Neal's madness ("the only people for me are the mad ones," Jack would write). In fact, Jack was a naturally shy man who never felt comfortable with strangers, only dropping his guard once he had grown to like and trust a person.

If Jack had not already known that his destiny was to hit the road and to explore the American heartland, to see and experience life for himself, the idea certainly took root as he listened to Neal's colorful tales of life in the golden west. Neal evoked Denver's mean streets through which he was pursued by pool hall hustlers, irate parents, jilted lovers, or the cops. Then there were the tales of incarceration and escape, life on the Uhl ranch, cross-country trips in stolen cars, and plenty of sex and drugs. It all came out in a life-affirming torrent of laughter and drama that convinced Jack he somehow had to share in some of this inspired lunacy. Whether or not Jack saw Cassady and his world as potential raw material for his own inchoate writing career is debatable. At this time Kerouac was working on what would become his first published novel, *The Town and the City*, a rather traditional novel modeled on the work of Thomas Wolfe, a work far removed from the picaresque and sometimes exaggerated tales of Cassady's life.

Certainly Kerouac was astute enough to realize that much of what Neal said was contrivance and invention intended to impress rather than inform, but concluded that his prime motive was to ingratiate and become involved himself with people like Allen (and like Jack himself);

besides, Neal's flimflam was so utterly seductive and flamboyant as to be irresistible.

Neal's response to this newly formed friendship was to dash off a letter to Bill Tomson in Denver. Tomson recalled that Neal referred to him throughout as his "younger brother" and to Jack as his "older brother."

"Neal looked up to Jack for his tenacity and for his intellectual competence," Tomson once suggested, adding that he believed Neal also found "companionship in Jack's energy."

Inspired by his rap sessions with Kerouac, Cassady fixated on the idea of becoming a writer himself. He approached Hal Chase for help. Chase declined but suggested that Neal approach Jack, who agreed to tutor him as best he could. By then both Neal and LuAnne had found work—he was parking cars at the New Yorker Hotel on 34th Street while she was working in a bakery in New Jersey. Ever the consummate time-juggler, Neal managed to fulfill his shifts at the hotel, pick up girls, score marijuana, and spend two nights a week with Jack, who was now staying with his mother Gabrielle in Ozone Park. (Neal broke down the initial resistance of this hostile and suspicious woman with his studied politeness.)

Neal also managed to keep LuAnne happy, but only in bed. Homesick and feeling lost in the big, scary city, she now had to put up with Neal's frequent absences. She grew increasingly angry and resentful. When Allen Ginsberg entered the picture, Neal began to spend even more time away from home.

Although Ginsberg had encountered Cassady at the West End in the fall of 1946, it was not until they met again at Vicki Russell's apartment on January 10, 1947, that he was struck by Neal's physical beauty. Ginsberg had been visiting Russell when Kerouac turned up with Cassady in tow. Kerouac would later describe the meeting of the two in *On the Road*, with Ginsberg as Carlo Marx. "Two keen minds that they are," Kerouac wrote, "they took to each other at the drop of a hat . . . the holy con-man with the shining mind, and the sorrowful poetic con-man with the dark mind that is Carlo Marx." Kerouac clearly felt left out.

In many ways Allen felt Neal resembled Jack, not just physically but also because, just as he had with Jack, Allen now found himself trading with Neal intimate fantasies and secrets about childhood. He told Barry Miles: "We were really interested in what was going on *inside*, without regard to whether it was practical or real, but more interested in the charm and the absurdity that everybody was having such an amazingly naïve secret life."

According to Allen, his relationship with Neal turned from friendship into a full-blown affair only a few nights after the encounter at Vicki Russell's, when he and Jack walked Neal home to the Spanish Harlem apartment and realized that it was way too late for Allen to go back to his apartment on 92nd Street or for Jack to make it back to Ozone Park. They decided that the most sensible solution was for them to stay the night. There were only two beds so Jack and Malkin took the double bed, while Allen and Neal shared a single. During that night they became lovers. Allen clearly reveled in the experience and celebrated the sex graphically in his poem "Many Loves," while Neal later confessed in a letter to Allen that he disliked homosexual sex but had affected lust "as a compensation to you for all you were giving me."

Allen's 1947 journal includes many entries about his affair with Neal. On January 21, for example, he wrote about his despair after spending "a wild weekend in sexual drama with Cassady." This despair was inspired by a growing fear that his homosexuality made him a freak and an outcast, or that he was perhaps mentally deranged for enjoying gay sex. He had at that time no experience of heterosexual intercourse but acknowledged that contemporary society prescribed it as "normal" while gay sex was "abnormal."

In time Ginsberg would, at his father's insistence, submit to extensive psychiatric treatment for this "illness" and even settle into a long-term relationship with a woman before finally admitting to himself that he was, indeed, resolutely gay.

• • •

On January 14, the increasingly unhappy LuAnne became caught in a snowstorm as she was on her way home to the New Jersey flat that she and Neal now shared. She lost her way, became disoriented, then frightened and tearful, as she wandered through Bayonne. When she eventually made it back home, Neal was out. LuAnne became furious, and when he finally did appear, she hit him with the worst thing she could conjure. Aware of his dread of police and prison, LuAnne told Neal that she had received a visit from some cops who wanted to talk to him about a marijuana deal he had made. Grabbing a few essentials, Neal raced off in a blind panic. After lying low for a couple of days, he sneaked back to the apartment, only to discover that LuAnne had left for good. Her patience exhausted, she had gathered up her own possessions, bought a bus ticket to Denver, and headed home. It goes without saying that Neal, hurt and angry, painted LuAnne as a villain in his account of her departure, maintaining a baffled "What did I do?" stance with his New York friends.

Neal devoted most of the next six weeks exclusively to Allen at the expense of Jack, who had devoted much of his own time to Neal's burgeoning ambitions to write or do something new. Kerouac did not seem to hold a grudge but was clearly uncomfortable with any overt displays of intimacy between Allen and Neal. On one occasion, Ginsberg told author Yves LePellec, he and Neal were sitting around talking with Jack. Neal was wearing only a short Chinese dressing gown and Allen kept his hand on Neal's thigh throughout the hour-long conversation. Eventually, Jack could bear it no longer and snapped, "Why don't you take your damn hand off his thigh . . . feeling him up all the time."

Jack and Neal seemed reconciled and reconfirmed in friendship when they met for another of their marathon rap sessions on March 3, the day before Neal would board a bus back to Denver.

Jack and Allen accompanied Neal to the bus station, each of them taking turns in a photo booth so the others could have a memento. Kerouac didn't like his picture, claiming that it made him look like "a thirty-year-old Italian who'd kill anybody who said anything against his mother." Allen removed his glasses but only succeeded, Jack thought, in looking sinister. Both of Neal's new friends had already voiced their intention to join him in Denver as soon as they could—Allen when the summer vacation from college began, and Jack when he could rustle up the fare from somewhere, but hopefully, as he put it, "when spring really bloomed and opened up the land."

Neal left New York dressed in a dark blue suit he'd bought for twelve dollars in a thrift store. On top of it he wore a present from Ginsberg—an overcoat that was part of a recent haul by Bill Garver, another junkie of Bill Burroughs's acquaintance who financed his habit through theft. In his battered cardboard suitcase Neal carried, along with his few personal possessions, a poem that Allen had written but which Neal intended to pass off as his own work when he saw Justin Brierly again. He had told Allen about his former mentor whom they waspishly renamed "Justin Mannerly."

Neal wrote a quick impersonal note to Allen during a stopover in Kansas City, all fussy detail about collecting a pair of forgotten trousers from a New York tailor and sending them on to Denver. He then penned a long impressionistic letter to Kerouac that knocked its recipient sideways with the verve and vivacity of its verbal riffs:

> Dear Jack:
>
> I am sitting in a bar on Market St. I'm drunk, well, not quite, but I soon will be. I am here for 2 reasons; I must wait 5 hours for the bus to Denver & lastly but, most importantly, I'm here (drinking) because, of course, because of a woman & what a woman! To be chronological about it:
>
> I was sitting on the bus when it took on more passengers at

Indianapolis, Indiana—a perfectly proportioned beautiful, intellectual, passionate, personification of Venus de Milo asked me if the seat beside me was taken!!! I gulped, (I'm drunk) gargled and stammered NO! (Paradox of expression, after all, how can one stammer No!!?) She sat—I sweated—She started to speak, I knew it would be generalities, so to tempt her I remained silent.

She (her name Patricia) got on the bus at 8 PM (Dark!) I didn't speak until 10 PM—in the intervening 2 hours I not only of course, determined to make her, but, how to DO IT.

I naturally can't quote the conversation verbally, however, I shall attempt to give you the gist of it from 10 PM to 2 AM

Without the slightest preliminaries of objective remarks (what's your name? Where are you going? etc.) I plunged into a completely knowing, completely subjective, personal & so to speak "penetrating her core" way of speech; to be shorter (since I'm getting unable to write) by 2 AM I had her swearing eternal love, complete subjectivity to me & immediate satisfaction. I, anticipating even more pleasure, wouldn't allow her to blow me on the bus, instead we played, as they say, with each other.

Knowing her supremely perfect being was completely mine (when I'm more coherent, I'll tell you her complete history & psychological reason for loving me) I could conceive of no obstacle to my satisfaction, well, "the best laid plans of mine & men go astray" and my nemesis was her sister, the bitch.

Pat had told me her reason for going to St. Louis was to see her sister; she had wired her to meet her at the depot. So, to get rid of the sister, we peeked around the depot when we arrived at St. Louis at 4 AM to see if she (her sister) was present. If not, Pat would claim her suitcase, change clothes in the rest room & she and I proceed to a hotel room for a night (years?) of perfect bliss. The sister was not in sight, so She (note the capital) claimed her bag & retired to the toilet to change——

This next paragraph must, of necessity, be written completely objectively——

Edith (her sister) & Patricia (my love) walked out of the pisshouse hand in hand (I shan't describe my emotions). It seems Edith (bah) arrived at the bus depot early & while waiting for Patricia, feeling sleepy, retired to the head to sleep on a sofa. That's why Pat & I didn't see her.

My desperate efforts to free Pat from Edith failed, even Pat's terror & slave-like feeling toward her rebelled enough to state she must see "someone" & would meet Edith later, all failed. Edith was wise; she saw what was happening between Pat & I.

Well, to summarize: Pat & I stood in the depot (in plain sight of the sister) & pushing up to one another, vowed to never love again & then I took the bus for Kansas City & Pat went home, meekly, with her dominating sister. Alas, alas——

In complete (try & share my feeling) dejection, I sat, as the bus progressed toward Kansas City. At Columbia, Mo. a young (19) completely passive (my meat) virgin got on & shared my seat . . . In my dejection over losing Pat, the perfect, I decided to sit on the bus (behind the driver) in broad daylight & seduce her, from 10:30 AM to 2:30 PM I talked. When I was done, she (confused, her entire life upset, metaphysically amazed at me, passionate in her immaturity) called her folks in Kansas City, & went with me to a park (it was just getting dark) & I banged her; I screwed her as never before; all my pent up emotion finding release in this young virgin (& she was) who is, by the way, a school teacher! Imagine, she's had 2 years of Mo. St. Teacher's College & now teaches Jr. High School. (I'm beyond thinking straightly).

I'm going to stop writing. Oh, yes, to free myself for a moment from my emotions, you must read "Dead Souls" parts of it (in which Gogol shows his insight) are quite like you.

I'll elaborate further later (probably?) but at the moment I'm drunk and happy (after all, I'm free of Patricia already, due to the young virgin. I have no name for her. At the happy note of Les Young's "jumping at Mesners" (which I'm hearing) I close till later.

To my Brother
Carry On!
N.L. Cassady

P.S. I forgot to mention Patricia's parents live in Ozone Park & of course, Lague being her last name, she's French Canadian just as you.

I'll write soon,

Neal.

P.P.S. Please read this illegible letter as a continuous chain of undisciplined thought, thank you,

N.

P.P.P.S. Postponed, postponed, postponed script, keep working hard, finish your novel & find, thru knowledge, strength in solitude instead of despair. Incidentally I'm starting on a novel also, 'believe it or not'. Goodbye.

Jack was thrilled by the way the very essence of Neal seemed to be conveyed in this headlong rush of narrative; he wasted no time in passing it around to his friends. He was particularly impressed by Neal's ability to render his speech patterns on the page. Jack could almost hear him telling the story.

By March 10 Neal was back in Denver and writing to request that Allen send a couple of Garver's overcoats for him to sell—his had become an instant fashion hit with the Denver crowd. He had seen LuAnne and persuaded her that it was probably best if she continued staying with her mother, found a job, and saved up "to pay Haldon back & such." Perhaps Chase had advanced LuAnne the bus fare from New York to Denver . . . or, equally possibly, it could have been money Neal owed Chase that he believed ought to be paid back, although preferably not by him. He wrote Allen that he was "seeking a room, then a job, then a typewriter, then some money, then to leave here in June."

Apologizing for the brevity of his notes so far, Neal further explained that, as he was not yet settled anywhere permanent and their letters might go astray and "fall into alien hands," he could not yet write freely to Allen, adding: "I & you must wait until I'm settled to begin to speak of other things—understand?"

If Ginsberg was living in anticipation of a love letter from Neal, he must have been gravely disappointed when he finally opened a long correspondence dated March 14 bearing the return address of 1073 Downing Street, Denver, where Neal had rented a room. Far from being filled with declarations of love and endearments, this letter dealt with mundane matters such as the depressing news that while Neal's rent was only six dollars a week, he still had to take his meals in cafés. Unable to find work, he was sinking into debt and pleaded with Allen to send the overcoats as soon as possible. He also reported that he was still trying to establish the precise status of his relationship with LuAnne who had, he claimed, "fallen into a complete apathy toward life."

"Her inability to meet even the most simple obligations is almost terrifying," Neal declared. "Her life is a constant march of obsessions. Her attitude toward everyone is so defensive that it constitutes continual lying, yet she still has many fellows who adore her & is, therefore, always getting drunk & has become very slipshod."

Neal's inability to sympathize with or understand LuAnne's confusion, dismay, and decline speaks eloquently of his lifelong tendency to distance himself from relationships whenever his partners became too demanding or problematic. He was apparently unable, or unwilling, to take into consideration either LuAnne's relative youth (she was still only sixteen years old), or the fact that she had every reason to have slumped into apathy after being all but abandoned by her husband more than two thousand miles from home.

In fact, LuAnne had a further reason to be confused. Neal had resumed having sex with her on a regular basis, something he neglected to mention to Ginsberg, to whom he wrote: "I need you now more than ever, since I've no one else to turn to . . . every day I miss you more & More." He concluded: "Let us then find true awareness by realizing that each of us is depending on the other for fulfillment. In that realization lies, I believe, the germ that may grow to the great heights of complete oneness."

Allen must have gathered that Neal had achieved at least one of his immediate objectives, since this letter was not written in what Neal called "my juvenil[e] scrawl" but on a typewriter. The machine in question was identified in Neal's letter of March 13 to Jack Kerouac as "an Underwood, office model, practically new and worth $75. . . . The only drawback to this typewriter is that it's only half mine . . . . the pardner in this is the best. You remember my speaking of Holmes?" we may infer from this (and a later reference in another letter to Kerouac to "my hot typewriter") that the machine was obtained—probably stolen—by Holmes and Cassady in Denver between March 9 and 13, 1947. Quite soon Cassady would be sharing another typewriter, this time an old German machine owned by Carolyn Robinson, an elegantly beautiful graduate student who was studying fine arts and theater arts at the University of Denver. Neal's acquaintance Bill Tomson had yearned for her but had blown his own chances when he'd unwisely introduced her to Neal Cassady the day after Neal returned to Denver. Carolyn was now being subjected to an all-out Cassady charm offensive, an assault few women could withstand.

10

THERE WAS NOTHING in Carolyn Robinson's upbringing to suggest that she would ever meet, let alone fall in love with, a man like Neal Cassady. They came from such different backgrounds and had lived such different lives that it is astonishing that their relationship lasted any longer than their first encounter in Carolyn's room at the Colburn, a residential hotel on Grant Street. It was, however, destined to turn into a marriage that would last for sixteen (often stormy) years, produce three children (each of whom Neal adored), and become one of the most remarkable love stories of the twentieth century.

The first eight years of Carolyn's life were spent in the comfortable security of East Lansing, Michigan, where her father, Charles Summers Robinson, was a member of the chemistry faculty in the Michigan Agricultural College—an institution his children irreverently dubbed the "cow college." His wife, Florence Sherwood, had been an English teacher until she married and devoted her time to tending to the incessant demands of her children: Jane, Joseph, Margaret, Charles, and Carolyn.

In 1931 Carolyn's father was appointed head of the biochemistry department at Vanderbilt University Medical School, in Nashville, Tennessee, and the family moved there, eventually taking up residence in the faded splendor of a plantation mansion, which they gradually restored to become a grand family home filled with books and paintings. The plantation's former slave quarters provided the Robinson children with many adventures as they explored the ruins.

Carolyn's eldest sister, Jane (who was ten years older), never lived at the Nashville house, having left home at the age of fourteen to be educated in Europe. Jane studied in Paris and Munich before returning to America and becoming a nursery school teacher; she was later to play a key role in her baby sister's life. While the Robinson family was outwardly respectable, with its comings and goings reported in the local society columns, there were some dark undercurrents beneath the smooth surface.

Carolyn's eldest brother—football hero Joe—began to sexually abuse her when she was ten years old. Then, one day, brother Chuck (who seemed to believe that his parents had produced Carolyn "just for him") set two of his friends on her, watching while they sexually assaulted her. Carolyn remained certain that neither of her brothers knew of the other's actions, and she would never have dared to tell her mother what was going on. Like many victims of abuse, she would live for some years with the guilty belief that it was her fault in some way, until she realized that her brothers were simply bullies—in some ways like their father, a strict disciplinarian and true Victorian patriarch whose word was unchallengeable law.

As Carolyn grew up she discovered that she had real artistic talent. Big sister Jane recommended that she apply for a place at the prestigious Bennington College in Vermont. Established in 1932 as a college for women (today it is coed), Bennington's campus spread out over five hundred acres of the Green Mountains; most of its classes took place either alfresco on lawns, or in converted barns and former farmhouses. Unorthodox and remarkably liberal for its time, Bennington was not the kind of place Carolyn's father considered suitable for a daughter he had wanted to become a teacher. However, for the first time in her life Carolyn dug in her heels, enrolled herself as one of Bennington's three hundred students, and elected to major in drama, a course that focused on the work and philosophies of the Russian actor, director, producer, teacher, and progenitor of the so-called "Method" school of acting, Konstantin Stanislavsky.

Although Carolyn did graduate from Bennington with a B.A. in that subject, most of her first year there was spent in the art department. She became interested in costume design, and since Bennington did not have qualified staff in this subject, six months of her final year—1943—were spent working in a New York fabric design house and immersing herself in the theatrical design archives at the city's museums. Carolyn's encyclopedic knowledge of this subject would later result in her initiating the theatrical section of Denver Art Museum when she moved there in 1946.

Carolyn Robinson thoroughly enjoyed her time in New York, even though while she was there she suffered the third traumatic sexual event of her young life when she was raped by a well-known radio singer whom she had been seeing platonically. Once again she maintained her silence, although understandably in male company she began to fear that a mere smile or pleasantry might trigger the wrong reaction.

When she returned home to Nashville after her studies, Carolyn came under pressure from her father to enlist in the military. Her brother Chuck had already done so, and her father saw no reason why Carolyn could not do the same. (Chuck had enlisted in the Navy and would rise to the rank of lieutenant commander; Joe Robinson had become an aeronautical engineer and so was not drafted.)

Reprieve came in the form of a move to Mills, the college in Oakland, California, where Carolyn successfully completed a three-month crash course to qualify for the post of occupational therapist in a military hospital in Palm Springs. Later, Palm Springs became a sybaritic playground for Hollywood's ultra-rich set. In those days, Carolyn noted, it was "little more than a couple of streets in the middle of a huge expanse of desert."

Carolyn found her work at the hospital simultaneously rewarding, taxing, and heartbreaking as she attempted to help badly wounded young men come to terms with the reality of returning to civilian life despite injuries that were often as much psychological as physical. However, her time there was soon to be made a living hell when she became the object of an army captain's psychopathic obsession.

A forceful man, the captain in question had once returned home from duty in the Pacific to discover his wife and her lover in bed; he shot them both dead, but an all-male jury deemed this action justifiable homicide, and he was allowed to continue his military career. Now he violently discouraged any man who dared to pay too much attention to Carolyn, actually beat up a junior officer who dared to ask her out for dinner, and openly threatened her when she made it clear she was not interested in him.

In 1945 her job in the hospital ended, and she returned once more to Nashville only to be followed to Tennessee by her manic suitor. Her nightmare did not end until he was posted to another state and the break was finally made in a brutally frank exchange of letters.

She was now free, well educated, and, at twenty-two, blessed with exceptional good looks. Her encounters with men, however, had so far been little short of grotesque. This, combined with a strict upbringing enforced by another overbearing man, had made her cautious, straitlaced, and proper. She would never have dreamed of getting involved with a married man, or of indulging in the casual sex of a one-night stand. Carolyn Robinson was both decorous and virtuous, and if her view of sex was not exactly jaundiced, it was at the very least wary.

Ironically enough, Carolyn's arrival in Denver came about as a direct result of her father's obduracy. Charles Robinson was still fixated upon the idea that Carolyn should become a teacher. Although he had rented a studio space for her in Nashville where she worked sporadically as a portrait painter, he insisted that she sign up with a teaching agency and, on learning that there were posts vacant in Denver, he urged Carolyn to head west. Her brother Chuck was already in Colorado working toward a Ph.D. at the University of Colorado at Boulder, and Charles Robinson imagined that brother and sister would be able to see one another frequently. As it turned out, that hardly ever happened.

Working as a substitute teacher, Carolyn was so terrified by the experience that she abandoned it and soon enrolled as a postgraduate student at Denver University. She was contentedly involved in her studies when she first met Neal Cassady.

Carolyn knew quite a lot about Neal Cassady's life even before she met him or knew who he was. Bill Tomson, in an attempt to impress

Carolyn, had already appropriated some of Neal's more attractively colorful life experiences as his own; he also told her about his charismatic friend, allowing Neal to retain some of his own history in these accounts as well as the fiction that he was a student at Columbia University. Carolyn quickly saw through most of Tomson's tall tales since he was obviously too young to have done half the things he bragged about having done. As for the mythical Cassady, a reputation as a womanizing car thief and former inmate of numerous detention centers and jails was hardly likely to dispose Carolyn toward him. She also learned that he was three years her junior. Therefore, when Bill Tomson arrived at Carolyn's hotel door one Saturday afternoon in March 1947 and introduced her to Neal, she was quite unprepared for the effect he would have upon her. Although she described the physical aspects of his appearance as "pretty average" in her memoir *Off the Road: Twenty Years with Cassady, Kerouac and Ginsberg,* she was instantly struck by the thoroughness with which he seemed to have appraised her with just "the sweep of his blue eyes." More prosaically, his thrift store suit "gave him a Runyonesque flavor," she recalled, "a dangerous glamour heightened by the white T-shirt and bare muscular neck."

After looking through her record collection for the Lester Young discs Bill Tomson mistakenly assured him Carolyn owned (she had, in fact, never heard of the great tenor saxophonist, and possessed mostly swing records by the likes of Artie Shaw, Benny Goodman, Harry James, the Nat "King" Cole Trio, and Duke Ellington), Neal selected something and placed it on the turntable.

No one spoke as the music played, but as Carolyn busied herself gathering up the pieces of a stage scenery model she had been creating, she was keenly aware of Neal's eyes fixed on her, unwavering and disconcerting. Despite her uneasiness she readily agreed to Neal's suggestion that she should take a break and go with them to collect some of Neal's possessions from one of his former lodgings. Carolyn had, in her own words, "a compelling desire to see more of this man."

While Neal collected his belongings, Carolyn and Bill Tomson sat silently in a cluttered, old-fashioned parlor. At one point, Neal handed her a typewritten love poem without explanation. Untitled, but bearing the inscription "by Neal Cassady," it struck Carolyn that, while she knew little or nothing about poetry, its author clearly did. She was duly impressed, but it would be some years before she learned that the poem was Allen Ginsberg's creation, supplied to Neal as part of some proposed trick intended to dupe Justin Brierly.

Carolyn then accompanied Neal to a small, shabby hotel on Downing Street where he deposited his suitcase on an unmade bed in a room already littered with items of feminine clothing and cosmetics. Then, without explanation, the trio headed for a café. While Carolyn and Bill waited on the sidewalk, Neal went in and immediately got into a heated discussion with a pretty young girl behind the counter. Her curiosity aroused, Carolyn asked an evasive Tomson for explanation. Reluctantly he told her that the pretty young girl was LuAnne, Neal's wife.

Carolyn was surprised by the strength of her reaction to this news, realizing just how interested she had become in such a short time. The fact that Neal was married put him strictly off limits as far as she was concerned. She decided that this strangely unsettling man would never play a significant part in her life.

11

DESPITE HER DISAPPOINTMENT, Carolyn found herself agreeing to Neal's suggestion that they all go to a music store and listen to some records. Although she walked as fast as possible, Carolyn recalled in her memoir, Neal always managed to stay ahead of her and Bill Tomson, "every now and then wheeling to face us, walking backward but never breaking stride. He shouted remarks and flashed his remarkable teeth, his light brown hair ruffling in the wind, his suitcoat flapping. He appeared caught up in observing everything and everybody on every side, but he had not ceased his intimate glances at me with those talking eyes. More than ever now I avoided his gaze."

In the record store Neal secured a copy of Benny Goodman's "Sing, Sing, Sing" from a sales assistant and, in the glass-sided listening booth, Carolyn had her first sight of Neal Cassady getting off on music. "He was passionately involved in every instrument, every note, every phrase," she wrote. "He shared his delight by insisting that I, too, become as engrossed as he, repeating nuances I might have missed, calling my attention to an impending riff, while—his face glowing in a wide grin—he exuded 'Aaaaah . . . hear *that*?' or, with his eyes closed, 'Listen . . . now *listen*, hear it? WhoooooweeeeEEE!' followed by gleeful giggling and shaking of his head while he clapped his hands on his bouncing knees in time to the beat."

At the end of what Carolyn recalls as being an exhausting two-hour session in the booth, Neal came up with the idea of having a grand dinner together that evening. They could meet at their favorite restaurant, he said, and Bill could maybe ask Al Hinkle and his girlfriend (Al was currently dating LuAnne's best friend Lois Williams) to come along as well. Not expecting anyone to demur, Neal rushed off before receiving a reply.

That evening Carolyn and Bill finally gave up waiting for their fellow diners and ate alone. They were drinking their after-dinner coffee when Al and Lois appeared, offering profuse apologies and explaining that Al had not received his invitation message in time to join them. Neal's absence, Al explained, picking his words carefully, was due to his only just having returned from New York, and to Neal and LuAnne getting "delayed" when she went back to their hotel room to change. However, Al continued, Neal had announced that they were all going to meet at Carolyn's hotel room to celebrate his homecoming.

Carolyn acquiesced, wondering why it had to be her room. Did none of these Denver residents have homes of their own? She raced ahead of the others so she could straighten the room. As everyone arrived, Carolyn was struck by the change in Neal's mood. Now grumpy, silent, and brooding, he slumped heavily and morosely into an armchair, not even responding to Al Hinkle's attempts to update him on events in Denver while he had been away in New York. For her part, LuAnne seemed determined to be the life and soul of the evening, laughing and chattering about how happy she and Neal were, showing off a diamond solitaire Neal had given her, and telling Carolyn that Neal had taken her to New York for their honeymoon. It had been really exciting, she said, and they had met such interesting people, including Allen Ginsberg and Jack Kerouac who, she added breathlessly, were writers.

When Carolyn asked how long Neal had been enrolled at Columbia, LuAnne appeared lost for a moment, but recovered her composure and continued: "Gee, I forget. But he came home just to marry me, and then we went back to New York together."

Meanwhile Neal left his chair and began pacing about, apparently deep in thought, pausing only to stare out of the window, his face a study in gloomy preoccupation. Then, much to Carolyn's relief, Al Hinkle called a close to proceedings because it was now very late. Everyone filed out and headed for the elevator except Bill Tomson, who dallied hopefully. Carolyn was about to shut the door when "Neal turned back abruptly and, taking a step or two toward me, raised two fingers in an urgent gesture. Then he spun around and joined the others."

Confused and puzzled, Carolyn eventually persuaded the ardent Bill Tomson that she really was tired. He left. Carolyn had washed her face and climbed into her pajamas and pulled her folding bed down from its closet. Then there was a soft knock at her door. It was two A.M. She opened the door cautiously and found Neal Cassady there holding a suitcase.

He came in, dropped the case, sat on the sofa, and explained that he and LuAnne were through. They had been separated for months, he claimed, and any hopes he might have had that they could be reconciled had proved fruitless. LuAnne had thrown him out of the hotel and he had fetched up at Carolyn's place because he had nowhere else to go. Philosophically he added that he had been foolish to marry LuAnne in the first place. She was way too young, but had felt sorry for her and her mother.

It was a convincing performance, Carolyn recalled in *Off the Road*, and so effective that she never thought to challenge Neal's tacit assertion that there was nowhere in the whole of Denver that he might stay. Instead, she mentioned LuAnne's earlier testament to the joys and wonders of her marriage. "Ah, yes, well, you know," Neal responded, "she was overwhelmed by you, and she wanted so badly to make a good impression." Then he added, "She is inclined to bend the truth now and again . . . it's a pity."

Carolyn was struck by a dread thought: the Colburn Hotel had a strict no-overnight-visitors rule. If anyone knew Neal was in her room, she too would be looking for a place to stay. When Neal told her that the night clerk was asleep and that he had walked up the flights unseen, Carolyn realized that if he left now he might still be observed. She felt she had only one option—to let this smooth-talking lunatic stay the night. She reluctantly offered Neal the use of her couch. It wasn't very long or wide, but it was his if he wanted it.

Never one to quit while he was ahead, Neal instead negotiated a place in her bed (arguing that it was clearly too wide for one person, so it seemed ridiculous to waste the available space). Assuming speechless Carolyn's compliance once more, Neal stripped down to T-shirt and shorts, got into her bed, and promptly fell asleep.

Next morning when he awoke he offered to help Carolyn with the stage model she had been working on when she had been interrupted by Bill Tomson's, fateful introduction. The work was again disrupted by Tomson, who was calling her from the hotel bar, insisting that she join him there. She did, only to discover that this was a ruse so that LuAnne could sneak into her room and see Neal alone. She found them there when she went back. She listened dumbfounded as LuAnne announced how glad she was that Neal had found Carolyn who was "exactly what he needed." Carolyn pointed out that she had made no commitment to Neal, and sent LuAnne on her way with a maternal pat and her best wishes. Turning to Neal she made him swear that he would make sure young LuAnne was properly looked after.

In these early stages of their relationship there is an almost comic quality to the disparity between Carolyn Robinson's demure and considerate behavior and Neal Cassady's astonishing dishonesty. As she wrestled with the implications of their burgeoning relationship, he continued to see LuAnne, having sex with her and others including two nurses, Helen and Ruth Gullion, who lived on Grant Street. (The Gullion sisters would be immortalized in Jack Kerouac's *On the Road* as the Bettencourts, and their occupations changed from nurses to waitresses.)

And there was still, of course, Neal's ambiguous relationship with Allen Ginsberg to be resolved. At this time Neal wrote a string of letters to Allen in New York, attempting to redefine that relationship from a distance of some two thousand miles. While insisting that he held Allen in the deepest affection, Neal spelled out a change in the terms of their engagement as early as March 30 when he wrote of his "confused sense of closeness":

"Also, I fear, therein lies our strength of tie to each other, I say I fear, for I really don't know how much I can be satisfied to love you, I mean bodily, you know I, somehow, dislike pricks & men & before you, had consciously forced myself to be homosexual, now, I'm not sure whether with you I was not just forceing [*sic*] myself unconsciously, that is to say, any falsity on my part was all physical. In fact, any disturbance in our affair was because of this. You meant so much to me, I now feel I was forcing a desire for you bodily as a compansation [*sic*] to you for all you were giving me. This is a sad state and upsets me for I want to become nearer to you than any one & still I don't want to be unconsciously insincere by passing over my non-queerness to please you."

We do not know exactly how Ginsberg reacted to this bombshell, for while he would keep and treasure all of Neal's letters to him, it would not be until late 1947 that Carolyn began saving Allen's letters to Neal. It is likely, though, that Neal's admission of "fakery" came as a devastating blow to Allen.

There was worse. In that same letter Neal proposed setting up a ménage à trois, through which Allen could perhaps "become truly straight." This arrangement (which Neal suggested might last from September to June and so allow him to sit in on French classes at Columbia) would see him, Allen, and a girl sharing an apartment. In so doing, Neal suggested, Allen would have more freedom than if he lived by himself "because of the pschological [*sic*] oneness we would obtain. If you grew tired of me, or the arrangement we could always not see each other, or move, or something. So Please, Allen give this a good deal of thought & even if your [*sic*] doubtful of its advantages, try & come to accept it, at least temporarily, in the next few months."

This letter marked the beginning of an absurdly quixotic campaign by Neal to change Allen's sexuality. Neal's belief that his proposed arrangement might "cure" Allen of his homosexuality is proof that Neal was no more enlightened on the subject than the vast majority of people in the 1940s, who viewed homosexuality as a sickness. Also, and as ever, there was an element of self-interest in the preposterous initiative: Neal had long been attracted by the idea of threesomes. Jimmy Holmes told Tom

Christopher that Neal "was always trying to get a third person involved" and recalled a night in a hotel when he himself had rejected an invitation to join in a threesome with Neal and a girl, but was encouraged to watch the couple having sex.

Meanwhile Neal's courtship of Carolyn Robinson was polite and well-mannered. In later years he would often refer to her as "my aristocratic darling," and it is clear that he liked to compartmentalize women into roles that they were then expected to fulfill. So, solicitous and thoughtful in all his dealings with her, Neal adopted a formally polite manner while attempting to win her completely. Carolyn recalls that there was no hint of sensuality in their relationship, only "a restrained affection, as though he considered our relationship to be on a higher plane."

For her part Carolyn was stimulated by the belief that she had at last found a man who could engage her intellectually. As the child of educators she had been raised in an atmosphere of logical thought and lively debate, and had always found it exciting and satisfying to follow arguments through to meaningful and clear conclusions. Her intelligence and wit had so far played little part in her encounters with men. With Neal, however, she was able to lower her defenses and enjoy mutual interests that she found preferable to sex. She was content to assume that a physical attraction would develop naturally as their relationship progressed.

The man who would spend much of his adult life trying to write an intimate autobiography seemed reluctant to tell her too much about his early life. However, Carolyn was appalled by those details of Neal's upbringing he was prepared to divulge. She saw his childhood as a Dickensian tragedy, although if she thought of Neal as poor Oliver Twist, she was very much mistaken—she was dealing with the Artful Dodger incarnate.

On April 10 Neal wrote again to Ginsberg, who had been distressed by his March 30 letter. This time Neal went to great lengths to take the heat out of the situation. In many ways this letter set most of the rules by which their relationship would continue, at least until Allen came to realize once and for all that Neal really did not reciprocate his feelings. As usual, the moods and undercurrents were confused as Neal worked unevenly through his feelings about Allen.

"I believe that instead of this being a complex thing it is rather a simple lack of knowledge," Neal asserted. "You naturally, presume that when I spoke of us living with a woman I meant that I select the woman, whereas, in reality, I meant that we find the proper woman. Now, this example shows a simple failure on my part to tell you these things and I believe it gives a proper slant to an understanding of the whole business."

Responding to a charge from Allen that he lacked emotional depth, Neal agreed, pointing out that even though he considered Hal Chase to be his best friend in Denver, he had only called him once since his return from New York and had only met with him briefly.

"I've brought this out," Neal added, "so you can see an example of my lack of compulsive, emotional need for anyone. Even women are the same, honestly, I'm pretty independant [*sic*] that way, on one hand it bothers me to think I'm unable to be affected emotionally as much as other people seem to be, on the other hand, this objectivity of emotionality, has, in my life, enabled me to move freely in each groove as it came, therefore, the prime difference of our respective personalities lies in this, and once fully realized, will I hope, tend to weld us together, rather than be a cause for conflict." Neal went on to explore this theme in a meandering speculative passage before suddenly reverting to a brisker, more practical tone.

"I'll tell you exactly what I want, giving no thought to you, or any respect or consideration to your feelings. First, I want to stay here and drive a cab until July, second, go to Texas and see Bill and Joan for a few weeks, third, (perhaps) dig New Orelans [*sic*] with Jack, fourth, be in N.Y. by early Sept, find an apt., go to college (as much as they'll let me) work on a parking lot again, and live with a girl and you. Fifth, leave N.Y. in June '48 and go to Europe for the summer.

"I don't care what you think, that's what I want," Neal pressed on. "If you are able to understand and can see your way clear to shepharding [*sic*] me around the big city for 9 months, then, perhaps, go to Europe with me next summer that's swell, great and wonderful, exactly what I want, if not—well, why not? Really, damn it, why not? You sense that I'm not worthy of you? you think I wouldn't fit in? you presume I'd treat you as badly or worse? You feel I'm not bright enough? You know I'd be imposing, or demanding, or trying to suck you dry of all you have intellectually? Or is it just that you are, almost unconsciously, aware of enough lack of interst [*sic*] in me, or indifference to my plight and need of you, to believe that all the trouble and helping and living with me, would not be quite compensated for by being with me? I can't promise a darn thing, I know I'm bisexual, but prefer women, there's a slimmer line than you think between my attitude toward love and yours, don't be so concerned, it'll fall into line. Beyond that—who knows? Let's try it & see, huh?"

Before he signed off with "Love and Kisses," Neal issued one last peremptory command: "you better not fight against it or any other damn thing, so shut up, relax, find some patience and fit in with my mellow plans."

If Allen Ginsberg had not been blinded by love he would surely have ended his relationship with Neal there and then, as well as canceling any plans he had to visit Denver. Neal, however, had saved the best for his postscript: "Say, it just occurred to me from out of the blue, probably since I'm in the act of closing, that you meant it when you called me a 'dirty, double-crossing, faithless bitch'. I've had your letter four days now and I just now suddenly saw that you meant it. Instead [of] mocking or admonishing you, I excuse you automatically, yet seek a hurt reaction inside myself, failing in this, I realize truely [*sic*] what an insensitive bastard I really am, here the most important guy in the world calls me that in all ernestness [*sic*], is honestly hurt and upset by me, and how do I react? do I feel guilty? do I beg forgiveness? hell, no! I'm so emotionally shallow I can only worry about my own lack of emotion in not reacting at all. That's my paranoia. ha! ha!"

Ginsberg was apparently not put off by this chaotic letter since during the next month or so Neal's correspondence to him returned cheerfully to plans for the summer, when Allen was due to arrive. They could work in a Central City hotel owned by Justin Brierly, Neal said, where "all anyone does there is drink, bang & fuck off in general." Neal's plan to become a taxi driver apparently failed because of his police record, so when Allen did finally step off the Greyhound bus in June 1947, Neal was employed by the May Company department store, driving a parking lot shuttle.

Meanwhile Neal continued to court Carolyn chastely, slipping away to make love and fight with LuAnne or to chase the Gullion sisters. He had managed to postpone telling Allen about Carolyn until his friend was about to leave New York.

At that point Neal wrote: "I have met a wonderful girl. Her chief quality, I suspect, lies in the same sort of awareness or intuitive sense of understanding which is ours, (yours and mine) chief forte. She is getting her Master's at D.U. For some strange reason she came to Denver last year, abandoning better places, because she could make money at DU. But she's not really as vulgar as she sounds. Her lack of cynicism, artificial sophistication and sterility in her creative make-up will recommend her to you. She is just a bit too straight for my temperment [*sic*]; however, that is the challenge, just as that is the challenge in our affair. Her basic inhibitions are subtle psychological ones tied up indirectly with conventions, mannerisms and taste; whereas, mine with you are more internal, fearful and stronger. She knows all about Theatre, draws a fine line, and is quite popular. Don't feel that I am overawed by her, though. I would have a justifiable right in being subjective to that. Somehow, my respect for her seems unimportant. I feel the only reason, reaallly, that she affects me so is the sense of peace which she produces in me when we are together. Secretly, she is the reason I am postponing the trip to Texas until later in the season—wait till you meet her."

Allen waited but when he did finally meet Carolyn the occasion had a distinct undercurrent of farce. Neither knew much about the other, so the situation was ripe for misunderstandings, assumptions, and talking at cross-purposes. Carolyn, for example, was under the impression that Neal and Allen had known each other for years, not merely for a matter of months. She also had no idea that they had been lovers, or that Allen was desperate to resume his affair with Neal. For his part, Allen was meeting a person whose existence had been kept from him until a few days earlier and whose presence in Neal's life made her a deadly rival, so it is understandable that his response was reserved when Carolyn greeted him warmly.

In *Off the Road* Carolyn described the Allen Ginsberg of 1947 as "a slim young man, close to Neal's height, with a shock of thick black hair and intense round black eyes encircled by dark-rimmed glasses. The narrowness of his jaw was emphasized by wide, full lips."

She was surprised by the deep, rich sonorousness of the voice that emanated from Allen's slight frame, and while the steadiness of "his owl-like gaze" made Carolyn self-conscious, she "sensed a note of sad kindness in his tone."

Carolyn decided that she would like to know him better. Her wish was immediately granted when Neal informed her that as Allen could neither stay with him nor afford hotel accommodation, he, Neal, had assured him that he could sleep on Carolyn's couch. There was one other alternative to explore, Neal said, but he was sure that he and Allen would be back in no time. Carolyn had been railroaded into an arrangement.

It was almost eleven P.M. before Neal and Allen returned, giggling and whispering outside Carolyn's door. They looked, she said, "like a pair of leprechauns, grinning gleefully, their eyes sparkling and very pink." To her astonishment both men began to undress. While Neal used the bathroom Allen helped Carolyn pull down her bed. It was not until Allen headed for the bathroom that she was able to challenge Neal. Surely he didn't mean to stay as well? Had he told Allen that they were lovers . . . that they slept together all the time? How could he?

Wrapping his arms around her, Neal launched into classic sweet talk: "Now, now, darling—isn't it about time?" he asked persuasively. "How much do you think I can stand? I've been a good boy, now haven't I? But you *know* how much I love you—please, darling, don't be upset, it'll be all right. What can we *do* with Allen here?"

The answer to his rhetorical question was quite a lot, as it turned out. Once it appeared that Allen had fallen asleep on the couch, Neal made his move, which was devoid of tender foreplay. Neal entered her, Carolyn recalled, like "an animal raging in lust. Crushed and bewildered I could only brace myself against the onslaught, fighting back tears and the threatening scream . . . even after he'd collapsed beside me, I felt chiseled from stone, except for the still-searing pain. My astonished ears heard whispers of glowing profound delight, and then he drifted off to sleep."

If Carolyn consoled herself with the hope that Neal might become more considerate in the future, she was wrong. Throughout their life together Neal's lovemaking was rough, even brutal, having everything to do with his satisfaction and little or nothing to do with hers. Carolyn contends that, years later, LuAnne admitted to the same experience, contradicting her earlier account to Tom Christopher that Neal was a gentle, patient, and sensitive lover when they first met.

Allen, of course, heard everything—as he did on other occasions when he was forced to lie feigning sleep on the couch, his head only a foot or two from the end of the bed. In his journal he recorded starkly: "Colburn Hotel Apt. Such terrible nights." Inevitably, this put a strain on his relationship with Carolyn, who remained blissfully unaware of the true nature of his relationship with Neal. It would not be until many years later that Allen admitted that he had misconstrued her murmurs of pain as being cries of pleasure, a misapprehension that only increased his anguish.

There would be even greater distress in store for Ginsberg when his money ran low and Neal found him a job (for twenty dollars a week) as a night-shift janitor for the May Company. Allen moved into a slum-standard red-brick rooming house on Grant Street, not far from the

Colburn. He sublet a dark, dank three-roomed basement there, which boasted little more in the way of furnishings than a small bed, a chair, and a candlestick. Worse, he was now seeing even less of Neal than he could bear while Neal maintained his busy social schedule. According to Allen's notes, Neal would share LuAnne's bed until one o'clock in the morning, dash over to the hotel to see Carolyn, and leave her to join Allen as he came off work. They would talk intensely (often fueled by Benzedrine, a drug Neal also persuaded Carolyn to try around this time) until six A.M., when Neal left to prepare himself for his jitney-driving job.

Given that Neal was also involved in other sexual adventures, it was inevitable that he occasionally failed to show at Allen's sad hovel and then added insult to injury by failing to contact him for days on end. Allen would toil away at the department store with his vacuum cleaner, alternately weeping and hallucinating that he could hear a phone ringing. Of course, when he switched off the vacuum the store was once again wrapped in nighttime silence and he would return to his self-pitying tears, a nervous wreck.

Allen's unhappiness did not render him incapable of artistic endeavor, however, and on July 21 he began work on a poem celebrating the birth of Bill and Joan Burroughs's baby in Texas. He also began to write the collection of poems known as *Denver Doldrums* and sketched out a descriptive prose piece that he later restructured to become the successful poem he called "The Bricklayer's Lunch Hour."

His talks with Neal—when the latter deigned to show—still concentrated on the "sacramental" side of their relationship. It was a subject that Neal still wanted to deny and avoid, especially when it led to Allen trying to press him into sex. Allen viewed Neal's behavior as outright treachery. He had only traveled to Denver to be with Neal, after all, and here he was, abandoned and lost. He began to make plans to leave, deciding that a trip to Texas was the best answer.

Allen was not the only New York connection to feel chagrined by Neal's behavior. Jack Kerouac had arrived in Denver in July, taking time out of a trip to San Francisco where he intended to join Henri Cru as a crew member on a merchant ship. Jack's relations with his former Horace Mann schoolmate and onetime fiancé of Edie Parker seemed to be cordial. On arrival in Denver, Jack called Hal Chase's home from the Denver Greyhound station, and a short time later Hal came to pick him up.

When Jack asked for Neal's address and phone number, Chase shrugged disinterestedly, making it clear that, as far as he was concerned, their friendship was over. Jack was never to learn why Chase pulled away from both Neal and Allen Ginsberg. As Kerouac noted in *On the Road,* "This was the beginning of [his] withdrawal from our general gang." Although Jack was made welcome at the Chase household for a day or so, he was also made aware that a room awaited him at a grand apartment owned by Ed White's parents. Allan Temko, who was visiting Ed White in Denver, was already in residence there with White, but they, too, answered Jack's queries about Neal with a distinct coolness. (Temko, who went on to become a respected architectural critic for the *San Francisco Chronicle,* was never charmed by Neal, of whom he said, "I thought he was criminal in the worst sense. That is I felt he would perform a criminal ripoff on anyone.") It seemed to Jack that there was a conspiracy afoot, with Chase, White, and Temko "generally agreeing" to distance themselves from Neal and Allen who, it appeared, had become "the underground monsters of that season in Denver."

Jack finally tracked Neal down through Allen who, learning that Jack was in town and staying at the White apartment, called him to arrange a rendezvous. Jack hurried over to Allen's squalid basement where he was given a crash course on Neal's activities of the past few months: his affair with Carolyn, his continued relationship with LuAnne, a sudden apparent enthusiasm for midget car racing, and Allen's continued unsuccessful attempts to get him back in his bed.

Jack was eager to see Neal again, so he and Allen made their way across town to the hotel where Neal and Carolyn had recently moved.

They'd left the Colburn in order to get a room with kitchen privileges. Jack and Allen climbed the stairs. Then Allen knocked on a door and ducked back out of sight, not wanting Carolyn to see him. A moment later Neal opened the door. Once again he was naked. Jack caught his first sight of Carolyn lying on the bed, "one beautiful creamy thigh covered with black lace." She had, Jack recalled, a look of "mild wonder" on her face . . . as well she might, given the forces at play all around her.

Neal was clearly delighted to see Jack. He introduced him to Carolyn and announced that it was now imperative for him to take Jack out and—as he had promised back in New York—fix him up with a girl. Noting Carolyn's unhappiness at this plan, Neal looked at his watch. It was exactly one-fourteen, he announced, and he promised to return at three-fourteen—not one minute earlier, not one minute later.

Meeting up with Allen in an alley, Neal spoke extravagantly of Helen, the Gullion sister he had selected for Jack, saying that he would have Ruth Gullion for himself. Arriving at the sisters' house and waiting until Helen returned from work, Jack called Bob Burford, a longtime friend of Ed White's in whom he had found a kindred spirit. Burford had called Ginsberg to let him know that Jack was in town and now rushed over to the Gullion sisters' house to join in the chaotic fun that Kerouac would describe in *On the Road* almost as if it were a scene from a frantic sex farce. After much confusion and an aborted attempt to move the action to Ed White's place (where Allan Temko barred the way, saying there would be no such "goings-on" in his friend's apartment), the company departed for Denver's downtown hangouts, after which Jack eventually found himself alone in the street with his last dollar gone.

Financial rescue for Kerouac came in the form of a telegraphed fifty dollars from his mother. Although he was offered work as a porter at a local market, Jack decided instead to immerse himself in experiencing as much of Denver—and Neal—as he could. During the next few days, however, Neal seemed engrossed in other matters, and when the time came for Kerouac to catch his bus to San Francisco some days later, he realized with a jolt that that he and Neal had not spent more than five minutes alone together.

Instead Jack had spent a couple of days exploring the district around Larimer Street, visiting the Metropolitan Hotel and imagining that every bum he saw was Neal's old man. A female midget newspaper vendor that Neal had told him about was still working the corner of Curtis and 15th, he noted. "I walked around the sad honkytonks of Curtis Street; young kids in jeans and red shirts; peanut shells, movie marquees, shooting parlors. Beyond the glittering street was darkness," Kerouac wrote in *On the Road*, "and beyond the darkness the West. I had to go."

Before he did he also managed to get involved in another riotous expedition, this time to the annual opera and arts festival at Central City, where he saw a production of *Fidelio*; he spent a night partying in a log cabin. The next day he watched a very drunk Bob Burford knock out one man, get them thrown out of a bar when he called a waitress a whore, and hurl a cocktail into the face of an opera singer. Jack also caught his first glimpse of Justin Brierly ("Denver D. Doll" in *On the Road*), in his role as effusive patron of the arts, shaking hands with everyone he met. It wasn't until Jack, Burford, Temko, and Burford's sister returned to Denver that Jack learned Neal and Allen had also made the thirty-five-mile drive to Central City. Allen recounted to him their adventures there, culminating in their return in a stolen car that Neal drove at ninety miles an hour down twisting mountain bends. What Allen did not say was that they had made the outbound journey by bus with Carolyn, but abandoned her soon after arriving. Distraught and hurt, she wandered around the festival until it ended. Only then could she find a ride home. When she got back, she found Neal sound asleep.

Carolyn would feature strongly in Kerouac's memories of Denver. They had hit it off at once, much to Neal's delight, and Jack went several times to watch her rehearse in two plays she had agreed to act in. He was complimentary about her performances and talked keenly about the plays. Both were shy, so they conversed mostly in generalities—comparing tastes in playwrights, authors, and movies, and their shared impressions of New England and New York. Carolyn was struck by Kerouac's perception and intrigued by his constant scribbling of notes in the little notebooks he carried everywhere to capture memories for his future writing.

One evening Jack suggested that Neal and Carolyn join him at a tavern. Neal fed the jukebox and, while Carolyn and Jack danced together on a tiny dance floor (Neal would not dance), darted around the room to talk to other patrons. Occasionally he would return to their table to discuss the merits of one of his jukebox choices with Jack, and they would lose themselves in animated conversation. "They were as much fun to watch as to listen to," Carolyn wrote. "Both mimics, they matched their words with facial contortions, vocal gymnastics, wild gestures, and every now and then broke up in laughter at the other's antics."

The only time she felt the slightest doubt about her dedication to Neal, Carolyn said, was when she danced with Jack, "for here was the warm physical attraction Neal lacked. This realization disturbed me and was difficult to brush away. Jack's manner was tender without being suggestive, although he did betray some tension. As though he had read my thoughts, he said softly in my ear, 'It's too bad, but that's how it is—Neal saw you first.'"

Along the way Jack also managed to meet and befriend Jimmy Holmes and Al Hinkle. As they sat with abashed smiles, Ginsberg declaimed some verses of his "Denver Doldrums." There was one last thing for Jack to do before he left for San Francisco. At White's apartment he finally had sex with Helen Gullion. Then, as he prepared to leave for the bus station, Jack got a call from Neal to say that he and Allen might join him in California. They never did, just as they failed to see Jack off as his bus headed out of Denver. Only Ed White, who had given Jack a ride to the bus depot, saw him leave.

Meanwhile, Neal and Allen had been planning to travel to Texas, where they could stay with Bill Burroughs. This formed only part of a busy, changing schedule Neal had invented for himself, which also involved trips to New Orleans, New York, and Europe. In the end an August trip to the Burroughs' new home in New Waverly, Texas, followed by a quick road trip to New York was all that he achieved. By the time he broke the news to Carolyn, she had news of her own. With her work in Denver finished, she had decided to take up the offer of Cyril Henderson, a British friend of her parents who worked in the Nashville city planning department. He and some other British exiles were heading out to Los Angeles for a vacation and he had written to ask if Carolyn would like him to make a detour via Denver to pick her up. She accepted eagerly, as she already had established some contacts in Hollywood and had long nursed ambitions to work as a movie costume designer. She was hesitantly explaining her decision to Neal when he confessed that he had decided to go to Texas with Allen. He then stunned Carolyn by admitting that Allen was in love with him.

Aghast, she deluged him with questions. Had he known this when he let Allen sleep in the same room with them? If so, that was sadistic—how could he be so mean? Carolyn had not in fact considered for a moment that actual sex might be involved and knew little or nothing about homosexuality. In any case, she assumed Neal's aggressive heterosexual activity precluded him from reciprocating Allen's infatuation.

Neal, in turn, was rather shocked when she offered no resistance to his Texas trip. She reminded him that he was not yet free to marry her and suggested that perhaps a little time apart would prove whether or not their love was strong enough for marriage. She still felt that Neal was the only man for her, but by then she also knew that coercion was not a strategy that worked for him.

Before she left, Carolyn had to fulfill an obligation: she had to appear in a matinee performance of Maeterlinck's *The Blue Bird* for a group of children on the very day Cyril Henderson and his friends were due to pick her up. She had stayed the night with a teacher friend who lived near the university campus and the movie theater where the production was being staged. Rising early the following morning, she returned to their hotel room, planning to share a farewell breakfast with Neal. Hoping to surprise him, she crept up the stairs and turned the doorknob as quietly as possible.

The surprise turned sour as Carolyn saw, on the bed, the naked sleeping figures of LuAnne, Neal, and Allen. Neal raised his head to mutter something, but, Carolyn says, she was already heading out the door, down the stairs, and out into the street, her mind numb and blank. The scene she had just witnessed kept returning to her as she performed in her role as "Light" in "Maeterlinck's sweet, allegorical, interminable children's play."

LuAnne had not, after all, wanted to let Neal go easily. She told Gifford and Lee that Neal broke the news of his imminent departure as they sat on the grass outside the Capitol building. She immediately burst into tears, telling Neal that she could not live without him. "I really and truly thought I would die," LuAnne said. "He started to leave and I grabbed him around the legs, and he tried to get up, and I was saying, 'Please don't leave me, Neal. Don't leave me.' And he kind of gave me a little shove and I fell down, and I stayed there, I was crying so hard. I thought he was gone.

"All of a sudden, I felt his arms around my shoulders and he said, 'I don't ever want to see you begging or crying like that for a man again.' He said, 'Come on. Let's go.'"

It was then, LuAnne claimed, that she, Neal, and Allen made their way to the hotel, and while the three of them did spend the night together, most of it passed with Neal pacifying her, explaining his relationship with Allen and telling her that his leaving for Texas "didn't mean that we were separated or anything."

LuAnne contended in her interview with Gifford and Lee that, when Carolyn made her early morning appearance, only she and Neal were in the bed. Moreover, Carolyn did not simply flee—she became angry and got involved in a verbal scrap with Neal. According to LuAnne, "Neal was, of course, jumping up and down, trying to explain to her. He had three of us. He had Allen, me, and Carolyn, all of us in the room and *was* trying to placate all three of us."

It hardly matters which version of these events you believe, although LuAnne's full account seemed to have a number of significant discrepancies in it. The outcome was the same: Carolyn left Denver in the evening of August 22 wondering if she had experienced nothing more than a summer romance and if she ought to be grateful that she had escaped from Neal in time. Neal and Allen began their trek to east Texas a few days later. Their own relationship was about to be tested to the limit and then changed forever.

12

Neal and Allen's journey to Texas took them only two days—not a bad hitchhiking achievement across vast expanses of open country where a passing vehicle of any kind was still a rarity. Along the way, somewhere in Oklahoma, they found themselves stranded at a crossroads with no ride in sight as darkness began to close in around them. They were in the middle of some deep metaphysical conversation when Allen suggested that they kneel in the road and swear to be lovers forever, if not physically, then spiritually. Neal complied.

The importance that Ginsberg attached to this episode would be confirmed by the number of times he referred to it in his writings. In "The Green Automobile," for example, he wrote:

> The windshield's full of tears
> rain wets our naked breasts
> we kneel together in the shade
> amid the traffic of night in paradise

Also, in an unpublished short story entitled "The Monster of Dakar," he recalled, "I hadn't imagined such a place or such an eternal vow: fidelity, union, seraphic insight, sights of America, everything I could imagine. He accepted it all, just a poor lost soul, an orphan in fact, looking for a father seraph and I was looking for a seraphic boy." Yet with the benefit of hindsight, Ginsberg would admit to biographer Barry Miles, "I realize he was obviously just being nice to me, humoring me."

The two travelers arrived in the east Texas town of New Waverly early in the morning of August 30, 1947.

The town stands on the main highway running southeast from Dallas to Houston. In those days the road was a two-lane blacktop, but it later swelled to become the six-lane Interstate 45 after the Eisenhower administration initiated a massive program to create a network connecting most major U.S. cities in the late 1950s. Bill Burroughs had recently acquired a ramshackle spread a few miles out of town. Set in an oak wood and an abandoned persimmon plantation, it was an ideal, isolated spot to grow the marijuana that he intended to sell in New York. In truth, the farm's ninety-seven acres were not fit for growing anything much more than cannabis sativa; the land had even rejected the opium poppies that Burroughs planted, and they grow in almost any kind of dirt. William Seward Burroughs was no farmer.

His farmstead was as rundown as the land on which it stood. It consisted of a teetering barn, a couple of sheds, and a heavily weathered cabin with a corrugated iron roof. Inside the cabin, Burroughs had erected partitions to make four rooms out of the original two large ones. Outside, he built a large wood frame on which stood a 700-gallon tank that collected rainwater from the roof. There was no indoor plumbing, but the creek was handy for bathing.

Soon after Bill had moved in, leaving a nearby citrus orchard in the sole care of a business partner, Joan and daughter Julie joined him in New Waverly. Burroughs also invited Herbert Huncke to join them. The strange little "family" was soon increased by one when, on July 21, Joan gave birth to a son, William Burroughs Jr.

Burroughs Sr. had quickly adopted the role of outdoorsman, busying himself fencing the property, cutting wood, and strolling over his land, a gun crooked in readiness on his arm, a small dog snuffling at his heels. He used the gun so often that locals at first believed that gangsters had moved in. Their relief was replaced by puzzlement when they found that the newcomers had relieved all the pharmacies for miles of their stocks of nasal inhalers. Despite her pregnancy, Joan had been using up to eight inhalers a day to extract the Benzedrine she needed. Huncke came to the rescue when he made a contact in Houston who could sell them a gross every couple of weeks. He also found a source for paregoric elixir, a camphorated tincture of opium painkiller that he and Burroughs substituted for morphine.

The routine at New Waverly rarely varied, according to Barry Miles. In *Ginsberg: A Biography*, he described it: "At 10:30 each morning, Bill would emerge from his room, wearing a suit and tie, ready to go and get the mail and local paper which he would then sit on the porch and read. Joan looked after Julie and little Billy and cleaned the cabin . . . Huncke's job was to fetch firewood for the outdoor grill and cook the steaks. He also wound up the record player on the porch and changed the needle from time to time, to play Billie Holiday records and the Viennese waltzes that Bill loved."

Herbert Huncke's physical condition and appearance were by now appalling, as he suffered from an undiagnosed skin disease. His presence further added to the weird Southern Gothic appearance of the gun-happy, Benzedrine-soaked Burroughs household.

When Neal and Allen arrived they found Huncke hard at work building a bed for them, cannibalizing some old army cots and cupboards to create a ramshackle structure generally deemed unusable for any purpose. Neal refused to assist, and so Allen—who was furious with Burroughs for not having considered their visit important enough to buy a proper bed—set to helping Huncke finish work on the makeshift one. During their stay Neal and Allen occupied what had been Huncke's room while Huncke himself slept out on the screened porch.

Neal would give his own account of the bed-building to Kerouac, later, and Kerouac would incorporate it in *Visions of Cody* (changing Allen's name to Irwin and Huncke's to Huck):

"And so . . . so we're out on the porch the first day and Irwin, his only concern was building this bed for where we was gonna sleep that night," Neal recalled as the tape recorder's spools turned. "And there was two cots, see, and that was what we were going to sleep on, but Huck and Irwin had the big idea to join the two cots, and that entitled [*sic*] a great deal of work, you see they were Army cots securely stapled together, and [they] had to break all that, and pull the front whole side of both the cots, and then put them together . . . by—terrible, *hard*, see. . . . Well, for *three days* he and Huck worked on that . . . in the front yard, you understand, see? And . . . Huck was queer about the whole thing, see, he was happy and queer . . . you know what I'm sayin [*sic*], he was eggin Irwin on, and Irwin asked when—and that was the reason he went to Dakar, see, because the bed was not a success [*laughter*]. Yes. Soon as we got in bed together—Oh, it never did get built and so finally had to just what we did [*sic*], 'cause we couldn't get it together, we collapsed the other end of both the cots and just slept on the floor [*laughter*], two cots on the floor, with scorpions, man, so it scared the hell out of you, see, you're only that far off the floor, and, ah, man, that was kind of a drag. "

While Allen would remember their visit as generally pleasant, he bemoaned the fact that Huncke's homemade bed meant that, as he told Barry Miles, he and Neal "didn't make out much, and that was the whole point of it. We were gonna go down there and I was finally gonna get satisfied for the first time." In fact, it took Allen no more than two days to realize that Neal was not interested in resuming their affair, or in sex with men in general, and that even the finest store-bought bed would not have made the slightest difference.

For his part, Neal felt Allen's emotional demands to be as much a turn-off as his physical ones. It got so bad that he could no longer bear for Allen to touch him. Allen decided to cut his losses, leave for New York, and resume his studies at Columbia, figuring that he could pick up a crewman's job on a New York–bound freighter in Houston. Neal busied himself helping Burroughs with chores—including erecting a new stretch of fence and building a dam.

In the first of a series of letters to Carolyn calculated to mend the bridges he had set fire to in Denver, Neal tried to persuade her to have him back. They were "the love letters of the century—any century," said Carolyn, who nonetheless failed to save them for posterity. Neal described the farm as "a crazy spot." He would use that same phrase when writing to Kerouac in the first of three letters he composed during the first two weeks, finally combining them to create one long missive.

The first, dated August 31, was obviously written in reply to a letter he had received from Jack, who was now working with Henri Cru in Sausalito as an armed security guard on the site of a construction company's dormitory facility. He had arrived in California too late for the merchant ship crewman's job that Cru had set up. Neal wrote:

> Dear Jack,
>
> Just received your letter; quite a real treat to hear from you.
>
> I've just eaten a huge meal; corn on cob, meat, sweet potatoes, peas, peaches, milk, 2 cokes. I'm too full to move or think. I sweat, I smell, I'm dirty.
>
> I'm scribbling away;
>
> Allen & I left Denver 2 A.M. Sunday & arrived here Tuesday dawn. Slept all day & night. Wed. spent in driving the jeep & getting supplies, talking to Bill & Huncke, getting supplies of tea from the garden etc. This is a crazy spot, but I anticipated that & can accept it with more kick.
>
> Bill has not received his money from his dad yet & we are unable to buy anything. For the last 3 days poor Joan & Huncke have had very little Benzedrine (2 tubes a day) to skim by on. The money should arrive tomorrow, then I shall drive Huncke & Allen to Houston, 90 miles away. [This was a typical Cassady exaggeration. New Waverly is only forty miles from downtown Houston.] Huncke will go in to restock on Benny & various other stimuli. Allen will go in to see if there may be a ship for him to ship on for a couple of weeks (to N.Y., say). I am going in to Houston to drive & dig the place.
>
> I'm building Bill a fence, repairing his garage, laying a cement floor, & damming up his creek with cement.

Your letters are really stimulating, but I find them hard to answer. All I can do is ramble on, for to come down to some one subject or . . .

[Neal continued his three-part epistle early in the morning of September 2.]

Woke up, determined to write; I have several plans in mind, but can't achieve pure certainty on any one of them. Will speak of them when I do, probably in my next letter.

What are you? A guard in a shipyard? How come? Did Henry [*sic*] set it up for you?

Page 2 of your letter was just right, how I wish I could explain myself to you that well, perhaps I may be able to soon. You're right, great & wonderful. *Please* don't feel I either misunderstand or misunderstand less; even worse—don't think; I seem to detect this, but can't believe it, for a moment I'm not sincere with you or that I enjoy your sadness. The only possible reason you could see me in that poor a light is because I'm confused & incapable, at present, of communing with anyone, even Allen. These things settle themselves if you don't push them. Jack, you must have patience with me.

[There was more hard news for Neal to impart when he settled down to writing the concluding portion of his letter on September 9.]

There's a whole week lost, huh? Well, I'm fully qualified to be excused when I tell you where it's gone.

I'll start with Sept. 3. Huncke, Allen & I went to Houston. Huncke went to buy supplies, just as I did, while Allen went to the Union Hall to find a ship. We all met around 4 P.M. Huncke was high & refused to come back here. So we fritted away some time trying to persuade him, but, being unsuccessful, we agreed to meet him at noon the next day.

Allen had gotten a messman's job on a freighter going to France in about 4 days. He decided to report the next day, so he & I came back to New Waverly.

Came dawn Sept. 4, off we rushed to Houston again. We meet Huncke & all 3 of us drove out to the ship to find the steward. Finally found him, he was drunk, so was Allen & Huncke. Allen agreed to come aboard next day & help feed the mess.

We got Huncke to come back with us this time & returned here. The next morning Allen told Bill it was his last day before shipping out, so could Bill give him enough money to rent a hotel room that night.

Huncke, Allen & I would spend that night there (Sept. 5) & at 6 A.M. Allen would depart from us & we would return here by noon the 6th. Bill agreed & off we went.

From the afternoon of the 5th to the morning of the 6th everything was really frantic. First we all got high (on assorted stuff) after an early evening of nigger joints, mad music etc. I told Huncke & Allen I'd see them later & took off in the jeep.

I found a mad woman, drug her back to the hotel room (Huncke & Allen were in the adjoining room) & fucked away. Allen was mad at me, Huncke a bit resentful of my using his room (he had a boy) & the girl was completely bewildered by all this. I passed out cold & didn't come to until 9 A.M. the next day.

The girl was a beauty & had been kicked out by infuriated Allen. Tough. We spent the day in a great hassle. Allen kept postponing going aboard the ship; Huncke kept refusing to leave Houston, & I kept urging more speed or Allen would lose his job; Huncke & I would never get back here in time to bring Bill & Joan ice, etc.

Sure enough, that's what happened; Allen not only lost his job for not showing up, but also was fouled up with the union. All of us returned, dejected, to the downtown area. Huncke still wouldn't come back here & so again Allen & I returned alone & promised to meet H. at noon the next day. That was just the start of more bullshit.

I'm going to cut this short; suffice to say, Bill was angry, (the meat had spoiled), 5 days had been wasted, & we were right back where we started.

The next day I took Allen back to Houston for the last time.

Huncke was met by us & we all sat in the union-hall 4 hrs with Allen hoping to get another ship. Well, he didn't, & the time came for Huncke & I to return here. So, after very tender goodbyes, he & I left Allen in the union hall, waiting to find a ship, reading Henry James & musing on his fate. That was the last we've ever seen or heard of him. Goodbye to Allen for now.

Incidentally, the girl I'd had that night is now in the nut-house, she was picked up, babbling, on the street the next morning. Too bad. Her beautiful body was matched by an idiotic mind. I feel truly sorry & wish I could see her again & perhaps could help her in some way.

Write me here. We leave for N.Y. in a month.

Am I excused for not writing sooner? This won't happen again. So write me, man & watch the answer fly back.

Your pal.

Neal.

P.S. I have a terrible pen, a cardboard box as a stand & a terrible looking handwriting, so please excuse.

N.

"writ by hand" is right

P.P.S. Have you heard from Hal? What's new? Although I know there's little that can be new with Hal.

P.P.P.S. Answer soon & call me down for all my bad habits that prevent me from writing a good letter. Give me pointers, pal.

Neal.

For once, Neal's account of a hectic few days did not stray into unnecessary embellishment. The only known diversion from fact lay in his description of his night with the sad, demented girl, who had only just been discharged from a local mental hospital. According to Huncke and Ginsberg in separate accounts, Neal had taken some barbiturates and these kicked in as he drove up to the front of the Brazos Hotel. Managing to steer the car into a no-parking zone, Neal brought it to a stop by hitting the curb and the girl had to drag him upstairs to the room he and Allen had reserved for their last night together. If Neal and the girl did have sex, it was entirely because of the girl's efforts—Neal was too stoned to do anything voluntarily.

Allen's fury when he returned and discovered them was terrible to behold—he had been betrayed, deceived, and—as he saw it—cuckolded. It is not surprising that he buried his head in a Henry James novel when the time came for Neal and Huncke to leave him at the union hall. After they had gone, he found a ship—a collier bound for Dakar, Senegal—on a voyage that would take twenty days to reach Africa, with ten more in port, and then take another twenty days to return to the United States.

Allen took the job, even though he knew this meant he would miss the start of the next Columbia term. Writing to his father (who was not aware of Allen's sexual orientation at this point), Allen promised to return to school in January 1948 and to use some of the money he was about to earn to buy his first course of psychoanalysis.

Neal stayed at New Waverly to help with the marijuana harvest. When things got slow, he stacked tin cans and bottles on a fence so Burroughs could try to shoot them. What with his regular intake of morphine, Benzedrine, and prodigious amounts of alcohol, Burroughs was not the world's finest marksman. Neither was his accuracy improved by the fact that he often took his potshots out across the yard from the comfort of a chair by the window of his room, or that he was notoriously nearsighted. On other occasions he would while away the time shooting with an air gun at used-up inhalers he had lined up on the mantelpiece. The New Waverly farmstead was "a crazy spot" indeed.

When the harvest was finally gathered, Neal took his turn driving Bill, Huncke, and the weed back to New York; for once it was Neal, so often the source of terror while driving, who was overcome with fear whenever the visually impaired Burroughs insisted on taking over the wheel. They finally made it safely to New York on October 2, and Burroughs immediately got down to selling his crop. When Joan Vollmer arrived from Texas by train, her dazed and drugged condition got her promptly admitted to Bellevue.

Neal hung around in New York with Burroughs, Huncke, Vicki Russell, and a jazz vocalist Kerouac would later call "Stephanie James" when he transcribed his taped conversations with Neal for *Visions of Cody.* Neal's take on her was that she was "a gone singer." Burroughs also mentioned her in his 1953 novel *Junkie,* calling her "Marian." Her real name was Stephanie Stewart, and it was she who presented Neal with a stack of jazz records that he would carefully transport to San Francisco. He stayed in New York for more than three weeks, hoping either to get news of Allen or to meet up with him in one of their old haunts. He was also able to persuade Gabrielle Kerouac to let him use Jack's vacant room in Ozone Park for a couple of nights, another testament to his charm in the light of Gabrielle's habitual antagonism toward her boy's buddies.

On October 29, only two days after Neal gave up and left for Denver (en route to San Francisco), Jack arrived from California and Allen finally returned from Africa. Crossed paths, missed rendezvous, and meandering detours would come to characterize the lives of Neal Cassady and his circle over the next two decades. For now, despite everything that had passed between them, Ginsberg had hoped to find Neal still in New York. Instead, he received nothing but "a harsh note" saying that Neal was going to marry Carolyn.

13

NEAL'S BUS rolled into San Francisco one cold and foggy evening in early November 1947. As she had promised, a nervous Carolyn was waiting for him outside her workplace. Neal was just as nervous, though he greeted her with a broad smile. Both were too shy to embrace. Carolyn took quick note of Neal's appearance—he was still wearing that dark blue New York thrift shop suit and T-shirt under his overcoat, and he was still carrying the familiar roped-together cardboard suitcase. Neal also had two cardboard cartons with him that contained the records that Stephanie Stewart had given him in New York. Carolyn says that her belief in his devotion was somehow reconfirmed when she learned that he had traveled all the way from the East Coast by bus, keeping his coat tucked under him at all times to make sure it did not get wrinkled.

Their reunion took place in San Francisco and not Los Angeles because Carolyn, after following up as many leads as she could in Hollywood, had come to two conclusions—first, that she was not destined to become the new Edith Head, and second, that she did not particularly like L.A. When she finally found a company that liked her portfolio, the people there could do no more than offer her the next job that became vacant—but they had no idea when that might be. Carolyn's sister Jane already lived in San Francisco, and she decided to join her there. Although Jane was delighted to have Carolyn stay, her husband was less welcoming. Carolyn found a job selling jewelry in a department store and then began looking for accommodation of her own. She found it "in a quaint house on Telegraph Hill with a wild woman who rented me a cot and a chest in the corner of her glassed-in front porch overhanging the bayside cliff." Carolyn's landlady, then in her seventies, was the widow of a painter. She dyed her hair platinum blond, boasted "claw-curled fingernails enameled in brilliant red," dressed habitually in Oriental pajamas, and drank gin from first light. As though to confirm her eccentricity for anyone still in doubt, she would also play the ukulele, strumming along to a radio that was invariably tuned between stations and emitting nothing but static. Much as she loved her new address and its breathtaking view of Oakland and Berkeley across the Bay, Carolyn was obliged by Neal's impending arrival to find more suitable accommodation on the other side of the water, in the Richmond district. She found an elegant two-bedroom apartment owned by a seafaring friend who was about to leave on a six-month voyage. It was ideal for a young couple who needed lots of time and space to themselves. Neal was genuinely impressed when he saw it for the first time.

That first evening, after dinner, Carolyn braced herself to ask the questions that had hung in the air between them since Neal's arrival. She knew that he had passed through Denver on his way from New York, so she naturally wondered if he had seen LuAnne. And, if so, had LuAnne gotten the annulment that Neal had promised she was arranging?

Neal was evasively noncommittal, suggesting that they leave that matter until the morning, so as not to spoil the evening. Anyhow, he went on quickly, to make his homecoming complete he had "a super-special, extry-ordinary, sen-sa-tional treat" for Carolyn. Why not stack the dishes in the sink and then come and sit down with him? Carolyn did, and then slipped into a brand-new nightdress and robe. When she returned to the lounge Neal was perched on the couch with a sheet of newspaper spread on the coffee table. On it, Carolyn saw, was a green mound of what seemed to be small vines, little round seeds and twigs. She was about to have her first experience of marijuana, all the way from New Waverly, Texas, via New York and Denver.

While he separated stems and seeds from leaves, Neal kept up an uninterrupted flow of persuasive patter, telling Carolyn, "You must have no fear, hear me? It is completely harmless, I promise you. All the tales you've doubtless heard are entirely false, perpetrated by Anslinger and his boys [Harry J. Anslinger, commissioner of the federal Department of Narcotics from 1930 to 1962] to keep up employment in the narcotic squads. All this does is heighten your sensory perception, awaken your own true awareness, and speed up your thought processes, while giving the impression that time has immeasurably slowed. You'll see more and see better . . . colors . . . patterns . . . you'll hear every note of every instrument, simultaneously. You'll be amazed at how much you usually miss. Oh, ho, ho . . . just you wait. You think you've heard music? You've never heard it until you hear it on tea."

And all this proved true for Carolyn. As they lay on the floor with the record player on, Carolyn says that every cell of her body vibrated; she relaxed into the glorious sensation of time expanding. Neal smiled at her and sighed. They were going to have a beautiful life together, he said. He could see them at eighty, sitting on their veranda, rocking in their chairs . . . and they'd never have to say a word. They would be so one, so in tune, that they could communicate with just a smile or a nod.

Neal eventually put Carolyn through a weeklong marijuana induction course. While she continued to enjoy the increased second-by-second awareness and the sensation of well-being that smoking dope brought, she was never able to get over her fear of being discovered in what was, after all, an illegal act. Carolyn's resentment at the thought of her mind being influenced or controlled by an outside agent eventually led her to give it up.

The morning after his arrival in San Francisco Neal opened a letter from Allen, who was hurt that Neal had not bothered to wait for him in New York, and angry at him for what he perceived to be the coldness of his note. He concluded: "I suppose I must say goodbye then, but I don't know how." It was certainly Allen's goodbye to Carolyn; Allen would not address her directly for several years and, when he did make mention of her in letters, consistently misspelled her name as "Caroline." Carolyn remains remarkably understanding about his stance, saying that it was only an accident of gender that put her where Allen wanted to be.

If Allen's letter wasn't a bad enough start to Neal's day, when Carolyn returned home from work she insisted on returning to the matter of the annulment. Neal admitted that he had stopped in Denver and had found LuAnne. Pacing the floor, he called LuAnne a bitch; she said that she couldn't—or wouldn't—get the annulment because she wouldn't have the money for three weeks. However, she'd promised that she would definitely do it. But what were a couple more weeks, Neal wheedled, when they had a whole life together to look forward to? It wouldn't be long, he swore, and he would keep putting pressure on LuAnne. Carolyn, who had no doubt that Neal was as keen to get married as she was, decided to accept his promise and put LuAnne out of her mind.

Later that day Neal wrote an apologetic letter to Kerouac, whose delayed return to New York on September 29 had been the result of an encounter with a beautiful Mexican American migrant worker named Bea Franco. Kerouac had met her in Bakersfield while traveling from Sausalito to Los Angeles by bus. They rode on together, staying first in a Hollywood hotel and then moving to Selma, California, where Jack tried—and failed—to make it as a cotton picker. Although he and Bea discussed settling down together in New York, their relationship ended the day Jack returned to Los Angeles once more, where another of his mother's fifty-dollar money transfers and a bus ticket to Pittsburgh were waiting for him. This two-week affair furnished Jack with the material for a short story, "The Mexican Girl," which would be first published in *The Paris Review* and later incorporated into *On the Road*.

"My conviction that Carolyn was enough, is, I find correct," Neal wrote, "so don't worry about your boy Neal, he's found what he wants and in her is attaining greater satisfaction than he's ever known."

There was progress, too, on the writing front, Neal reported. "Since arriving I have begun to note little thoughts, actions, etc. written them on scrach [*sic*] paper and along with my attempt to recall all my past life and record it in a semi-outline (similar to a diary) is, I'm sure, enough writing to occupy my time this winter."

From this it would seem that Neal had begun to sketch out the beginnings of what would eventually become *The First Third.* Equally important, Neal felt, was a breakthrough in his approach to writing. He told Kerouac: 'I am finding it easier to led [*sic*] a more productive life, having escaped the fixation on my need-to-write (have you?). I now find I'm relaxed enough to start plugging away at it; this seems to fit my temprement [*sic*] to a greater extent than the old, frantic, unreasoning drive—which, when not let out, started to rot in my gut; sterility followed."

Some time in the next few weeks Neal received another letter from Allen, apparently written from the depths of despair. Now living alone in a small furnished room on West 27th Street, Allen was devoting his time to consuming vast amounts of Benzedrine and trying to perfect the art of writing rhyming couplets. If the stanza he included in this particular letter is anything to go by, Ginsberg still had a lot of work to do. An extract from a longer poem he called "The Creation of the World," it featured these maudlin lines:

> This was such grace, to think it is no more
> I cannot mock in dignity, but weep.
> And wherefore dignity? The heart is sore;
> True lovers have no dignity to keep,
> And till I make departure from this shore,
> My mind is sorrowful and will not sleep;
> And mockery is no good, nor mind is, nor
> Is meditation, sadness is so deep.

Allen went on to tell Neal that he could now admit that he knew "more or less consciously that all the 'purity' of my love, its 'generosity' and 'honour' [*sic*] was, though on its own level true, not at all my deeper intention toward you, which was and is simply a direct lover's."

In other words, however much he had dressed up his feelings with protestations of 'holy' and 'sacramental' love, Allen was admitting that his fundamental interest in Neal was, and had always been, purely physical.

Allen asked Neal what he had to do to get him back. "I will do anything," he promised. "Any indecencies any revelations any creation, any miseries, will they please you. I am lonely, Neal, alone, and always I am frightened. I need someone to love me and kiss me & sleep with me; I am only a child and have the mind of a child. I have been miserable without you because I had depended on you to take care of me for love of me, and now that you have altogether rejected me, what can I do, what can I do?"

His desperation now in full control, he continued: "I have adjusted my plans to yours, my desires to your own pattern, and now I do ask—I pray—please neal [*sic*], my neal come back to me, don't waste me, don't leave me. I don't want to suffer any more, I have had my mind broken open over and over before, I have been isolate and loveless always. I have not slept with anyone since I saw you not because I was faithful but because I am afraid and know no one."

Neal decided not to reply to this or the next similar letter, which again saw Ginsberg alternately pleading, threatening, and groveling. Within a few months Neal's sense that this would all blow over was proven correct, and the two men returned to more amicable exchanges and a more ordered friendship. What Neal did not know was that Allen's despair deepened during this time because of the fact that his mother's mental deterioration worsened; he had no option but to authorize her doctors to carry out a prefrontal lobotomy. It was a dreadful decision for him and his brother Eugene to make (their parents had divorced, and Louis Ginsberg now had nothing to do with Naomi), and so it was left to the twenty-one-year-old Allen to sign the appropriate forms.

Now convinced that nobody loved him, Allen also dived into a bout of promiscuity as aggressive as it was sad. In his own words, he became "more actively queer," trolling gay bars and telling Kerouac that he had become "one of those people who goes around showing his cock to juvenile delinquents." He was also able to coax Jack into having sex again, especially when Kerouac was high on Benzedrine, and was particularly triumphant when he persuaded Jack to give him a blow job.

While this sad episode was unfolding, Neal and Carolyn were taking every advantage they could of San Francisco's vibrant arts and social scene, attending concerts, plays, and lectures; going to the zoo, the movies, galleries, and Chinatown; playing board games at home; or simply sitting and watching the sailboats in the bay.

Carolyn was thrilled by Neal's ability to absorb the nuances of every situation and elaborate on them with reference to other areas of life, literature, philosophy, or history. When they attended the theater (a novel experience for Neal) he could barely sit still, so engrossed was he in every aspect of the play and the actors' roles. Describing this newly acquired love of the stage, Neal told Kerouac: "I do love to do take-offs on everybody: Chaplin, Barrymore, etc. I feel the urge and jump up and act out, stage, direct, costume and photograph an entire Class B movie . . . Scene after scene rolls out; one coming from another, and soon I'm portraying everybody from the script writer to the temperamental star; from the leader who arranges and conducts the music for the soundtrack to the stage hands who rush in and out with the sets."

In November he wrote Kerouac, breathlessly: "I saw the great, one and only, Thomas Mann [the German Nobel Prize–winning novelist and essayist; author of *Death in Venice* and *The Magic Mountain*] day before yesterday. He gave a terrific lecture on 'Nietzsche in the Light of Modern Experience.' It was not a simple rehash of stock thought and inept handling of our Friedrich, but rather, pushed into the real 'rarified [*sic*] air' of true understanding; not abstract nonsense and trashy, trite inquiries into his motives, etc . . . but honest dealment with the problem."

There was, Carolyn says, only one cloud in what she called "the glorious and fulfilling days of our first two months." Sex with Neal had not improved to the extent she had hoped, but she resigned herself to this flaw in an otherwise idyllic life. That life became better still when, early in November, Neal at last found a job—with a service-station chain that had come up with a headline-grabbing and extremely successful approach. As Carolyn described it, "Their idea was for five men to hit a car at once and see how fast they could service it, including washing the inside of the windows and vacuuming the floors."

It was, she says, exactly the kind of challenge that Neal loved, even if he disliked the company's high-pressure sales methods. He threw himself into this new career, memorizing the voluminous sales literature and procedures, out-working, out-smiling and out-cheering his workmates. His bosses were suitably impressed and rewarded him with frequent raises.

On the afternoon of December 1, 1947, Neal and Carolyn were sitting at home, playing a leisurely game of chess. It was a Monday, Carolyn's day off work from the department store. She was relaxed and untroubled, quietly anticipating a rosy future with Neal. Then the doorbell rang. Standing on the stoop were two young women. It took Carolyn a moment to realize that she was looking at LuAnne and her friend Lois Williams.

As Carolyn recalled, "This LuAnne was not the little girl in pigtails I had last seen. Here was a beautiful, sophisticated young woman, well groomed and chic. Her hazel eyes were shadowed by thick black lashes, her complexion waxen smooth, her wet red lips curved in a stunning smile over those glistening perfect teeth, all framed in a huge white fox-fur collar. She was breathtaking."

Regaining her composure, Carolyn invited them in. They teetered on high heels into the next room, where Neal just stared as LuAnne advanced, her hand outstretched. Neal did not take it. LuAnne explained that they had arrived a few days earlier with someone called George, someone Neal was supposed to remember. George (Murphy) had been nagging and nagging LuAnne to marry him. Without going that far, she had accepted his offer of a trip to San Francisco—on condition that she could bring along Lois as her chaperone. LuAnne laughed at her little joke, but Carolyn noticed that the more LuAnne twinkled and chattered, the surlier Neal became. Always the courteous hostess, she invited LuAnne and Lois to stay for dinner, so they could bring Neal up to date on events and friends in Denver.

LuAnne continued to bubble throughout the meal, apparently oblivious to Neal's ever more curt replies and deepening frown. Carolyn was amused—LuAnne was "evidently doing some getting even, and I had to admit that Neal deserved it. She played her cards well and got just what she wanted: Neal was angry on all counts."

Carolyn believed that LuAnne posed no threat to her now solid relationship with Neal, for they were as inextricably tied to each other as any married couple. There was only one question in her mind—had LuAnne obtained that annulment yet?

It turned out that LuAnne had not.

14

DESCRIBING THE NEW remodeled LuAnne to Jack in a letter a few days later, Neal wrote: "She is quite changed, affected a more sophisticated air, came on hep and moved with improved poise. After some preliminary skirmishing we reverted back to old naturalness of relationship and it was with great difficulty I finally managed to extract the commitment of desire to gain an annulment from her. The process of becoming legally free now rests on money. After the 5th I'll have some and forward it to her mother in Denver to start the divorce.

"I think, dear Jack, we've underestimated money. I predict a lucrative year for me, since I'm goin' to make money one object of this year's struggle. Hear me?"

Carolyn, who now saw most of Neal's outgoing letters, did not pick up on Neal's phrase "the old naturalness of relationship." If she had done so she would have been spared much shock and heartache when she finally learned the truth. Neal and LuAnne were having sex again, simply picking up where they'd left off only five months earlier.

Before Carolyn learned of this latest duplicity, she and Neal spent a blissful Christmas together. He was astonished as goodies began arriving from members of the Robinson clan—home-smoked country ham from Tennessee, cheese from Canada, Carolyn's mother's annual English plum pudding, and a huge box of cookies, most of which miraculously survived their journey through the mail intact. Neal was visibly touched when each package contained a little something especially for him, for it made him realize that Carolyn's family had accepted him as a member. It was not, however, a situation with which he was entirely comfortable, as he confided to Allen in a letter he wrote on December 30, the contents of which he kept from Carolyn, for good reason: "On December 1st

LuAnne came to town and since then has been a constant thorn; she is with an old beau and a girlfriend and together they all live in a downtown hotel. Since she doesn't work (although the other two do) and does nothing, even read, she has much time to come by my station in his car, call on me at home in the morning while Carolyn is away and before I go to work; in short, my efforts toward an annulment have been little rewarded. However, now that I've at last (during several emotional scenes) made it plain to her that all is finished, she has again promised to have her mother gain our legal separation.

"I am moving by myself again because Carolyn has practically gotten married to me in the eyes of her family, and unless I break quickly things may become drastic."

That same letter also contained Neal's stated plan of returning to Denver, locating his father and his sister Shirley Jean, and setting up home with them. It would remain an unfulfilled mission.

Neal's inner conflict and intention to break from Carolyn was exacerbated by LuAnne's continued presence in San Francisco and his growing hatred of the service-station job. He broke out in hives, a painful condition that recurred whenever he allowed—or caused—his life to become too complicated.

It was on January 7, 1948, that Neal wrote Jack a letter that would alter the young author's approach to writing in the future and help him adopt a more relaxed, naturalistic style. Until then, Kerouac had followed existing accepted rules in the creation of his work-in-progress, *The Town and the City.* He was now nearing the end of two and a half years' labor, which would result in a novel that contained more than 300,000 words.

In this letter, which Jack would later cite as the principal spur for the change of direction that would help him find his own voice, Neal admitted that his earlier optimism about making a breakthrough and acquiring the discipline necessary to write had proved premature. He was now "not sure that the roots of the impulse to write go deep enough." However, he added, if he found that writing became a "must," as Kerouac had, "even my most indifferent and trivial hours must become an expression of this impulse and a testimony to it."

Then came the key passage that so greatly influenced Kerouac: "I have always held that when one writes, one should forget all rules, literary styles, and other such pretensions as large words, lordly clauses and others phrases as such—rolling the words around in the mouth as one would wine, and, proper or not, putting them down because they sound so good. Rather, I think one should write, as nearly as possible, as if he were the first person on earth and was humbly and sincerely putting on paper that which he saw and experienced and loved and lost; what his passing thoughts were and his sorrows and desires; and these things should be said with careful avoidance of common phrases, trite usage of hackneyed words and the like. . . . Art is good when it springs from necessity. This kind of origin is the guarantee of its value; there is no other."

It is hard to say what specifically inspired or influenced Neal Cassady to set out his views about writing in this memorable and lucid passage. A long list of books he was planning to read or reread compiled ten months earlier included the work of several writers—Evelyn Waugh, e. e. cummings, and Albert Camus among them—who would have had little time for spontaneous outpourings of the sort Neal was advocating. Auden, Rimbaud, Wyndham Lewis, Eliot, and Yeats also featured in his list. Not included, although not necessarily unknown to Neal at this time, was Ralph Waldo Emerson, whose preoccupation with self-reliance (and religion and transcendentalism, both of which would interest Neal later in life) might well have struck a chord with someone who survived a tough and opportunistic Denver upbringing. More significantly, it was Emerson who referred to art as "the old tragic Necessity" in an essay on the subject, and also gave us the quotation "Classic art was the art of necessity." Either line might have prompted Neal's own much-quoted line about art being good when it springs from necessity, but whatever its inspiration, Neal's theory sounded most plausible to Jack Kerouac. It came, however, too late and perhaps in too abstract a form to influence

The Town and the City in any significant way. Some three years later Neal would write a virtuoso letter that put this theory into dazzling practice, with immediate and radical repercussions for Kerouac's own writing.

Meanwhile, Neal's physical and psychological condition continued to deteriorate. He admitted to Carolyn that LuAnne had taken to visiting him at the service station (though he still did not admit to the resumption of their sex life), and he mentioned his rage over the fact that she was still stalling in the matter of the annulment. He readily agreed to Carolyn's suggestion that he quit his job and find something less demanding, but she ascribes the marked and rapid improvement in his physical condition to the fact that he had also bought his first car—a twenty-year-old Chevrolet with its original engine, paint job, and upholstery. He had made a down payment of $100 toward the sale price of $225, he told Kerouac. The result was, he added, "I'm broke and in debt up to my ears."

Trying to rectify that state of affairs, Neal found work selling encyclopedias, but it took him only a few days to realize he was singularly ill-suited for the job. Then one evening during dinner, Carolyn announced she was pregnant. Although she had expected to have a family with Neal one day, she says, this was not the way she had anticipated it happening. She suspected that he would be no more thrilled than she was but had faith that he would stand by her. They would work it out together.

In fact, Carolyn was more concerned at the shame her condition would bring on her family. It would also, she knew, confirm her mother's reservations about her daughter becoming engaged to a man the family had never met. Neal soothed Carolyn's fears, but the next day he announced that he had figured out how they could "take care of it." Seeing how crushed and upset she was by this—so clearly horrified at the thought of an abortion—Neal nimbly changed strategies, gathered Carolyn in his arms, asked her forgiveness, and protested his love for her and their unborn child. Eventually mollified, Carolyn accepted his apologies and protestations. "I believed him again and felt relieved," she wrote, "pushing back the question of why he hadn't discussed the idea [of abortion] with me first."

Carolyn began to make plans for Neal's birthday, which fell on February 8. She knew that he attached great importance to such anniversaries so, despite an extremely limited budget, set about making the event as memorable as possible with a special dinner consisting entirely of Neal's favorite dishes. Carolyn had to work on his birthday, and when she left the store, she expected to find Neal waiting for her at his usual parking spot in a loading zone. She was more puzzled than alarmed (maybe the car had a flat, or perhaps he had a surprise of his own up his sleeve), but when there was still no sight of the Chevy after a bone-chilling twenty-minute wait, Carolyn, ill at ease, decided to take the streetcar home.

It was not quite dark when she walked down the block toward the apartment. She was relieved to spot Neal's car by the curbside. She had passed it and was turning up their walk when a movement in the back seat caught her eye. Carolyn went back and peered in. It was Neal. Alarmed and confused she pulled the door open, asking, "Darling, what is it? Why . . . ?"

"Go away!" Neal barked, his tone gruff, hateful, and chilling. It was only then that Carolyn spotted the silver revolver in his left hand. Slamming the car door shut she raced into the apartment. She described her panic in *Off the Road*: "I was shaking now, violently. I paced rapidly around the rooms in an effort to control my pounding heart and chattering teeth. A gun! Neal with a gun! He'd always felt as I did—violence of any kind sickened me, but firearms terrified me. . . . How and where could Neal have found one? And, more important, why? I didn't know how to unravel the nightmare, nor what to do next. I sat down, desperate to calm myself and think constructively."

Neal came in slowly, the pistol dangling in his hand, his face ashen and drawn. Slumping down on a chest beside Carolyn's chair, he held out the pistol, handle first, and pleaded with Carolyn to shoot him. "Please," he implored her, "You do it . . . help me. I've tried all day. I can't do it."

Fearing for his sanity, Carolyn took the gun and placed it on the highest bookcase shelf she could reach. Neal sat rocking, his head in his hands, not responding to Carolyn's anguished questions until she asked where he had gotten hold of the gun. Leaning back against the wall, Neal admitted that it was Al Hinkle's—he had seen it in the glove compartment of Al's car and stolen it. Al had bought it in Texas, or so he believed.

Carolyn grabbed the phone and dialed Hinkle's number in Oakland, where he had moved a few months earlier to find work with the Southern Pacific Railroad.

When Al answered, Carolyn only had to say, "It's Neal," before Al responded, "I'll be right over."

While they waited for Al to drive the ten or so miles from Oakland, Neal calmed down and stood to stare silently out the window. After what seemed an interminable silence, and still staring out into the dark, he finally spoke. "Please, Carolyn, forgive me," Neal pleaded. "I didn't mean to frighten you. I really am sorry. I'm OK, don't worry. I haven't lost my mind, though I thought I had for a while."

Neal crossed the room, knelt beside Carolyn and laid his head on her lap. Unable to make sense of this scenario and unwilling to disturb the fragile peace that seemed to have descended on Neal at last, she gently stroked his hair until they heard the sound of Al Hinkle's racing footsteps outside. Neal opened the door, adopting an obviously fake jocularity as he explained to Al that he and Carolyn had merely been having "a little family crisis."

Challenged by Carolyn, Al conceded that the pistol was his. Taking it down from the shelf and removing the bullets, he said he had been wondering what had happened to it—he had forgotten to lock his car and was afraid someone had stolen it. He justified his ownership of a gun by explaining that he had simply seen it in a pawnshop window in El Paso and bought it on impulse. "Guess it's a leftover from my cowboy hero days," he offered lamely. Fascinated, intrigued, and frightened in equal measures, Carolyn picked up the gun to examine it. The moment her finger came into contact with the trigger, it released. Carolyn dropped the pistol, even more frightened by the thought that Neal's finger had been crooked around that hair trigger.

Al Hinkle calmed them both down. Eventually, he suggested that he and Neal play chess. Carolyn left them to it, heading for the kitchen to prepare dinner. Even if Neal's birthday had hardly been what she might call normal, she was determined to create the illusion of normality.

It would be twelve years before Carolyn learned the unsavory truth about that day, when Al and LuAnne finally supplied the details. Al told Carolyn that Neal had called on him in Oakland early that morning, hoping that his always-sensible friend could help lift the depression that was enveloping him. For once, Hinkle was unable to help. Tormented and desperate as to how to handle the problem of LuAnne, Neal spotted Al's gun, pocketed it, and drove to LuAnne's hotel. According to LuAnne, Neal had awoken her, threatened her with the gun, and demanded that she accompany him to Denver to get the annulment. Playing for time and hoping to change his mind, LuAnne coaxed him into bed. Realizing what she was up to, Neal dragged her out, forced her to get into his car, and drove to a deserted stretch of beach. He then beat and raped her, LuAnne said, and when he finally allowed her to crawl back into the car, he drove her back to the hotel. Ordering her to go back to her room to change and pack, Neal said he would be back at noon to drive her to Denver. LuAnne did shower, change, and pack, but then fled to the safety of a boyfriend's apartment. She was gone when Neal returned.

It is not difficult to imagine Neal's fury when he realized that LuAnne had escaped. A host of other emotions must have followed, including remorse for what he had done to her that morning and anger at himself for letting her fool him. Self-disgust and dark despair followed.

No matter how many options he considered, and no matter how many solutions he tried to find, things just seemed to get worse. He had no job, no money, and no sense of self-worth. His wife would not release him from the marriage that stopped him from marrying the woman who now carried his child. Worst of all, most of his travails, woes, and worries were the result of his own actions. He had no one to blame but himself, and now he had a loaded gun. He could end it all.

In an interesting footnote to this incident, years later Al would admit that Neal had not stolen the pistol—Al had given it to him to scare LuAnne into coming with him to Denver. Asked why he had never confessed the truth to Carolyn, Al simply said: "I knew she'd be mad at me."

Unsurprisingly, Neal was distracted and unhappy in the days following this bleak episode, spending his time reading and writing as Carolyn tried to match her moods to his. When he was ready to talk, she learned that Neal had tried to kill himself on a number of occasions in the past. Each attempt had ended the same way, with Neal consumed by self-disgust.

Jimmy Holmes would confirm this suicidal obsession, relating to Tom Christopher how Neal once tried to borrow a rifle belonging to the father of his friend Bob Speak. Another time he took out an insurance policy and promised to draft a will naming Speak the sole beneficiary if he would lend him his car. Neal intended to crash the car and kill himself by driving it at an oncoming vehicle. Speak refused, just as he had turned down Neal's request for the rifle. Whenever Neal became really depressed, Holmes said, he would pick a route with lots of blind corners and drive at high speed across those bends on the wrong side of the road. Nothing ever came of these suicidal excursions, Holmes said, "but he did that quite a lot, and that scared me too."

Following the latest crisis Neal decided to drive to Denver at the end of February and persuade LuAnne's mother to begin processing the annulment. He would also pick up some of the belongings that Carolyn had left in Colorado. He would be back in a week, he promised Carolyn. Despite her reservations, Carolyn agreed when she saw how much his mood was lightened at the thought of taking positive action and returning to the open road. The next morning he drove her to work before speeding off. While he was gone Carolyn gathered up her courage and wrote her mother, advising her of her imminent grandmotherhood. As she feared, the reply was condemnatory and scathing. Carolyn was an irresponsible, wanton woman, her mother said, who had brought dishonor on the family. When Neal returned from Denver, Carolyn said he found "a pitiful hausfrau awaiting him." He tried to change her mood with a funny, frantic account of his trip.

Apart from achieving a remarkable driving feat ("Thirty-three hours, baby—just think of that! It's two thousand eight hundred and ninety-four miles, y'know!" Neal boasted), he claimed to have had one desperately dangerous adventure at the top of the Donner Pass when his Packard (he had part-exchanged the Chevrolet in one of eighteen changes of vehicle in less than two years) stopped dead in subzero temperatures. Neal had not thought to fill up with antifreeze. He had sat shivering in the car for seven hours—or so he claimed—wondering if his now redundant death wish was going to be fulfilled, when a bus hove into view. Snowplows had succeeded in opening up the road behind him. Taking pity on Neal, the bus driver used his vehicle to give Neal a push, enabling him to coast down the other side of the mountain. With his windshield wiper broken, Neal said he'd been forced to drive the rest of the way to Denver with his head out of the window in freezing temperatures. It would have been a remarkable story, if true. In common with many of Neal's tales, there was certainly some truth in the account, but it was buried in a fair amount of needless embellishment. As ever, Al Hinkle supplied the facts when interviewed for this book. Al was in fact a passenger in the Packard on Neal's return journey from Denver. He had gone there after the suicide scenario and now offered Neal gas money for a ride back. The route back to San Francisco initially took him north into Wyoming, after which he headed west through Utah via Salt Lake City, and then roughly southwest across Nevada, crossing into northern California near Reno. The Donner Pass is some thirty-five miles southwest of Reno and had nothing to do with what really happened:

> The day we left Denver it was like ten below zero. We didn't get an early start, [so] it was dark when we left. Neal had picked

> up some girl who wanted to go to Oakland—he had hooked up with her for a couple of days. So the three of us get in the Packard and take off. This girl didn't even have a winter coat, and we get up to Greeley [northern Colorado] and there's no more cars on the road. By now it's maybe fifteen below zero. Neal had put some cardboard up by the radiator and he got the engine too hot. And there we were, dropping down in to Wyoming, when the car stalled. If we'd had any sense we would've been scared.
>
> So Neal has me take my railroad lantern out and put it behind the car, and we had some railroad fuses, flares. The only thing we'd seen was a Greyhound bus that we'd passed about an hour before. And that's the next thing that came along, that Greyhound bus, and he stopped for us, up there on that hill, and pushed us down in to Laramie, which was about 10 miles away. I think he pushed us the whole way. It was either push us or leave us out there to die . . . they don't do that kind of thing nowadays. We were just lucky I guess. Anyway we got into Laramie and the block wasn't cracked, so after the thing thawed out we put in some antifreeze and just carried on and we made it to California—we made it all the way over the desert, then the Sierras and into Oakland. I think Neal drove the whole way. And I don't think we pulled over any place, he just drove on. He must have been on something.

Neal's account is full of discrepancies. His claim to have driven 2,894 miles (from San Francisco to Denver and back) in thirty-three hours was nonsensical on two counts: to have covered such a distance in the time he claimed, Neal would have had to average eighty-seven miles an hour—a formidable achievement for a driver in ideal conditions, let alone one making the trip in the depths of winter on regular tires with no snow chains. Factoring in his supposed seven-hour stopover in the Donner Pass (which reduced his actual driving time to twenty-six hours) he would have had to average 111 miles per hour. Neither does Al Hinkle remember Neal being forced to drive with his head out of the window (there was, indeed, no call for Neal to do so), but this detail does bear a remarkable similarity to events when Neal and LuAnne fled Nebraska in 1946, going to New York in that stolen car. In this, as in so many of Neal's tall tales, a favorite detail becomes transplanted, or quite separate incidents are conflated in a parody of truth that echoes the technique of the fiction writer. Never much of a fiction writer in the conventional sense, Neal was certainly an inventive storyteller in his conversations and letters where he was not so much economical with the truth as wildly creative with it. No wonder he advocated the sort of writing that simply echoed spontaneous speech. Trivial anecdotes like that of the stranded car might amount to little in themselves, but their cumulative weight does combine to invite skepticism about any of Neal Cassady's uncorroborated claims.

With the matter of his annulment hopefully now in hand and his failed suicide attempt no longer fresh in his mind, Neal relaxed a little and began preparing for the birth of his and Carolyn's child. He also started looking for a new job.

It was dependable Al Hinkle who came up with the answer Neal was seeking. He was going to join Al on the Southern Pacific Railroad (SPRR), working on the company's freight trains transporting fruit and vegetables from California's citrus groves and farms. The money was good, Neal knew, having seen Al's wage slips from his first season with the SPRR. The job sounded interesting, challenging even. Most important, it did not sound like it could ever be boring.

15

AL HINKLE'S CAREER with the Southern Pacific Railroad had begun as a result of circumstances so colorful and dramatic that they sound more like part of Neal Cassady's life than that of levelheaded, steadfast Al. Early in the summer of 1947, Al's father, a sergeant of detectives with the Denver Police Department, had gone to California on two weeks' vacation and left his smart downtown apartment untended. Al had a key and promptly moved in a motley collection of friends and associates, including a couple of girls who had just been released from reform school. LuAnne was also present, although Neal was off seeking work in Colorado Springs.

Hinkle explained: "Neal had an opportunity for a really well-paid job as a carpenter [there] and he had no place to leave LuAnne, so I promised Neal that [she] could have one of the bedrooms by herself. I think she was true to him while he was gone, but . . . he came back early. I think he was worried about LuAnne, because a couple of her ex-boyfriends would come over and bring the booze and the whatnot . . . dope."

As the date of his father's return loomed, Al organized a Herculean cleanup of the apartment.

> Well, the girls from the reform school sure knew how to work. They cleaned the place spick and span, but we didn't have money to do the laundry, so all the sheets and pillow cases were bundled up, dirty. And there wasn't a crumb of food left in the place. But I had to hide from my Dad, to give him a chance to cool off.
>
> We never got in to trouble with the police department during those two weeks because we kept it quiet—it was a nice

> soundproofed apartment. The landlady, I discovered, was kind of sweet on my dad. She did come to the door a couple of times and did ask, "Who are all these people? . . . I noticed a lot of bottles going out into the trash," but she was kind of nice.
>
> So I went to Pederson's Pool Hall, and was thrown out of there. They said there were detectives looking for me. I was successful in hiding out for three weeks, but came my grandfather's birthday, I had to go see him. I checked the street and checked the alley, to see if my dad's car was there, but I didn't see it. And, of course, my dad was in there, waiting for me.
>
> So, after he'd read the riot act to me, he said I had two choices: I could go to jail or go to California the next day. I wouldn't have had a record, but would have done some time. So he bought me a ticket, and that's how I came to be in San Francisco. I had an uncle there who was a ticket collector on the railroad, and he'd told me that he could get me a job any time I came out. So I had a nice job waiting for me. Of course, I didn't see my uncle till my money ran out—I had to see San Francisco first.
>
> Like he promised, he got me the job—I started on September 11, 1947, and there was at least one month there I made twice the money my dad made as sergeant of detectives. He was making 175 or 180 bucks a month, a lot of money in those days, and I made 325, maybe 350. I was working out of San Luis Obispo. I went down there September 11 to January 3rd without taking a day off. On the road, on the freight trains, we went to Watsonville one way and Santa Barbara the other. Then there were local trains, locals over at Guadalupe. . . . I loved it, I really did.

Al introduced Neal to his uncle, who promised to put in a word for him. This was to be no shoo-in, however, for no matter how well-connected applicants might be, there was a strictly observed protocol before applicants were taken on. Initially, a new man worked off what was called "the extra board," a system whereby runs were either fill-ins on regular runs if someone failed to show up for work, or men were needed for extra nonscheduled trips. Under this scheme, new men signed on at the bottom of a list, only moving up as trains and crews were matched or eliminated. "When your name reached the top of the extra board," Carolyn explained in *Off the Road*, "you were obliged to accept whatever job was next in line. This added a certain sense of suspense and adventure."

The principal drawback to this system was the need to be available by phone at all times—miss a call and you went back to the bottom of the list. The upside of this arrangement was that men could end up working more hours at a higher rate of pay than on scheduled runs.

Every newcomer started work on freight trains and, during the slack winter season, could be laid off. This was precisely what had happened to Al Hinkle. Some men simply found other work during that period, while others saved enough to tide them over. Only when you had enough years under your belt, and enough seniority, could you become a brakeman on passenger trains. There was even more time to serve before you rose to the rank of conductor and could hold down your choice of regular job, either on freight or on passenger trains.

The runs that Neal and Al worked lay between the extremes of Bakersfield and San Luis Obispo to the south, and the Bay Shore yard in San Francisco to the north. During the peak summer months the most common "local" runs picked up farm produce from the Salinas and Santa Clara valleys, but at any given time they could find themselves on a two-week "hold down" anywhere in the network.

After a crash course in the official handbook of signal lights (in order to disguise his color-blindness), Neal successfully completed the examinations necessary for him to enroll in the SPRR's two-week training program, an unpaid probationary period that could very well end with an applicant being deemed inadequate and unemployable.

Neal had been pressuring LuAnne's mother once more about the annulment, and when he returned home on March 29 he found, much to his delight, that the paperwork was finally in place. He would drive LuAnne to Denver and get her to sign it. Neal attempted to calm Carolyn's fears about his spending more time alone with LuAnne by saying that she was now engaged to a sailor—although neither LuAnne nor Neal had much respect for wedding bands or indeed engagement rings. When it came to Neal, however, Carolyn was always easily reassured if she wanted to be. She waved goodbye to him the next morning, as the Packard noisily confirmed its weariness.

A few days later Neal was back, delayed by a minor accident on the way into San Francisco but having at last secured the annulment. Neal and Carolyn already had a marriage license. LuAnne had stayed in Denver, which further added to Carolyn's relief at the outcome of the trip.

Over a celebration breakfast Neal took Carolyn's hand. "So now, my one-and-only," he pronounced, "you and I will blast down to the courthouse tomorrow morning and get hitched at last, eh wot? Hey, baby? You 'n' me forever, like I said, right?"

If it was not the most lyrical of proposals, it *was* what Carolyn wanted to hear; and if there was a portent in the fact that the date on which she finally became Mrs. Neal Cassady was April 1, she did not care to consider it.

On the appointed day, Carolyn rose early and dressed in a light green woolen dress her mother had made, over which she wore a navy coat lined with the same fabric. The matter of Neal's outfit was simply solved—he only had one appropriate suit along with a white shirt and a couple of ties, all purchased for him by Carolyn when he had first gone jobhunting in San Francisco. His New York thrift shop suit stayed in the closet.

Carolyn headed downtown to Post Street and the White House department store where she had agreed to meet a woman, a casual acquaintance, who sold and collected antique jewelry. When this woman learned that Carolyn was getting married, she insisted on providing Neal and Carolyn's wedding rings. All Carolyn had to do was call to say when they were needed; she had done so and they agreed to meet at ten A.M. by the side entrance to the White House. As Carolyn waited for the woman (who was late) she decided to escape a chilly wind by crossing the street and going into the Woolworth's store. While in there, she saw a display of fake diamond rings and felt pleased that she did not have to resort to five-and-dime costume jewelry on her big day. Carolyn returned to the meeting place only to spot the woman she was waiting for diving into Woolworth's and emerging a few minutes later. She came over and pressed her gift on Carolyn with effusive good wishes for the future. Carolyn had to feign delight as her gaze fell upon two rings from the cheap display she had just casually dismissed as being beneath her. She took a cab to City Hall in forlorn spirits.

Her mood lifted at the sight of a smiling Neal, dressed in a suit and waiting at the curb. He presented Carolyn with three gardenias, which she promptly pinned to the lapel of her coat. During the wait to see Judge Clayton Golden she showed Neal the horrible rings they were to wear, and then joined him in a bout of what she described as "those irrepressible giggles that one gets at a time of great solemnity."

At the end of a perfunctory wedding ceremony, it was Carolyn who had to fumble in her bag to find the ten-dollar fee the judge demanded, but, once outside, Mr. and Mrs. Neal Leon Cassady howled with laughter as they ran into the plaza, scattering pigeons and pedestrians. Neal said they could not simply go home—they had to redeem the day somehow.

"If that judge hadn't fleeced me, I'd ask my wife to join me in a glass of champagne and an elegant lunch," Neal pronounced grandly, ignoring the fact that he was not the one who'd paid for the service. Pooling resources, Neal and Carolyn discovered that they could afford no more than a snack at a crowded, grimy diner across the street. The celebratory champagne turned out to be a bottle of beer apiece, but Neal was at his most attentive and charming, and Carolyn sniffed her gardenias happily.

As they left the diner, Neal spotted a small grocery store. "Hey," he said cheerily, "I think we have enough for a six-pack, by gum. We'll have a celebration yet!" They took a streetcar home, as the Packard had finally succumbed following Neal's trip to Denver.

Neal and Carolyn's wedding may have passed unremarked in San Francisco, but on April 12 Carolyn's family's hometown newspaper, the *Nashville Tennessean*, reported the event in its society page, under the headline "Miss Robinson, Mr. Cassady Are Married."

"Dr. and Mrs. Charles Summers Robinson announce the marriage of their daughter, Carolyn Elizabeth, to Neal Cassady of San Francisco, Calif., son of the late Mr. and Mrs. N. L. Cassady of Denver," readers were told.

"The marriage was solemnized on Thursday, April 1 in San Francisco. The bride was graduated from the high school department of Ward-Belmont School in Nashville and from Brennington [*sic*] College in Bennington, VT. She attended Mills College in Oakland, Calif., and the University of Denver in Denver, where she did graduate work in art. Mrs. Cassady studied art in Nashville with the late Miss Pearl Saunders.

"Mr. and Mrs. Cassady will make their home in San Francisco. Mr. Cassady attended Columbia University in New York and holds a position with the Southern Pacific Railroad in San Francisco."

The two pieces of misinformation contained in this item (that both of Neal's parents were dead, and that he had attended Columbia) originated from Carolyn. At this stage in her relationship with Neal she still labored under the misapprehension that Neal Sr. was dead. Similarly, she had no idea that Neal's connection with Columbia University existed only in his imagination and his friendship with former Columbia students Kerouac, Ginsberg, Hal Chase, and Ed White. The truth would only emerge later and gradually.

There was to be no honeymoon for the newlyweds, even if they could have afforded one, for the next day Neal began the two-week course of unpaid railroad training trips. His concern about this arrangement had been assuaged when Al Hinkle offered to cover him financially.

"I wanted so bad to get Neal on the railroad that I persuaded him to give up his job parking cars and take the two-week student trip out of San Francisco—working out of the freight yard at Bay Shore," Hinkle recalled. "He didn't want to do it, so I had to guarantee him what he was making parking cars, which was twenty-five per week, or something. I said, 'I'll give you the twenty-five dollars.'

"No, it was worse than that, because I told him, 'If you don't get to work right away I'll continue to pay you the twenty-five bucks . . . until they call us back to work.'

"And it turns out that was the case, because he completed the student trips and they still didn't have any work for us. So we finally went down to Watsonville, and they have a seniority board down there. Every once in a while they would wheel them in, and that would be the day you started on the railroad. So we went down there and stayed in a dormitory for three or four days.

"Neal couldn't stand it, so he goes back to San Francisco . . . and the day he goes back to the city we get called. They called him to go to work, and he wasn't there, so I took the job. I worked a couple of days, and then he came back. The train-master there kind of liked Neal and kind of liked me both, we were pretty good kids, and he told us they needed some brakemen over at Bakersfield. He said he'd hold two spots for us if we wanted to go to work there. So that's what we did."

What Al did not know at the time was that during his return to San Francisco a dejected and desperate Neal had announced that he had decided to go to sea instead. Carolyn was aghast . . . the baby would be born without him . . . how would she be able to cope? Neal agreed that it was a grim prospect, but it would only be until the railroad picked up. Anyway, he would send her all his pay . . . what else could he do?

Two days later, Neal came home a full-fledged ordinary seaman, carrying papers and an identification card bearing a photo of him taken on a boardwalk under souvenir banners of San Francisco. Two days later he announced that he had signed on with a ship bound for Arabia. It was just then—with Carolyn maintaining a stoic silence, though she felt as if a rug was being pulled out from under her feet—that Al called to tell Neal to get back to Watsonville. There was work to do if he really did want to be a railroad man.

16

WHILE NEAL was hard at work learning the tricks of his new career, and beginning to earn what Al Hinkle describes as "beaucoups money," Carolyn was left trying to eke out an existence with—at one point—no more than five dollars to her name. Her situation was further complicated by the arrival home of the nautical friend whose apartment she'd been living in. He announced that he was marrying a woman who already had a flat and so was moving his possessions out of his apartment.

He left Carolyn rattling around in a set of rooms now boasting only a bed, a fold-out couch, a storage chest, and a kitchen stove. Not that she had anything to cook on it, nor any pots with which to cook. Recalling her sister's tale of how she had once subsisted on a diet of peanut butter and lettuce, Carolyn did likewise, adding milk for the sake of her unborn child. When her finances dwindled even further, she was forced to accept the paltry $2.50 that a record store offered for the Cassadys' prized record collection (holding back a few Billie Holidays and Nat "King" Coles for overwhelming sentimental reasons) and the twenty-five cents she received for a mink-dyed muskrat coat she had hauled from store to store in the midst of a heat wave. That quarter did no more than pay her carfare home, but she was determined not to carry the coat—a relic from her college days—one more yard.

Looking back on this chapter of her life, Carolyn is appalled at the privations she was forced to suffer. At the time, she says, "I was proud to be enduring for 'us.'" Her ordeal was somewhat mitigated by daily loving letters from Neal. He helped her to put her suffering into context, she says, with his descriptions of the grueling work schedule he was forced to maintain in exhausting conditions. Bakersfield, too, was sweating through a heat wave. There was relief of sorts when he was sent to work on a potato local in Pixley, a town so small that Carolyn couldn't find it on a map (it is, in fact, some thirty-three miles north of Bakersfield on Route 99).

This job saw Neal rising at the relatively late hour of 8:30 A.M. but working through from 9 A.M. until 7 P.M. He was, he told Carolyn, sleeping in a company train car, taking his meals in a local café, and devoting his spare time to reading, writing, thinking, and smoking. There was an unexplained delay in Neal's first paycheck, and Carolyn's position had become extremely precarious when Al Hinkle arrived with the much-needed funds. Al had been moved from Bakersfield to the Southern Pacific's San Francisco depot after a crippling bout of hay fever, and he now found relief in the sea breezes that wafted across the bay.

Al told Carolyn how impressed he was at the amount of work Neal had found and correctly predicted that he would be pretty well off by the time he was through. At the end of June, when the Pixley job ended and Neal returned to San Francisco, he and Carolyn would end the briefest of house-hunting expeditions by renting an apartment on the appropriately named Alpine Terrace, a precipitously steep hill overlooking Castro Street. "Had we been less hurried," Carolyn remarked in *Off the Road*, "we'd have noticed it was at least six blocks uphill from the nearest market or Laundromat. But once again love made all things possible, and I was eager to build a nest for Neal and our child."

During his railroad holdovers Neal had resumed his communications with Ginsberg and Kerouac. He'd written Allen to let him know about his marriage and Carolyn's pregnancy, receiving in reply a short note that told him: "Now, I suppose I should congratulate you . . . So O.K. Pops everything you do is great. The idea of you with a child and a settled center of affection—shit . . . my mind isn't made up into anything but complete amused enthusiasm for your latest building."

Neal was hurt by Ginsberg's tone and in late June wrote him, "Since I've not let you see myself of late, you are, of necessity, way, way, way off base in much of your letter. . . . You should congratulate me—as you would congratulate me on, say, buying a car, or some such impersonal object. Everything I do is not great. I see no greatness in myself—I even have no conception at what is greatness. I'm a simple-minded, child-like, insipid sort of moronic and kind of awkward-feeling adolescent. My mind doesn't function properly. The child and Carolyn are removed from my consciousness and are on a somehow, secondary plane, or, i.e., not what I think of, or dwell on, or am concerned about, except in a secondary way. If you do have complete amused enthusiasm for this latest building, your [*sic*] being enthused about the wrong thing, at best, the secondary thing."

Allen's letter contained the important news that Kerouac had finished work on his first novel, *The Town and the City*. Allen had read it and reported: "It is very great, beyond my wildest expectations. I never knew. But I will let him tell you himself." Allen also wrote enthusiastically about the possibilities he perceived in "the vast realistic vision" of Neal's letter.

Neal was quick to reply: "Oh bullshit, dear Allen, bullshit. I spoke of no 'vast realistic vision.' What possibilities? I'm ill man, why, why, do you speak of realization, expression? I wrote for a month straight—what came out? terrible, awful, stupid, stupid trash—it grew worse each day. Don't tell me it takes years. If I can't write one good sentence in a month of continuous effort—then, obviously, I can't realize, or express."

Neal was successfully hiding from Carolyn his ambivalence toward marriage and impending paternity, for although he longed to father a child, he shied away from the implications of the role, especially as he had only the example of his own father as a measure and feared that he too might prove a failure. However, he could not resist revealing his doubts and true concerns to Allen. After confessing that he hated words as a communication medium ("they are too much"), and preferring the immediacy of music ("I love music I live music I become truly unaware of all bullshit of life only when I dig it"), he closed: "Let us stop corresponding—I'm not the N.C. you knew I'm not N.C. anymore. I more closely resemble Baudelaire."

In contrast, Neal elected to write positive upbeat letters to Kerouac, saving all his doubts and insecurities for Ginsberg. This may have been because he did not want to crush Kerouac's overwhelming optimism about *The Town and the City*—and the crucial role he still maintained Neal had played in its completion. Even so, when the mood was upon him, Neal was still capable of writing long, tortuous confessions to the man who most admired his writing style.

Neal was in Pixley on June 16 when he wrote Jack the following long and revealing letter:

> Dear, dear Jack; my good, good friend:
>
> With no preamble I begin by stating, simply—I've nearly gone crazy the last ½ yr.—so, please try & understand that fact (tho you know not the cause) & do be good & kind & forgive me.
>
> Your letter to me lay unanswered in my suitcase, each time I'd start a reply I'd have to quit, either because it became a foolish love-note & plea for your sympathy, help, understanding & forgiveness, or because in describing any tortures I'd become too overbalanced or too distastefully, incoherently mad.
>
> Having already tried several times to relate my ache & distorted vision of flesh & latest & most terrified stupidities to you—& failed each time I tried; I quit—instead, comes an unimportant or chronological table of unimportant developments—which are, strangely, entirely removed from my being—almost as if I were telling of another person—I begin:
>
> Jan. 12—Bought a 1941 Packard club coupe, blue, spotlight, heater, radio, overdrive, seat covers, 6 cylinder. 80 top speed, paid $1195 for it, $100 down, $75 a month. Raced 14,000 miles in 85 days—gave it back.
>
> Jan.20—Quit my job at McKales—was really out of my head at this time—got so saturated with grief would tear across busy blvd. intersections at 50, right thru the stop sign—hoping to get hit.

Feb. 8—My birthday—tried to kill myself again—stole a 38 caliber revolver—several times had it to my temple—tried for 14 hrs.—sweat, nausea, fear—couldn't pull the trigger—drove in a ditch & lay in back seat—tried to cry—couldn't—disgusting.

March 1st—Drove to Denver—2894 miles in 33 hrs no sleep—stuck on continental divide 7 hrs at 8 below zero—no anti-freeze in damn radiator—no chains—tried to freeze myself—got too cold & finally stopped a bus & got pushed.

March 5th—Returned to Frisco, made it in 36 hrs thru Wyo. & Utah—picked up young girl—caught crabs from her—drove her from Greeley to San Francisco—left her in hotel—meet her 2 weeks later & drive her (Joy is name) to Sacramento to a whorehouse & she's there now—whoring & eating cock—the bitch.

March 20th—Had wild, wild, wild experience—meet young nigger boy, 25—he has 30 yr old sugar mama—she tells me she loves his beautiful cock—can't do without it—3 times they do it—every other *hour,*—every day. I stay there & get high & dig great music.

March 22—Meet a girl, who, I'd swear, is truly a virgin—or at least, unexperienced—take her to nigger's house—she's really a good girl—I think—3 hrs later she's a little drunk & then, started the greatest show—she does dance for us—she takes off pants—leaves on dress & silk stockings—she stands on head & does splits—she's moaning all the time—mumbling "I love cock, your cock,—eat me, on my food, in my mouth, ease it, feel it, oh." She's always moving, she gets on knees by side of bed & tears open nigger's pants—lifts out long black beauty—jacks & kisses it—moans—then spreads nigger gal's legs—kisses her black, hairy twat—jumps on, beating it, the bed, laying on bed, spreads legs to impossible split, asked to be tied down & raped, nailed, ripped, eaten, bitten—grabs mine & swallows it—try to talk—can't—she's glazed-eyed—lost, spreads her cunt—grabs nigger's ears—forces him down—nigger gal grabs me—4 way orgy—goes on for hours—nigger fucks dog-fashion as she kneels on bed & blows me—as I blow nigger gal—etc.—etc.—name is Susie—mad nymph.

March 30th—Drive to Denver again—heartaches. Make it in 37 hrs; get divorce from LuAnne.

March 31st—Drive back—lots of car trouble—go for *46 hrs* straight driving—*without sleep.* Have wreck as I approach Frisco, went to sleep at wheel—lucky, wreck was minor.

April 1st—Marry Carolyn—she becomes my second wife.

April 2nd—Start on railroad—5 days on local, 5 nights on local—trip to Santa Barbara & return.

April 10—Give car back—paid total of $200.00 on it.

April 17th—Finish student trips on railroad—no pay for it.

April 27th—Go to Watsonville—hoping to get started to work—don't.

May 6th—Get tired of sitting in Watsonville, can't get work—railroad not busy enough yet—decide to go to sea—know marine division of Standard Oil Co. boss—see him—he fixes me up.

May 8th—I'm now a full-fledged Ordinary Seaman—papers & all.

May 10th—Start to go to Arabia on "Cheveron," a motorship—get last-minute chance at railroad—decide to work on road until I'm cut-off next January '48—then go to sea until April '49—then return to railroad.

May 17th—Finally will start to work—got call to go to Bakersfield—went.

May 19th—Am in Bakersfield—work for first time in 4 months (except for 2 weeks as book salesman with wild character named Sinex—tell you later).

May 20th to June 6th—Daily routine is this: 15 hrs in Bakersfield—8 hrs on road—10 hrs in Fresno—14 hrs on road—15 hrs in Baker again, then repeat, repeat.

June 7th—Got call to go to Pixley, Calif. & work on potato-shed local—good job—went.

June 8th to June 16th—Daily routine is this: Up at 8:30 A.M.—work from 9 to 7 P.M.—sleep in outfit car here, eat in café across street—read, write, think & smoke.

That's it, Jack, a brief, partial resumé of my last 6 months—leaving *out* entirely any reference to my *cause* of neurosis. I tell you briefly—it's a girl—not Carolyn, or Susie—you know. Whether you know anything of my lost being or not, I know you are my older blood-brother & feel always better as I realize this. Enuf.

My dear, sweet, great little wife—my perfect Carolyn (she's changed, she's great) is now 7 months along & will present me with my fifth (5) child the last of August. This child, unlike the other 3 boys and a ?—(don't know) I shall keep, raise, & glory in—needless to say, dear Jack—if my baby is a boy—I shall name him after you—& Allen. If it is a girl—I can't, for a name like Jacqueline, or some such thing, is unbearable to think of.

I make no attempt to answer your letters; I'm insisting on a copy—with autograph—of the great, perfect & loving tome of yours—please believe Jack, I can suspect the sweat you've developed to achieve this thing—I am trying to write too, you know. But, I've new visions I hide—Not the writing so much, as—oh, well,—tell you later, if I can.

You understand, of course, that I want only too much to speak of these things to you, but, you've no idea unless I present a faint semblance of structure & these mad & wild terrors are unworkable as yet—anything I'd say would be pre-

> sented in my limited vocabulary & become misunderstood by you, & deemed trite, wrong or foolish—I feel like Joyce—a new world of words—Don't feel I believe I need new words to merely translate my private knowledge—I need it to preach a new psychology, a new philosophy, a new morality. That's what we need—a new morality, philosophy & psychology—what a task—how can I expect to speak in a letter?
>
> I'm presumptuous, foolish & very unwise, I feel no need to make demands, or no right to attempt to—all I feel for you stems not from hero-worship (as it used to with Hal, & partially with Allen) but, rather, from a simple feeling of your being an "older blood-brother"—that's all.
>
> This madness has been unlike any I've ever known, *entirely* different—I feel as if I've never had any life before—I do childish things—I think in new, distorted, over-balanced levels. I burn with agony—I sense a loss of most all wisdom I've ever had. When I see a girl I tremble—I spit,—I'm lost.

On June 27 Jack replied: "How wonderful it is to recall that months and months ago, years ago, you were here in Ozone Park tempting me and taunting me and pushing me to continue writing *Town and City*, and I went on blasting away at it just to impress and more to please you. That was the turning point of the novel . . . that was when I got to doing it, toward getting it done, wham, wham, wham.

"And guess what? IT IS NOW FINISHED . . . IT IS IN THE HANDS OF SCRIBNER'S. What an amazing thing to realize that *you*, more than anyone else, can be said to be the biggest pitchfork that got me howling and screaming across the pea-patch toward my inevitable duties. It's that wonderful Nealish creativeness that did it. Others may criticize, others may hurt me, others may suggest darkly, others may not care, others may watch without emotion—but you yell and gab away and fill me with a thousand reasons for writing and getting a big story done."

Jack's excitement at the manuscript of *The Town and the City* being considered by Scribner's was inspired in great part by the possibility that it might cross the desk of Maxwell Perkins, the company's most illustrious editor. Perkins was the man who'd discovered and worked closely with Jack's literary hero and model, Thomas Wolfe, in the 1920s and '30s, and was even then refining the work of Ernest Hemingway, the most famous and successful of Scribner's authors. If Perkins did in fact cast an experienced eye over *The Town and the City*, he was not impressed. Scribner's decided to pass on putting Jack Kerouac into print for the first time and it would not be until 1950, after his novel had passed through the hands of a number of other publishers, that Harcourt, Brace helped Jack realize his ambition to become a published author.

Jack himself knew nothing of this, of course, and had begun making grandiose plans for spending the vast royalties he was certain his novel would make when Scribner's launched it on an eager public. "I've made up my mind to become a rancher," he told Neal in what would be the first of several vague ambitions to work close to nature. "I've learned all about it in books, and I am going to learn the rest this summer working on ranches in Colo., Ariz., or Wyo. All I want is 300 head, a spread that cuts enough alfalfa for them, a winter pasture, two houses for me and whoever joins me in partnership, etc. etc. Just a small outfit that me and a partner can run without hiring cowhands. Also grazing permit for a national forest . . . if not that, I'd need a fortune to buy my own grazing land wouldn't I."

Grudgingly allowing a hint of reality to enter his reverie, Jack suggested that if his royalties failed to match this daydream, he would have to consider renting or leasing a suitable spread. In any case, he added, he would "proceed to live a good life in the canyon countries, lots of forage, trees, high sharp mountain air . . . and marry a Western girl and have six kids."

After naming his initial choices as partners (his boyhood friend Mike Fortier—who would be renamed "Fournier" when he appeared in Jack's later, Lowell-inspired novels—and his brother-in-law, Paul Blake), Jack cautiously added: "and even you if you ever wanted to *settle* and do something consecutively for years, maybe your whole life. Why roam around. . . . Why not roam from a base? Think of it. Well, right now this is just a dream, but so was the novel when I started it and you were around to prod me."

Neal responded positively to Jack's cowboy dream, telling him: "I know your mother (you must bring her) and Carolyn would get on together famously—and for us to build a ranch, a great spread, together, would be better than renting rooms for $50 the rest of our lives."

He and Jack would continue to swap ideas on this subject, with Carolyn's the only voice to be heard advocating caution and good sense. The idea, inevitably, foundered on the rocks of harsh reality, although, in retrospect, Jack and Neal's planned living situation sounded like nothing so much as a precursor to the rural hippie communes of the 1960s.

In contrast to Ginsberg's grudging congratulatory note concerning Neal's news of Carolyn's pregnancy, Jack was honestly thrilled. "Now allow me to congratulate you with all my heart and love on your marriage and impending birth of a child," he wrote. "Carolyn is an amazing girl—I talked to her in Denver, you know—and now that she has become great, as you say it so wildly, that initial difference between the two of you must undoubtedly be ironed out, that is, her kind of serenity, and your restlessness and blood-brother craziness. I am truly so glad."

There was now a change in Neal's spirits. He told Jack: "For the first time in more than three years my soul has faltered in its black, purposeful dash to sick ruin. It's not a cycle . . . for God has once again touched my seed—it blossoms, I blossom." Confiding in his creative endeavors, Neal added: "I am working seriously on a short thing about a man digging—oh, well, if I finish it I'll talk about it . . . I have a little thing I've done. If you'd give time I'd be pleased to send it to you for an opinion you could give."

It is not known whether Neal did send his "little thing" to Jack (and there was certainly no feedback from Jack in any of his letters), but Kerouac had already put his opinion of Neal's writing skills and potential on record in his "ranch project" letter of June 27, when he signed off, "Your letter, by the way, was so good that I suddenly realized that you and I may be the two most important American writers someday. That is according to my judgment."

With *The Town and the City* completed, Kerouac began sketching out ideas for two new projects. One was a fantasy he called *Dr. Sax* and was largely inspired by the talks he'd shared with Neal and Allen about their childhood fears and fantasies, and of course his own memories of radio thrillers like *The Shadow*. The other was a freer-styled piece that began as a pen portrait of Neal that Kerouac entitled "On the Road" but would later become "Visions of Neal" and then *Visions of Cody*. He began to draft ideas for the novel that this would feature in, originally seeing it—like *The Town and the City*—as a sprawling family saga. At this stage the character loosely based on Neal was given the name "Vern Pomeroy." There were to be many changes before the novel we now know as *On the Road* would be completed, during which time Vern would become Dean and Pomeroy would become Moriarty, the family-saga storyline would vanish, and the narrative would concentrate, instead, on the freewheeling, feisty, fun-loving fool who had meant so much to an impressionable Kerouac.

As the date of Carolyn's delivery neared, Neal experienced another dramatic and positive change in his spirit. On August 4 he wrote Ginsberg: "Two weeks ago, if one can place a time on such things, I came out of the cauldron cleansed. I'm stronger; better in every way. I enumerate: Looking first at the outward manifestations of my activities and interests; I work with zest, function perfectly at it, am not prone to bitching, etc. I get things done . . . but, simple accomplishment, I utilize time more fully, having only 8-12 hours at home every 24-36 hours I, yet, am more creative than previously. I see all shows worthy, (for example, 6 months ago I didn't deem even theatre worth a block's walk) art museums, concerts, etc. also, (this is most important) I can, once again, walk into a hip joint, smell hip things, touch hip minds—without crying. As for self-improvement: I'm starting music lessons soon; I'm all set up, if necessary, to get psychoanalysis . . . but, perhaps, more interesting to you—I am writing daily; poorly done, poorly executed, woefully weak ice words I string together for what I try to say, maybe, only one paragraph, maybe differant [*sic*] subjects each day, maybe, crazy to try (for I seem to get only further embroiled in style) but, I am trying."

Reviewing that last paragraph, Neal decided he came across like "any tea-head who is swearing he's cured," adding perceptively: "Marajuana [*sic*] and psychology seem not to mix well in most cases, the neurosis is first heightened, then fought; any solution becomes intellectual, invalid, and fluxuates [*sic*] for the period of time that each individual's make-up allows involvement. Some never stop, or, perhaps, reach partial alleviation, and then, let things ride. Conversely, marajuana and psychology are necessary if one is to become awakened . . . It follows, therefore, that why most tea-heads fail, is lack of strength with which to temper their insight into their own soul. A Ginsberg soul with a Kerouac spirit is needed."

Ginsberg rebuffed Neal's plea for help to improve his writing style with the response: "I can't give you any advice on writing. I myself stopped all literary creation with the few imperfect poems that I enclose. I mean to take it up again, but not till I know what I am doing . . . I don't know much technique. I have always suspected reality in the masters, so I have imitated them . . . my poetry has not been my own, but it has been good poetry, as poetry goes, because it was sincere. It will be my own in the future."

Neal began musing anew on the matter of names for his first legitimate child. On August 20 he wrote Ginsberg: "All my previous offspring have been boys, but all of Carolyn's family have had girls first;—at the beginning I presupposed I'd be content with only a male, however, after a degree of thought, I would be as pleased with a girl. If it is a boy I shall name it: Allen Jack Cassady. I anticipate him always signing his name thus: Allen J. Cassady. Gradually the rather strange sound of Allen Jack will be modified & the middle name, Jack, fall into the oblivion most middle names do fall into & become simply 'J.'—now that's alright—Allen J. Cassady.

"If my child is a female I have decided to name her: Cathleen Jo Anne Cassady. This decision required much effort—but, listen on a while yet. I could not call her Jackquline [*sic*]—& there's no good feminine name of Allen—turning then to the child's (perhaps) wishes I thought that although Cathleen Cassady is too stock as an Irish type (she would find it difficult to look Irish anyhow with her father only 1/2 and her mother 1/10 Irish) it would please her vanity in her romantic stage & earlier in life as a young tom-boy (& later in college) she'd be known as simply 'Jo'."

There was a great deal more of this woolgathering, probably little of which interested Ginsberg, although he was surely flattered to have Neal promising to name his son after him. He would have been less flattered had he known that Neal had already told Jack, three months earlier, that he planned to name a son after him.

As it happened, Neal and Carolyn's first child was a girl. Cathleen Joanne Cassady was born at 12:29 A.M. on September 7 after Carolyn sweated painfully through eight hours of labor that were accomplished without the benefit of anesthetic—a young intern explaining that the hospital was trying to do without that week, adding: "Besides, we think women should have this experience." Carolyn assumed that by "we," he meant men.

Neal had been at home when Carolyn's water broke, so he was able to beg a lift to the hospital from a railroad friend. Carolyn would have appreciated his presence and support during the next few hours, but in those unenlightened days fathers were not allowed to attend births. Her only contact with Neal came in the form of flowers and a loving note, which she kept and still has. Carolyn assumed Neal would use the enforced separation to play the field, an assumption she held until she revisited his correspondence while preparing her collection of unpublished letters for publication and learned that he actually spent his time visiting libraries and art galleries.

Completely besotted with Cathy Jo (as she instantly became known), Neal made up her formula, fed and bathed her, changed diapers, took the wash to the laundry, and read the recently published *Baby and Child Care* by Dr. Spock with all the enthusiasm he usually saved for racing form guides. As Carolyn recalled, "While he fed her a bottle, I beamed at the sight of that tiny pink mound no longer than his forearm nestled against his bare, muscular chest. He was beside himself with delight in her, repeating often, 'I never knew . . . I never knew.'"

Writing to Kerouac in October, Neal was still clearly a smitten father. "I can't tell you the blubbering glee I've been gurgling since Cathleen's arrival (and before)," he enthused. "She's a month old today, has gone out into the world 3 times . . . and is thriving in general. She's now 21 inches long and weighs 8lbs, 8ozs. I love her like mad." Neal also suggested that his daughter's arrival had changed him in quite dramatic fashion. "I used to be indefatigable," he said. "Sex drove me . . . now, I like music and am sterile. Maybe my girl, Cathy Jo, will continue to make me content and strong."

Ginsberg's response to the news of Cathy Jo's arrival was much warmer than the one he had written when Neal first told him of Carolyn's pregnancy. "If you send me some details surrounding the psychic atmosphere of her birth, I'll write you a triumphal ode," he offered, adding generously, "I've put little Cathy in my will . . . I'm seeing my lawyers tomorrow. She will inherit zillions of dollars when I die. P.S. Blessings on my daughter-in-law for a change, and on you, too, son." Allen's postscript was a rare but welcome gesture of warmth toward Carolyn, although when he died in 1997, Ginsberg did not name Cathy or either of her siblings as a beneficiary in his most recent will.

During November Neal was, as he knew he would be, laid off by the SPRR for the winter. He found himself in the unique position of having a fairly healthy savings account and time on his hands until the following spring when he expected to receive his callback. It was a potentially deadly combination, as his subsequent actions would prove.

Neal began to make plans to drive to New York to visit Jack and Allen. There were two obstacles to this scheme, no detail of which he shared with Carolyn. He must have known that she would raise all kind of sensible objections, not the least of which would be to his abandoning of wife and infant daughter as the Christmas holidays neared. Then there was the fact that he would need to make a sizable dent in the family's reserves to buy a new car—certainly a purchase that had not factored in their prudent financial planning. He decided not to share his plans with his wife, although he happily shared them with Al Hinkle, who seemed very keen on the idea—all the more so since he saw a place for himself in Neal's scheme. Al had become involved with Helen Argee, a young woman who had already agreed to become his wife; Manhattan would surely make a great honeymoon destination. Al and Neal were in fact laboring under the misapprehension that Helen had substantial funds at her disposal, enough for her to underwrite the journey with food and gas money.

Neal confronted Carolyn with the fait accompli of a shiny new Hudson saloon car less than twenty-four hours after Al's sudden revelation that he had a fiancée, a person of whose existence Carolyn had heard no previous hint but whom she now learned he was due to marry only two days later. Carolyn had assumed that Al, like most men, would have chosen a pretty young thing for himself; she was surprised to be introduced to Helen Argee, a stolid Mother Earth figure of indeterminate age (she was, in fact, only twenty-two), her rich brown hair tied back in a bun. To add further years to her appearance, she wore a tailored brown suit.

The two women circled each other warily, Helen answering Carolyn's polite questions grumpily, her body language making it obvious that she would rather be anywhere else. (It was not until much later, when the two became good friends and confidants, that Carolyn learned Helen's initial reserve was due to her dislike of Neal as well as to her natural shyness.)

Raised by a strictly religious father as a Seventh Day Adventist following the death of her mother, Helen had never seen a movie or worn make-up until she was twenty, and her social skills were minimal.

Carolyn had no reason to suspect anything when Neal left the apartment the next morning, saying that he had to help Al prepare for his nuptials. So her shock at his return behind the wheel of a two-toned (metallic maroon and gray) automobile was understandable. So was her fury, for there they were, as she later recounted, "living in a cardboard dump with orange-crate bookcases, yet we had a brand new car, no savings, no income, a new baby, and he was talking about driving clear across the country."

This last item of information was revealed as Neal tried to calm Carolyn down after she ran back into the apartment. She reported him as saying: "Now, now, Carolyn, look here, you don't understand. Al and Helen are getting married tomorrow, right? They have to have a honeymoon, but they have no car. Now, then, Jack wants to come out, but he hasn't the money to get here. So, see, ol' Cass to everybody's rescue. We'll kill both birds with one basket, so to speak. I'll whip over to New York to get Jack, break in the new car, and at the same time Al and Helen get their honeymoon, see? But the best part is, Helen is loaded. She's paying all our expenses! It's a free ride, don't you see?"

Asked if Helen had paid for the car as well, Neal reluctantly conceded that he had bought it—or at least made the down payment. Naturally, he added hurriedly, it was really for Carolyn . . . for her and the baby, so she could take Cathy to the doctor, or to the store. As Carolyn began to realize that Neal had used up pretty well all of their precious funds to buy the Hudson, he tried to reassure her by saying that he could easily make that much back in a couple of months when he returned to the railroad the following spring. The monthly payments on the car were practically nothing, he said, and he'd find a temporary job as soon as he returned from New York. Everything was going to be all right. Carolyn's panic turned to fury when Neal revealed that this honeymoon trip would start the following day, right after Al and Helen's wedding. What was she supposed to do, she demanded? How would she and Cathy get by without any money? Neal had already worked that out. A workmate called Ardo had agreed to look out for them while he was away, he said, and would fetch groceries if Carolyn gave him a list . . . and he would take the wash too. Neal would pay him back when he got a job—anyway, he'd only be gone a week . . . two at most.

Neal then invited a tirade of righteous anger and effusive tears when he appealed to Carolyn: "Don't I deserve a vacation after I've worked so damned hard?" It was the wrong question to ask a woman who had made no demand for a honeymoon of her own because she knew that it was financially impossible, who had had to endure the indignity of trying to get a decent price for treasured belongings from pawnbrokers and indifferent dealers just to raise some grocery money, who had been forced to survive on a diet of peanut butter, lettuce, and milk while pregnant, and who had recently endured an eight-hour labor without the help of anesthesia.

Neal continued to throw clothes into a suitcase while Carolyn bombarded him with tearful recriminations. He was a bastard, she told him, who was finally showing his true colors. If he had a heart it was made of stone. He was nothing but selfish, and all he did was take advantage of people . . . but she should have known, because he was nothing but a guttersnipe! When Neal finally turned to face her, Carolyn felt that her degradation was complete, for he was also weeping, his face contorted. "I have feelings too, you know," he said quietly. As if on cue, baby Cathy woke up and began crying. Carolyn carried her to the kitchen and mechanically started fixing a bottle of formula. When she returned to the sitting room, Neal was waiting, one hand extended, the other clutching his suitcase. Carolyn backed away, hissing, "Just go, if you're going. Get out, now! I never want to see you again—not ever!"

Recalling the next few moments in *Off the Road,* Carolyn wrote: "I listened to his departing steps, the closing apartment door, the closing front door, the front steps, the engine starting and the roar of the departing car—the breaking cord. Gone. Really gone."

17

SO IN MID-DECEMBER 1948 Neal Cassady did indeed leave home for New York on the trip that, with a combination of tactlessness, unfounded optimism, and duplicity, he had first arranged and then presented to Carolyn as a done deal. Housebound, broke, and with a new baby to care for, Carolyn was expected to get by with occasional help from Ardo, one of Neal's railroad coworkers. He turned out to be a trusting youngster who had clearly fallen for the Cassady charm and who entertained no doubts that his hero would return and repay him for the groceries he would regularly buy and bring to her apartment at 109 Liberty Street. When, in an ill-judged attempt to cheer her up, Ardo showed Carolyn a postcard he had received from her absent husband, it achieved the opposite effect when she noticed the Denver postmark. Denver meant LuAnne. Belatedly, Carolyn realized that LuAnne's continuing hold on Neal put a new complexion upon recent upheavals, his ostensible suicide bid, and this current contentious cross-country journey.

"Can't you see he's using you too, Ardo?" she asked her trusting benefactor bitterly. "He'll never pay you back . . . how can he? Who knows if he'll ever even come back?"

Neal was intermittently in contact by phone. Whatever logic there had been in his initial rationalization of the trip—buying a car he could not afford so that he could take the newlywed Hinkles on a honeymoon trip—evaporated when, in the course of one of his phone calls home, he revealed that the bride had been deposited in Tucson, Arizona, while the groom had stayed on the road with him.

In a new twist, the latest objective of the trip was to transport Jack Kerouac's mother and her effects from North Carolina to New York. In fact, although Carolyn could not know it at the time, there was a kind of Cassadian logic in the revised plan: Helen Argee, now Hinkle, had disliked Neal's driving so much that she quit the road trip in Tucson, preferring to use her new husband's railroad pass to travel to William Burroughs's new home in Algiers (a community within the city of New Orleans on the west bank of the Mississippi River), where she would wait to be collected by the returning party of Neal, Al, and Jack. Much later she would describe parts of the trip to Carolyn Cassady:

"[Neal] picked up a woman and her child on the way. The child was epileptic or something, and Neal was simply fantastic. I've never seen anyone be that nice. I had to sit on Al's lap, mind you. . . . I lasted until Tucson, and then I had just had it. I insisted I had to have a bath, and Al must get us a hotel room. When we got the room Al and I talked and I told him I was less than enchanted with our honeymoon and wanted out."

Free of Helen, Neal and Al immediately drove north from Tucson to Denver, where they collected the newly engaged but still ready-for-anything LuAnne. They then headed east for Rocky Mount, North Carolina, where Jack's sister Nin lived and where Jack and his mother were spending the holiday season. Neal, Al, and LuAnne arrived at Rocky Mount on Christmas Day.

Meanwhile, back in San Francisco, Carolyn was mortified to find she would have to tell her sister Jane about Neal's defection since she had been invited to her home for Christmas dinner. Carolyn took Cathy, and although her sister tried to boost her spirits, the domestic situation at the Liberty Street apartment now had an almost Dickensian shroud of gloom hanging over it. After a meal that was festive in name only, Carolyn went home to that empty apartment to unwrap Christmas gifts.

"When I entered my own, dark close rooms, so permeated with memories of Neal, weakness and fear threatened me again," she later wrote. "The task looked too great. I had no motivation even to attempt it."

Meanwhile, in the east, Neal was exercising his almost superhuman talent for long-distance driving. After their Christmas dinner, Neal, Al, and LuAnne drove to Jack's home in Ozone Park, Queens, New York, taking some furniture with them as part of the ad hoc relocation plan for Gabrielle Kerouac. Then Neal and Jack drove back to Rocky Mount, collected Gabrielle, and returned to New York with her. It was another hard 2,000 miles on the clock but, once achieved, it allowed Neal, LuAnne, and Al to stop traveling and celebrate New Year's by moving into Allen Ginsberg's Manhattan apartment on York Avenue at 78th Street. From there they planned to sally forth and enjoy the city.

If John Clellon Holmes's fictionalization of the Ginsberg apartment in his novel *Go* (1952) can be taken as accurate (and Holmes would say in 1976, "I am amazed now to see how slavishly [*Go*] hews to real events and real people"), then it was a fourth-floor apartment at the back of a building with a dingy stairway smelling of garbage and populated by stray cats and the odd drunk. From this inauspicious lodging the trio prepared to see in the New Year by attending a series of parties thrown by members of Ginsberg's set. During the process they would encounter several colorful figures, including the now freed killer Lucien Carr and John Clellon Holmes himself. Holmes later reworked his vivid first encounter with Cassady (renamed Hart Kennedy) in *Go.* The transparent nature of the novel is such that most of the other pseudonyms hardly need explanation.

Holmes (Hobbes in the book) is visited by "Hart, Pasternak, Schindel, and Hart's first wife Dinah, whom they had picked up in Denver on the way from San Francisco." Hobbes puts on a bop record to break the ice, and Hart "stood by the phonograph in a stoop, moving back and forth on the spot in an odd little shuffle. His hands clapped before him, his head bobbed up and down, propelled, as the music got louder, in ever greater arcs, while his mouth came grotesquely agape as he mumbled: 'Go! Go!'"

Soon, though, Hart becomes impatient and tells Hobbes that they came over especially to meet him: "'but you see, we've got to get ten bucks somewhere to keep going. You understand, for food and things. Now, if you can let us have it, that'll be great! Ed here . . . Ed Schindel,' and he reached for Schindel's arm without shifting his gaze from Hobbes, 'he's getting a check, see. Back pay on the railroad where we were working in Frisco. Positively be here by Friday. So you'll have it back in just a couple of days. We've been everywhere, all of Gene's connections and everyone, but we couldn't raise it.'

"'Well . . .' Hobbes stumbled.

"'It's just a loan, see. We're just borrowing. You know, I've got my first wife along, and we've got to get located. You understand.'"

As soon as Hobbes and his wife reluctantly agree to lend the money, Hart has no more use for them.

"'That's great!' Hart said, a brief, easy smile relaxing his lips. 'Now look, man, we ought to be cutting out.'"

New Year's in New York was so diverting to the out-of-towners that on January 10, 1949, Al Hinkle wrote his new bride (who was still languishing chez Burroughs in Algiers) that she must join them. "I am certain we must stay in NY for, at least, one month. Acting on this certainty I herein enclose $15 for you to come to NY at once."

Both Neal Cassady and Jack Kerouac occasionally affected the speech mannerisms of W. C. Fields for a joke, and here Al Hinkle seemed to have adopted a letter-writing style reminiscent of Fields's florid spoken delivery; perhaps it was a private joke but it hardly sounds like a natural communication from Al to his twenty-two-year-old bride. On the same day—and almost certainly using the same envelope—Neal wrote to William Burroughs in a solicitous tone saying they would not now be coming to Algiers until the following month, by which time they would have accumulated some money, "otherwise we would burden you with our hungry mouths when we visit you."

Quite why the visit was any longer deemed necessary is not clear since Helen Hinkle had simultaneously been told to come to New York on the bus and therefore would no longer need to be picked up. Perhaps Neal had always intended to visit socially even before the Burroughs home had been promoted to a way station for the disgruntled bride.

However, either the two letters never arrived or they arrived too late, because Burroughs wrote to Ginsberg rather briskly insisting that Al should come and get Helen as soon as possible. So, on January 19, 1949, Neal, Jack, Al, and LuAnne reluctantly drove from New York to Algiers, where they stayed briefly with Burroughs before the Hinkles suddenly decided to relocate to the heart of New Orleans itself. There they found themselves an apartment in the Vieux Carré and dropped out of the trip altogether.

• • •

Neal was still capable of bouts of self-criticism in his letters to Carolyn. Before leaving New York he had sent her a conciliatory letter, which ended with: "I wound all the people I love—why?" And, despite Carolyn's skepticism, he did come back. In the last week of January the heroic Hudson rolled into San Francisco, bearing not only Neal and Jack but also LuAnne; her engagement was to Ray Murphy, a San Francisco resident. Neal naturally did not bring either of his traveling companions to Carolyn's apartment until he had tested the emotional waters with a phone call. Not for the last time, Carolyn was a grudging pushover, pretending to take him back purely out of consideration for her desperate situation (it had come down to a matter of survival), but all the time secretly hoping for the best.

"Why wasn't I like the other women who got hurt or betrayed once and that was that?" she wondered. "Turn it off, go on to someone else, pride and honor intact, the lesson learned?"

Encouraged, Neal cautiously produced Jack, who moved in with them despite his knowledge of Neal's duplicity with LuAnne, which inhibited any kind of relaxed conversation with Carolyn. This was only the second time she had met Jack.

Neal immediately took a job selling aluminum cookware, probably for the sake of the gesture rather than in any real expectation of success.

A salesman who had once failed to sell encyclopedias, he would now fail to sell pots and pans. Ever the optimist, he wrote Ginsberg: "[I] have a good job, but since all I sell is on a commission basis I'm not sure of any money, in fact I've made no money yet, just laid out almost 10 dollars to get started."

At night he and Jack frequented the San Francisco jazz clubs, seeing, among others, blind British jazz pianist George Shearing and Detroit-born Slim Gaillard, a cult figure from vaudeville who was at that point in his long and eccentric career a jive singer and as such seemingly outside the Cassady/Kerouac favored realm of bop and jazz. Gaillard's most famous number was "Flat Foot Floogie," a novelty song containing a verse that Neal might well have adopted as his own anthem: "Whenever your cares are chronic, just tell the world, 'go hang.' You'll find a greater tonic, if you go on swingin' with the gang!"

For whatever reason, Gaillard made quite an impression. Along with the corresponding Kerouac/Cassady evening out, he eventually resurfaced in *On the Road*: "One night we suddenly went mad together again; we went to see Slim Gaillard in a little Frisco nightclub. Slim Gaillard is a tall, thin Negro with big sad eyes who's always saying 'Right-orooni' and 'How 'bout a little bourbon-arooni.' In Frisco great eager crowds of young semi-intellectuals sat at his feet and listened to him on the piano, guitar and bongo drums. When he gets warmed up he takes off his undershirt and really goes. . . . Dean stands in the back, saying, 'God! Yes!'—and clasping his hands in prayer and sweating. 'Sal, Slim knows time, he knows. . . .'"

The brittle atmosphere in the Cassady household finally shattered when LuAnne, now installed in San Francisco and waiting for fiancé Ray to return from a trip, blithely telephoned to speak to Neal. Carolyn took the call. Jack was out at the time but when he returned a little later he found Neal furious, and Carolyn distraught and tearful. Anxious to distance himself from the worsening atmosphere, Jack lost no time in catching a bus back to New York. Neal drove him to the bus station in the

Hudson (which was now in imminent danger of being repossessed), and Carolyn told her husband in no uncertain terms not to come back. He did, of course, a few days later, sporting a fractured thumb, the result, he said, of hitting LuAnne in the head.

"That thick-skulled bitch . . . *she's* just dandy!" he reported bitterly, saying that affair was now over for good. Carolyn drove him to Mission Emergency where misfortune turned into low comedy as LuAnne herself suddenly appeared outside the hospital and, after chatting to Neal affably enough, spotted Carolyn in the Hudson (this had been Carolyn's first—and last—opportunity to drive "her" car) and came over to engage her in conversation in the sweetest terms. This slightly surreal exchange between the two Mrs. Cassadys went unexpectedly well and even continued at the Cassady home while Neal was kept waiting for treatment at the hospital. A curious affinity emerged between the luminously pretty LuAnne and the beleaguered Carolyn, who felt that her own considerable beauty, eroded by despair, was no match for that of her predecessor. Yet Carolyn took bitter comfort in her rival's cheerfully dismissive criticisms of Neal, also learning in the process that since LuAnne's fiancé was due back in San Francisco soon, the recently concluded road trip had been, from LuAnne's point of view, simply a way of getting from Denver to San Francisco for her impending marriage. If this was true, it was almost certainly one of the most convoluted lifts in the history of American travel.

Neal was duly sent home from hospital, but came back deeply depressed because his injury meant he could not work. He was not able to support his family, reimburse Ardo, or keep up payments on the Hudson. Incredibly, this complicated trip—that cross-country spree of shifting plans and endurance driving—had taken only a little over four weeks.

The day after his injury Neal dumped the Hudson on a side street. The finance company did not have his address but he was already two payments behind, and it was only a matter of time before they tracked down both Neal and the car. Soon thereafter Neal suddenly shaved his head, an action for which he offered Carolyn no explanation. He then resumed writing his autobiography.

Carolyn agreed to have Neal stay home and tend to Cathy while she went out to work. Almost immediately she secured a job working for a Hungarian radiologist. "When he asked if I could begin at once," Carolyn wrote, "he also tactfully inquired if I'd like an advance on my salary. Evidently, my wedding outfit had lost its glamour."

If the outfit had, Carolyn had not, and before long the doctor began to show more than a professional interest in her.

"I will take care of Cathy as long as Carolyn will allow me," Neal wrote in an uncharacteristically maudlin letter to Allen Ginsberg in mid-March. "My life's blood she is, lovely and perfect—she wakes at this very moment, I stop to kiss her."

In what was to prove an eventful spring, Ginsberg would soon have more pressing matters on his mind than Neal's domestic arrangements. Criminal activities were afoot. At the beginning of March, William Burroughs had been arrested in New Orleans on charges of possession of guns and narcotics. Escaping imprisonment on a technicality, he moved his family to Pharr, Texas, near the Mexican border. Then on April 22, Allen Ginsberg, along with fellow members of Joan Vollmer's Manhattan circle Herbert Huncke, Vicki Russell, and Russell's hoodlum friend Jack Melodias, was arrested for handling stolen goods. After a series of low-comedy events involving a car crash that happened while the quartet was attempting to flee from cops (who were not even intending to chase them), Allen was implicated in receiving the stolen goods that had been piling up in his York Avenue apartment, courtesy of Jack Melodias, aka Little Jack Melody. In the end Ginsberg's father successfully argued for Allen to be sent to the Psychiatric Institute of Columbia Presbyterian Hospital instead of prison, which was where Huncke, Russell, and Melodias wound up. John Clellon Holmes would include a thinly disguised version of the incident in *Go.*

With money from the sales of *The Town and the City,* Kerouac suddenly and rather unexpectedly decided to move his family to Denver, partly in the spirit of a romantic dream to make a life out West, partly because, as he succinctly put it in a letter to the writer Alan Harrington after the car chase incident involving Ginsberg and the others, "all my geniuses (are) in jail." On May 15, 1949, Jack wrote Hal Chase saying that he had "just arrived in Denver" with "the definite feeling of . . . finding my world at last . . . the East is really effete. When a cowhand got on the bus at Hugo, and smiled at all of us in there, a whole busload of people, I knew that he was more interested in mankind than 10,000,000 New York School and Columbia professors and academicians."

Ironically, Neal Cassady, a real westerner, prodigious car thief, and user of marijuana, was quietly writing his memoirs and being a relatively well-behaved house father while his respectable literary friends were out acquiring criminal records or pursuing romantic cowboy dreams. Afternoon father-and-daughter walks in the park with Cathy would soon be a regular occurrence, and the presence of LuAnne surreptitiously in tow marked the extent of Neal's misdemeanors while Carolyn was at work. Neal's great love for Cathy was unquestionable and without ulterior motive. This unconditional love meant he was uncharacteristically diligent when looking after her.

"With her he was wonderful and conscientious," Carolyn wrote simply.

Then Neal developed osteomyelitis in the bones of the broken thumb, and this threatened to extend his period of enforced unemployment while necessitating further treatment with penicillin (which Carolyn injected in order to save on medical bills).

Carolyn worked until June when personal relations with her employer worsened. "My lack of cooperation with the doctor's amorous advances eventually caused him to become unreasonably picky and demanding of my work," she recalled. "So when Neal declared he'd been idle as long as he could stand it and wished to go back to work I was overjoyed to be able to give my notice." Neal had managed to get employment as a mold man, curing recapped tires for Goodyear. Soon, though, Carolyn took another job to supplement Neal's income. "I found a job with two doctors who shared an office, one a male surgeon, the other a woman general practitioner," she wrote.

They had moved into 29 Russell Street in the spring of 1949. This was a three-level house on a quiet street near Russian Hill, not a glamorous neighborhood but one within easy reach of some of Carolyn's favorite San Francisco locations: Fisherman's Wharf, Chinatown, and Telegraph Hill. This and other news Neal related in a very long—and ultimately very significant—letter to Jack Kerouac dated July 3, 1949.

It took Neal three weeks to write the letter, and parts of it would eventually become far more famous than *The First Third* ever would. Kerouac would use long sections almost verbatim in the published version of *On the Road.* In Kerouac's seminal work Carolyn became Camille, Cathy became Amy, and Neal was Dean Moriarty. Even Neal's employer, Goodyear, was recast as Firestone (disguising one genuine proprietary name with another instead of giving it a fictitious handle), but the events, the words, the rhythms, and the speech patterns were all Cassady's. Kerouac recycled the saga of the broken thumb, Neal's conceit about the elaborate cocktail of racial genes that made up Cathy/Amy ("thirty-one-and-a-quarter-per-cent English, twenty-seven-and-a-half-percent Irish, twenty-five-percent German, eight-and-three-quarters-percent Dutch, seven-and-a-half-percent Scotch, one-hundred-percent wonderful"), and even retold an anecdote of Neal's youthful skirmish with a Kansas law enforcement officer who spotted him carrying stolen license plates hidden under his clothes.

"My first arrest was for license plates. Wait, forget for a moment the above paragraph, I feel like a remembering of things past," Neal wrote before launching into a more detailed reminiscence.

When Neal's alter ego, Dean Moriarty, reenacts Neal's Proustian flashback, it is triggered not by biting into an evocative madeleine but by recognizing a familiar stretch of highway, and although the location changes from Kansas to Nebraska, the account he gives to Sal Paradise is an almost verbatim version of the story in the letter: "I had a twenty-dollar Buick back in LA, my first car, it couldn't pass the brake and light inspection so I decided I needed an out-of-state license to operate the car without arrest so went through here to get the license. As I was hitchhiking through one of these very towns, with the plates concealed under my coat, a nosy sheriff . . . found the plates and threw me in a two-cell jail with a county delinquent who should have been in a home for the old since he couldn't feed himself . . . I made the most magnificent speech of my life to get out of it . . . he let me go."

In the same long letter Neal recounted that LuAnne had finally gotten married: "Ray Murphy has sharpened a sword and is dashing about town trying to find me so he can cut my throat. I've had two narrow escapes; he got to Liberty Street soon after I moved, and three days ago he finally got my phone number here and called to try and find the address. If the prick does manage to find this house and is foolish enough to attack me I'll kill the bastard."

Neal told too how he had dreamed of Slim Gaillard; how he had just read Norman Taylor's *Flight from Reality* (a prescient 1949 examination of what were not yet known as recreational drugs); and how Carolyn was now pregnant with their second child. Her response to the pregnancy, discovered a mere two weeks after starting her new job, was one of shock. "I had been so extremely conscientious in following the doctor's directions for birth control," she wrote. "This time Neal acted happy, perhaps trying to make up for the first time, or perhaps because he found such a source of joy in Cathy. For myself I felt trapped, half wanting another child of his, but mostly afraid of being more dependent on Neal when I was still trying to resist him."

Though she was pregnant, Carolyn managed to prolong her employment even after the surgeon felt that her condition would be detrimental to his practice; the female doctor moved into her own office one floor above and employed Carolyn to type and count pills.

"I could watch the people and the pigeons below in Union Square," she wrote, "and I could still ride the cable car. My defenses relaxed, and again I saw that our marriage might recover. By now I should have learned to fear the calm more than the storm."

Jack responded to Neal's long letter on July 28, 1949, with a substantial missive of his own from Denver. It was introduced with the ominous opening line: "Dear Neal—Let me put it in a real great elaborate way."

The letter is divided into eight chapters headed with Roman numerals until Kerouac tires of the device ("Enough of chapters"). It opened with the news that a recent display of heat lightning over the plains prompted him to look both east ("New York, Allen, etc.") and west ("Frisco, you, etc.") and to conclude, "I had a desire to go in both directions at the same time." He writes of an imminent $1,000 advance from Harcourt, Brace, and asks if Neal would like to go to Italy with him.

Neal responded by inviting Jack to come and spend some time at the Cassady home on Russell Street. Jack did not reply but simply turned up there late one evening in August 1949.

• • •

The reunion of Jack and Neal reminded Carolyn of two schoolboys playing hooky. "They exulted in each other," she noted, fulsomely characterizing the effect as "a drawbridge between me and Neal being drawn up, enclosing them in their castle of delights and leaving me sitting wistfully on the opposite bank, filling the moat with tears."

She was still working and would come home and make dinner only to see Jack and Neal get up from the table and set off on a night's carousing. Her disapproval was obvious, and even when grudgingly invited along she still felt excluded. "I was a fifth wheel, like a bratty little sister who big brother has to take along with his friends," she recalled of those nights when a neighbor was pressed into service to sit for Cathy while Carolyn tagged along with the boys. Shabby nightclubs, strippers, and an endless search for marijuana in the cigar stores and bars of predominantly black neighborhoods were not Carolyn's idea of a good night out, and she soon detached herself from Neal and Jack's nocturnal adventures. Pressure built, and Carolyn felt she could not discuss anything with her husband, while Neal and Jack were an inseparable entity. In the end she threw them both out. Somewhat to her surprise Neal did not resist this time—which is what she had expected and even counted on—he simply went with Jack. A farewell note dictated by Neal to Helen Hinkle (Neal's infected thumb was now inhibiting his penmanship) made Carolyn believe that this time he had finally gone for good.

"Won't ever bother you again," wrote Neal's amanuensis. "I won't come back in a month to make you start it all over again—shudder shudder!

"I am going to Denver, Detroit, and New York City and won't ever come back to Frisco. Incidentally, I'm not going to see LuAnne—don't know where she is." The letter, written on a page torn from a 1947 calendar, was accompanied by three dollars.

• • •

In fact, Neal Cassady had not left San Francisco for good, although he would not return for almost a year. The intervening period was as turbulent as any in his life while Carolyn's stoical determination to carry on without him might have proved impossible but for the companionship of Helen Hinkle. Helen too was alone as her husband Al had gone traveling with his friend and Neal's old pool mentor, Jimmy Holmes; they were bound for Portland, Maine, for reasons no one could fathom. As a result the two women now formed a close friendship. Helen moved in with Carolyn for a while, choosing to stay on for a time out of friend-

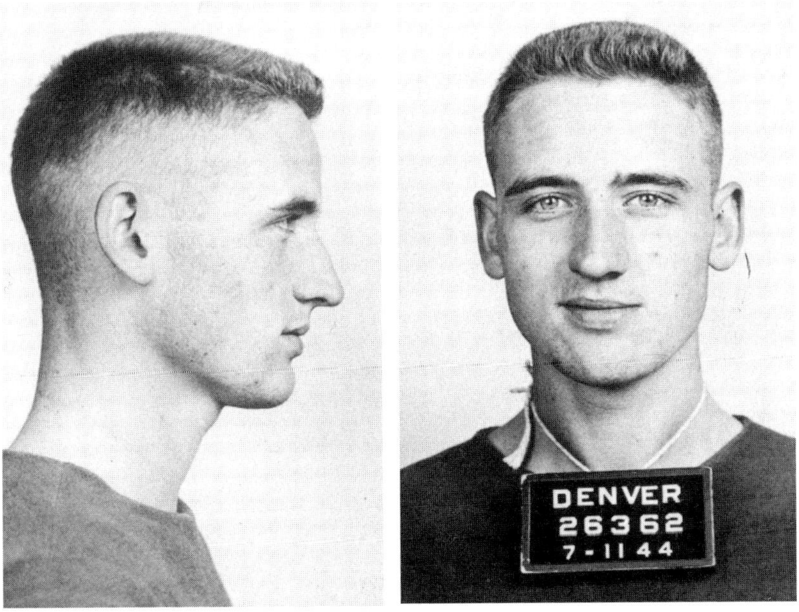

Neal Cassady, Denver reform school, 1944. *Photo courtesy of Carolyn Cassady*

LuAnne Henderson, 1946.

Photographer unknown, but possibly Neal Cassady

LuAnne's high school graduation photo, 1946. *Photo courtesy of Carolyn Cassady*

Carolyn Robinson sketching an actor in the Nashville Community Playhouse, where she was the head of the make-up department. *Photographer unknown*

Neal holding Jami, San Francisco, 1950. *Photo by Carolyn Cassady*

With Cathy Cassady and Jack Kerouac, San Francisco, 1952.
Photo by Carolyn Cassady (above)

With Carolyn, San Francisco, 1952. *Photo by Jack Kerouac (left)*

With two conductors on the Southern Pacific Railroad, around 1952.
Photographer unknown

San Francisco, 1952. *Photo by Carolyn Cassady*

With Cathy and John, San Jose, 1952. *Photo by Carolyn Cassady (above)*

San Jose, 1952. *Photo by Carolyn Cassady (left)*

With Jami and Cathy, Mallory Valley Farm near Franklin, Tennessee, 1953.
Photo by Carolyn Cassady (above)

With Carolyn and John, Los Gatos, 1956. *Photographer unknown (right)*

Los Gatos, 1962. *Photo by Ettore Sottsass*

With Anne Murphy, 1963. *Photo by Allen Ginsberg (above)*

At a party at the Grateful Dead country house for members of the University of California LSD Conference, 1966. *Photographer unknown (next page)*

ship even when Al returned and asked her to come back home. Despite the inauspicious atmosphere of their initial meeting, Helen and Carolyn became very close, and Carolyn greatly appreciated Helen's sacrifice and support at this crucial time.

"She was marvelous with Cathy and a sympathetic companion," Carolyn recalled. "Her great sense of humor prevented us from becoming completely depressed or desperate. We wouldn't have said we were happy and we grumbled about our fate and the worthlessness of men, but usually we ended up laughing when the melodrama threatened to become a farce."

So Helen stayed through a Christmas that for Carolyn was otherwise even worse than the previous one, and until late January 1950, when Carolyn gave birth to her second daughter, Melany Jane, at the end of a normal working day at the doctor's. ("I completed all the unfinished business in the office," Carolyn noted, "then took the cable car home. I had a cup of coffee with Helen, packed my bag and called a cab.") Melany Jane would be known as "Jamie," spelled "Jami" in later years when the abbreviated spelling seemed a more fashionable variant for the dancer she wanted to become. (This book uses the *Jami* spelling except when quoting from letters that favor the original spelling.)

Then Carolyn had received another bolt from the blue, courtesy of Neal—a call from a woman named Diana Hansen in New York who chattily introduced herself as Neal's new lover and who, also being pregnant with his child, was now anxious to join the growing list of Mrs. Cassadys. To this end, would Carolyn divorce him? Neal had asked her to ask.

Utterly shocked and mortified, Carolyn demanded that Neal should make the request himself. He soon did, via a typewritten letter probably composed by his new lover but unequivocally signed by Neal himself. Carolyn hired a lawyer, divorce proceedings were started, and the redoubtable Helen Hinkle agreed to serve as Carolyn's witness.

• • •

Diana Hansen was a fashion model who had an apartment on Manhattan's East 75th Street. (Carolyn Cassady questions whether Diana ever was a model at all, mainly on the grounds of her heavy physique, something usually described by less partisan observers as "statuesque." In fact Carolyn, who was often quite astonishingly gracious and sympathetic to LuAnne and other women in Neal's life, never took to Diana.) On graduation from Barnard College, where she had majored in philosophy and aesthetics, Diana married her English literature professor, Ted Hoffman. That marriage had ended by the time Neal Cassady met her at a party soon after he arrived in New York. At the time, Neal was staying with Jack for a few days in Gabrielle Kerouac's new apartment in Richmond Hill. Neal moved in with Diana almost immediately. When Diana discovered she was pregnant by Neal, his divorce from Carolyn was deemed imperative, which led to that first of many phone requests from Diana to Carolyn. The divorce suit was filed exactly one month after Jami's birth, and Carolyn appeared in court in June 1950. When the judge asked where the philandering husband was, Carolyn's lawyer announced that he was "In Mexico getting married."

This was untrue. Neal had discovered that he and Diana would have to wait another year for any interlocutory degree to become final, and he'd consequently gone to Mexico to get a quickie divorce.

That trip, like so many others, acquired diversions and secondary agendas along the way. Neal drove to Denver and picked up Jack Kerouac and a young acolyte called Frank Jeffries. The subsequent excursion was eventually transmuted into a central strand of Part Four of *On the Road*, an aromatic, evocative portrait of Mexico as an exotic escape route, a land of hedonism, something close to paradise for men who did not believe in it. Here, according to Kerouac, they arrive at the threshold of heaven: "Then we turned our faces to Mexico with bashfulness and wonder as those dozens of Mexican cats watched us from under their secret hatbrims in the night. Beyond were music and all-night restaurants with smoke pouring out of the door. 'Whee' whispered Dean very softly. . . . 'It's the world,' said Dean. 'My God!' he cried, slapping the wheel. 'It's the world!'"

Once again the point of Neal Cassady's adventure somehow became secondary to the seductive vagaries of the itinerary . . . which led to the question of whether the seductive vagaries had not in fact been the real point of the adventure all along.

The divorce document Neal eventually brought back (after a week of hot nights full of high jinks, drink, drugs, sex, and at least one casualty in the shape of a fever-bound Kerouac, whom he abandoned at William Burroughs's home in Mexico City), was described by John Clellon Holmes as "twenty sheets of foolscap studded with red seals." These papers, which looked impressive, were in fact invalid. Not that this fact inhibited the wedding that took place between Neal Cassady and Diana Hansen in Newark, New Jersey, on July 10, 1950. This bigamous ceremony was witnessed by Allen Ginsberg, John Clellon Holmes, and Alan Harrington (author of *The Immortalist* and the model for Hal Hingham in *On the Road*). One hour later Neal himself was once again on the road . . . or this time on the rails, to be more exact.

Neal was going back west, his trip subsidized by a Southern Pacific Railroad pass, on board a train bound for California, ostensibly going there to maintain his seniority with SPRR by reprising his work as a brakeman based in the city he had vowed never again to visit. Always prepared to try any line of work no matter how unsuitable when the need arose, Neal Cassady saw working on the SPRR as a uniquely appropriate employment. It was dependable in that it was a job for life from which one could not be fired except in extreme circumstances; and despite its bewildering rules and regulations and unpredictability—the layoffs, the systems of priorities, status, and sliding pay scale—it suited Neal much better than anything else, because those changing schedules, stopovers, and the constant travel gave him opportunities to juggle friends and lovers in a way that a deskbound job never could have done. Now SPRR had drawn him back to California again. Once there his first port of call was 29 Russell Street and the woman he had said he would never bother again.

He arrived on Carolyn's doorstep on July 14, just four days after his nuptials. She attempted some small talk, but Neal ignored it.

"(He) walked slowly and softly around the house," Carolyn noted, "gazing reverently at everything like a man returned from the dead. Barely audibly he said, 'Oh darling . . . you don't know how great it is to be home.'"

18

NEAL CASSADY'S RELATIONSHIP with Diana Hansen is in some ways harder to fathom than most of his other known affairs. Certainly she was striking looking, educated, and not quite as penniless as she would frequently claim to be when calling and writing to Carolyn Cassady. (Diana actually came from a wealthy family in Tarrytown, upstate New York.) Carolyn noted waspishly, "At least twice a week [Diana] would telephone, spending $25 to tell me how broke she was." In fact, although Diana did have financial problems, including an escalating income tax bill, it was always tacitly assumed that family money would come to the rescue eventually; hers was therefore a different kind of "broke" from Carolyn's.

An affair had seemed inevitable once Jack Kerouac had introduced Neal to Diana. "I saw him score," said John Clellon Holmes in Barry Gifford's oral biography *Jack's Book*, speaking of the night at a party when Neal Cassady felled Diana with a killer smile and promptly moved into her apartment. "She'd never seen anything like Neal, who came roaring into her life." Holmes spoke too of the love nest Neal and Diana shared at 319 East 75th Street, an apartment in which the shades were permanently drawn, colored lamps turned on, and Neal customarily wore nothing but a short kimono while Diana hovered adoringly.

"All she wanted was for him to love her and she was willing for anything," said Holmes simply. Neal found temporary work in a New York parking lot while this affair flourished through the fall and winter of 1949 and 1950; Diana assumed he had informed his current wife of what was happening. Of course he had not, which made the first of Diana's many phone calls an extra shock to Carolyn. Things moved rapidly even as a stunned Carolyn was reluctantly organizing the divorce from San Francisco.

All the signs were that Neal intended to try to make the relationship with Diana work, and he certainly seemed to be devoting a lot of effort to ensure the planned marriage was legal. Looked at another way, perhaps Neal's trip to Mexico, ostensibly undertaken to obtain the all-important divorce, was after all primarily motivated by a wish to go traveling with Jack again and obtain marijuana. Or perhaps, like Diana, Neal really did place a lot of importance on making sure that their child would not be born out of wedlock, however the marriage panned out. Whatever the reason, there remains the suspicion that it was something more than a wish to maintain his seniority with Southern Pacific that made him leave Diana for California just two hours after they were married. Had he made the right decision in marrying her? In a letter to Jack Kerouac shortly after he arrived in San Francisco, Neal summarized his return from the Mexican trip and subsequent events: "21 days of solitude in NY except Di at night, during which 2 full ozs disappeared. Long hassle to decide futures—then, finally, 4 day & nite trip across country on Streamliners from passes SPRR gave me via telegram to return to work here in SF."

From San Francisco Neal wrote letters to Diana that were loving but, by his standards, awkward and often strangely oblique.

"It's very hard to write," began the first. "All across the country I've thought of sentences, parts of paragraphs etc., which would go in my first letter. Instead, this—what can I say?" The letter concluded: "I only have one attitude toward you, anything that's everything about you in itself returns to its structure & is the one way I think of you. The only thoughts are ones of love. Must catch train."

When Neal attempted to move back in with Carolyn at Russell Street, she flatly refused. Accustomed to getting his way with women, Neal seemed more annoyed than disappointed by this.

"You've really gone too far this time, Neal," Carolyn told him. "I've had enough, and I've a good start on my independence. I certainly don't want to 'start all over again, shudder, shudder,' as you said in your farewell note."

Neal reluctantly moved into a skid row hotel but spent most of his free time at the family home, playing with his two daughters (this was the first time he had seen Jami), and turning on "the old charm, devotion, helpfulness, kindness, and consideration I'd loved him for in the beginning," according to Carolyn. Meanwhile he was attempting to persuade Diana to move to California as part of a scarcely credible plan whereby he would spend six months with her followed by six months with Carolyn, so as to be able to make an informed choice as to which woman to favor with his long-term affections.

In the summer Carolyn was obliged to terminate her employment when the woman doctor who had hired her moved to a distant new office. This doctor would generously verify that Carolyn was suffering from postpartum depression (a condition, she noted dryly, from which Carolyn should be suffering even if she was not), so qualifying her to receive disability insurance payments. These payments gave Carolyn time to be a homemaker and also to launch herself into a correspondence course in illustration, paid for by her parents. It seemed like a welcome opportunity to develop a career as well as a degree of independence—independence both for its own sake and as a much-needed symbol of freedom from Neal.

Jack Kerouac's novel *The Town and the City* was finally published, and Jack sent a copy to Russell Street, although by this time even he was dissatisfied with what some reviewers saw as a pastiche of his favorite author Thomas Wolfe's *Look Homeward, Angel.* Carolyn, however, read it and enjoyed it and was tempted to write in a conciliatory tone to Jack, whom she had evicted so peremptorily; in the end, it was a temptation she resisted.

At about this time Neal moved from his San Francisco hotel to Watsonville, in the Pajaro Valley just south of Santa Cruz. About a hundred miles from San Francisco, Watsonville was a railroad town that provided dormitories for SPRR workers. He immediately summoned Diana to stay with him for a couple of weeks in an apartment he would rent for the occasion in uptown Watsonville, beginning on August 20. His plan was to lay the foundation for a more permanent arrangement that would, eventually, place the two Mrs. Cassadys, for the purposes of comparison, at either end of a hundred-mile subsidized railroad line ("How many men have ever had it so good?" inquired Carolyn wryly). To this end, on August 12, Neal wrote pregnant Diana with comically complex instructions as to how to find him in Watsonville, where she duly visited him. During her stay she wrote for her husband a quasi-legal document stating that it was her "wish and command" that Neal should indulge himself unrestrainedly with "all women possible" and should have "a totally free hand in his selection . . . including female children," the arrangement expiring on "the date our relationship of marriage is severed." She signed it "Diana H. Cassady."

At the end of her Watsonville sojourn Diana contacted Carolyn in San Francisco asking if she could stop by on her way back, and saying, "I want to see Russell Street and the house I've heard so much about, and Cathy and Jami." Carolyn had always found Diana's unwelcome attempts to be friendly quite unstoppable—and so it was again. Despite being firmly told not to visit, Diana contrived (or so Carolyn believed) to miss her Saturday flight back from Oakland airport, telephoned again, and begged to be allowed to stay at Russell Street overnight. She arrived at the apartment, irritating Carolyn beyond endurance with her unwelcome chumminess ("She jabbered on and on about Neal as though we were all in some delicious conspiracy together," Carolyn recalled), cooing over the children and staying the night. Mayhem ensued early next morning when Neal dropped in, assuming that Diana was now safely back in New York. Suddenly faced with an unwelcome collision of two worlds he had painstakingly sought to keep apart, he argued violently with Diana, and was lambasted by Carolyn. One might think that this encounter would make him drop all plans to ingratiate himself with each woman by claiming lack of interest in the other. In fact he did nothing of the sort, and in this was supported by Diana who, in a subsequent letter to him from New York, dated September 15, made light of the incident in her characteristically breezy way: "I dropped a note to Carolyn thanking her for putting me up Sat. night, apologizing for my 'breakdown' & asking her about what kind of diapers are best. . . . As for the Sun. A.M. we don't have to discuss it because I think I understood. It was just so painful and unpleasant, and I, for one, was completely worn out from the battle with the airlines."

Neal had returned to the Watsonville apartment he had rented for Diana's visit but, after inviting LuAnne there for a spell, soon tired of their constant squabbles and abandoned that apartment in favor of moving back to San Francisco. He now rented another apartment in San Francisco's Divisadero Street in the Haight-Ashbury district.

He made the move on September 19 and described it in a letter to Jack Kerouac dated September 25: "I've got a great bachelor 3 big room apt. with everything, refrigerator etc., and I only pay 35 a month and I go to Carolyn's and we understand each other and things in general are fine, except worry over Diana and her coming child and what to do about it."

It seems Neal was considering bringing Diana over again in December, this time to live with him and so put into practice the first installment of the two proposed six-month trial periods. However, the plan disintegrated for no clear reason. Carolyn discouraged it mainly on the grounds that a nearby Diana would be even harder to repel than the one who still phoned her long distance with unwanted confidences and requests. In any event, on October 17 Neal put off Diana (now sequestered with her disapproving family in Tarrytown) in a long letter containing more than a hint of emotional blackmail: "I'm convinced you can't come out here now, that one thing is sure even if it kills you to stay with MAMA. But what if we split up? . . . So although I know how awful this all is to you; how you'll rebel, there's really nothing you can do about it, so may as well relax and spend your free time fixing up for baby and working on your ideas for business which is equivalent to me trying to write and Carolyn trying to draw even while living through this period."

Neal unilaterally reduced the trial periods from six to three months and suggested to Carolyn that their three months could begin immediately if he moved back into the Russell Street house; anyway he could no longer afford the rental on the Divisadero Street place. Grudgingly Carolyn said yes. Although she stipulated that he must sleep on the sofa and behave properly, this was really a self-deceiving acquiescence, as Carolyn's later admission confirms: "I was happy only when he was around showing an interest in me. To fortify my position I accepted dates . . . even though I had no conversation to offer, having been so immersed in Neal and in staying alive . . . my deep belief that Neal was the only man for me had still not changed, try as I might to deny it, and I found it all too easy to slip back into a married feeling with him."

Established once more in the Russell Street household, Neal had again resumed writing *The First Third*, now with the aid of a new piece of technology he hoped would make the process easier: a Webster Electric 109WE Ekotape recorder. Oxide-based magnetic tape recorders like this were a relatively new phenomenon in 1950, and would soon replace the inferior wire recorder. Wire recorders registered the audio signal onto a spooled length of glorified piano wire resulting in a very narrow dynamic range and frequent transport problems. The fidelity and reliability of the new "tape" recorder was far superior.

In retrospect audio tape would seem to have been the ideal medium not only for fast-talking Neal, but also for Jack, whose typing speed always lagged behind his mental outpourings. Indeed Neal tried to persuade Jack to acquire a similar machine, deploying all of the salesman's flair he had so signally failed to demonstrate when selling encyclopedias and kitchenware: "A tape recorder . . . a gone instrument which reproduces so flawlessly (you can hear a clock ticking from way over in the next room when you play back recording) and so cheaply and so effortlessly, and the tapes last forever and don't break, can save any part or all of anything recorded."

Neal's idea was that he and Jack could exchange really long audio letters unrestricted by having to write them down. Interestingly, Neal was so enamored of home recording that he also set about taping his own readings. These included the prologue to Thomas Wolfe's *Of Time and the River* as well as a few of his own marijuana-fueled conceits including "A Hi Hour with Proust" and flights of verbal fancy based on Major Hoople, a pompous newspaper cartoon character whom Neal voiced as W. C. Fields. Carolyn, to her regret, didn't save the tapes.

On October 20 Diana Hansen joined the major league of Cassady-circle letter writers with a twenty-two-page riposte to Neal's denial of the six-month trial period she was due to begin with him in San Francisco. But she had already been overtaken by events. On October 27 Neal was summoned by SPRR to work for several weeks in San Luis Obispo, a town located halfway between San Francisco and Los Angeles. There he would lodge with Al and Helen Hinkle—Al was already stationed there—and make runs to Santa Barbara and Watsonville. Two days before he had to go, he telephoned LuAnne—now Mrs. R. T. Murphy and seven months pregnant—with a view to arranging an assignation. However, when she resisted Neal gave in. As he wrote to Jack Kerouac in a letter dated November 5, 1950, "I got so heartsick I let her beg off meeting me & so lost her again, as I had done last on May 31, '49." His almost adolescent precision about the date and time seems to suggest that LuAnne continued to exert an exceptional emotional hold on him.

During Neal's time in San Luis Obispo, he and Carolyn exchanged letters that skirted around the possibilities of a life together. From Carolyn a letter beginning: "First know that I love you all I want in life is to be your wife & the mother of your children—but I want all that this implies. Foremost it means I want you as a husband and a father—and all that this implies." This drew from Neal a long reply so ambiguous in its intellectualizations that even Carolyn, hungry for his words, was forced to conclude: "Insofar as I could follow his thoughts, this letter did little to reassure me, and it made me vaguely anxious and confused in a new way."

A letter from Allen Ginsberg dated October 31 contained a description of Bill Cannastra's colorful death on the New York subway and the philosophical issues he felt it raised. Cannastra had been the most extreme figure among the young Turks in "subterranean" New York; his chaotic loft was a magnet for confused seekers of undefined destinies, and his passing surely must signify something . . . or so Ginsberg reasoned. John Clellon Holmes's *Go* told the story of Cannastra's death as a grim farce in which the drunken prophet of the subterraneans boarded a downtown subway train and then inexplicably attempted to climb out of a window as it pulled out of the 23rd Street station. Too late he tried to retreat, only to be dragged out of the window upon impact with the wall of the tunnel, falling beneath the train wheels. He was dead when they freed him and, Holmes notes in a deadpan grace note, "the trains on that part of the line were held up for thirty-six minutes."

Ginsberg's letter concluded with a paragraph containing the lines, "Heard little from Diana, she seems worried about future, etc., as well she might. . . . So you're back with Carolyn, eh? . . . Jesus, what the hell are you all after in each other?"

Neal now seemed to be writing mainly when high on marijuana or Benzedrine, a state that better suited writing to Jack or Allen (who welcomed the buzzy tone of ambiguity and spontaneity) than to Carolyn (who was more interested in practicalities). Jack received a thirty-six-page letter that had been written on November 5 containing Neal's protean thoughts on everything from Cannastra's death and his own sudden craving to own a flute to a pornographic reverie that anticipated a foursome involving himself, Jack, and two vaguely sketched girls ("like 'em skinny").

Back at Russell Street Carolyn was briefly being entertained by a friend of her brother's, a man named Bud, who had an expense account but also a wife and five children. No romance was planned or assumed, but Carolyn enjoyed being taken out. She also enjoyed the attention, and so Bud became, at least in family conversation, an emotional stick with which she could beat Neal when he returned from San Luis Obispo.

Meanwhile things were happening in New York. On November 7, Diana gave birth to a boy, Neal Junior, eventually to be rechristened Curtis Neal. Ten days later Jack Kerouac stunned everyone by unexpectedly marrying Joan Haverty, a young woman ungraciously described by the best man at her wedding—Allen Ginsberg—as "a tall dumb dark-haired girl just made for Jack."

The newlyweds stayed with Jack's mother in Queens for a while and then moved into Cannastra's old loft. Joan, who had previously had a brief relationship with the recently deceased, had since taken over the lease.

For the autumn issue of *Neurotica* magazine, John Clellon Holmes collaborated on an article entitled "The Myth of the Western Hero" (the article was credited to Alfred Towne, a pseudonym for the combined authorial efforts of Holmes and the magazine's editor, Jay Landesman). It was an assured and playful account of how the western movie was currently assuming a cultural reading that had never been applied to the sort of innocent cowboy flick that Neal loved as a boy.

"The western film, and its hero, is fast becoming America's number one candidate for the cultural analytical couch," it began. "Reach, stranger, reach way down deep into your unconscious. Unholster your impotence and blast the big bad man. Clear your name, stake your claim and go home happy. . . . Escape from the subtle psychological anxieties of today into a Utopia populated entirely by outlaws, rustlers, dance hall girls, gamblers, weak-willed sheriffs, and ferocious Indians, is like a vacation from Sodom in Gomorrah. If it's innocent fantasy you want you might as well miss that stage coach. For the western, to the contrary, merely simplifies reality so that you can handle it."

The authors also asserted that *Red River, Duel in the Sun,* and *The Outlaw* have plots that "are fantastic in their blatant homosexuality, and it takes no psychiatrically oriented audience to understand it."

All this inspired Neal sufficiently to write to Holmes on November 20 (five days after his return from San Luis Obispo) with sincere approval and some of his own youthful reminiscences, including those accounts of his competitive bike deliveries with Ben Gowen and chicken-rustling activities quoted in Chapter 5.

"I read your Myth of the Western Hero in 7 of Neurotica and got a real boot out of it," Neal wrote to Holmes. "Even tho you write such stuff to eat (and so whenever one begins to praise any of it you depreciate it all and so belittle yourself that one is tempted to accept your deprecation and not deal with it seriously), I only wish I could come up with anything that can approach your 'trash.'"

Neal obviously felt admiring and envious that his own heartfelt writing could not even match the quality of a Holmes potboiler, although whether or not he was specifically drawn to the subject matter of the cowboy myth is debatable. Despite his Denver upbringing and a tendency for others to see in him a cowboy spirit, Neal Cassady never seems to have affected a cowboy persona; he hated guns and, as we shall soon see, was decidedly uncomfortable around horses. It is more likely that it was the confidence of the prose, the perceptive identification of those movies' homosexual themes (years before it became fashionable to deconstruct popular entertainment in this way), and even perhaps the reference to *Duel in the Sun,* a notorious movie that featured an overripe performance from Jennifer Jones, whose looks had made a particular impression on Neal.

In the paragraph that follows his initial praise of Holmes, Neal changes stylistic gears rather abruptly: "In the beginning, when the Faustian land was still without cities it was the nobility that represented, in the highest sense, the nation. The peasantry, everlasting and historyless, was a people before the dawn of culture and survives when the form of the nation has passed away. The Nation, like every grand symbol of the culture, is intimately the cherished possession of a few: those who have it are born to it, like men are born to art or philosophy."

There are four paragraphs in this grandiose vein, presumably intended to show Holmes that, despite the self-deprecation of the earlier paragraph, Cassady was capable of handling Big Ideas. In fact, to the astute observer it showed that his tendency toward petty larceny was still alive and well because, as Dave Moore has pointed out, the four paragraphs are partially edited and completely unacknowledged quotations from Oswald Spengler's *Decline of the West* (1928). Toward the end Neal reviews his own letter. "Goddam my soul, John, I just stopped for the first time to reread this letter. What a bunch of blabbermouth junk, poorly thought out, worse in construction and pretentious as hell."

It is hard to disagree with Neal's self-assessment, which makes it particularly ironic that one of his best and most influential pieces of writing was also produced at this time. As *The First Third* progressed only fitfully, on December 17 Neal sent a prodigious and highly influential letter to Jack Kerouac; it had taken him three drug-fueled days to write. Now the stuff of literary legend, "the Joan Anderson letter," as it came to be known, was in its entirety probably about 13,000 words long, although only a 5,000-word extract survives. How this came about is uncertain, although there is circumstantial evidence to suggest that the "extract" was in fact an incomplete copy made by Kerouac in April of 1952 when he apparently intended to type up the whole letter during a visit to the Cassadys. "I am typing up the entire Joan Anderson chapter of Neal's to stone Carl [Solomon] with," he confidently wrote to Allen Ginsberg at the time—incidentally revealing that he assumed the letter to be a chapter of Neal's memoir. Later he implied in a letter to Carolyn that he had been "sposed" to type it up during that visit but that this intention had been interrupted by a falling out that triggered a parting of the ways—Kerouac would be given a lift to the Mexican border while the Cassadys drove on to Tennessee. It is therefore quite possible that Kerouac did type up around 5,000 words of the letter and that this was the partial typescript that survived following the loss of the original. That original was lent to Ginsberg who in turn loaned it, along with other papers, to one Gerd Stern, a poet who was also the West Coast representative of Ace Books. Later Stern always denied losing Neal's original or any part of it, claiming he returned everything to Ginsberg. Since Stern lived on a houseboat in Sausalito, the rumor persisted that most of "Neal's letter" had accidentally fallen into the San Francisco Bay. This version of the story would suggest the original was lost after it was returned to Ginsberg. If the typescript theory is correct, no one seems to know what happened to the original letter or at what point the typed portion became the source of the surviving "extract."

Despite all of which, if there was a single moment when it became clear (at least to future readers) that Neal Cassady's greatest writing talent lay in the epistolary form, this was it. Misleadingly published in 1964 in John Bryan's magazine *Notes from Underground* as "The First Third" (a confusion compounded when the self-same extract reappeared as "To have seen a specter isn't everything . . ." in the 1971 City Lights' edition of *The First Third* proper), this fragment even formed the insubstantial basis for a 1997 Keanu Reeves movie, *The Last Time I Committed Suicide*, in which Neal is played by Thomas Jane. The original letter prompted its recipient to respond with effusive praise for "your wonderful 13,000 word letter . . . I thought it ranked among the best things ever written in America and ran to Holmes & Harrington and told them so; I said it was almost as good as the unbelievably good Notes From Underground of Dostoevsky . . . I say truly, no Dreiser, no Wolfe has come close to it; Melville was never truer . . . It is the exact stuff upon which American Lit is still to be founded."

In a sense it would be. The exact degree of influence that one writer may exert upon another can never usually be quantified, but little over twelve weeks after receiving Neal's letter, Kerouac made a start on a new book that would effectively be completed in three weeks and would owe nothing to *The Town and the City* nor to the literary model of Thomas Wolfe. Kerouac had found his muse in the shape of the man he had first met in New York in December 1946 and who had now shown him a spontaneous style of writing—loose, rolling sentences studded with pin-sharp descriptions and vignettes—that perfectly suited his ambitions to create a written equivalent of "crazy jazz" rhythms and riffs.

The surviving section of the Joan Anderson letter deals with Neal's recollections of a girlfriend whom he abandons not once but twice, first as she recovers from aborting his child in the hospital, then as she recuperates afterward. Her physical resemblance to the luminously beautiful 1940s and '50s movie actress—and star of *Duel in the Sun*—Jennifer Jones seems to be the main attraction for Neal, but that is insufficient to make him commit to her, despite the generous efforts of two of her friends to help the couple make a life together. Neal's story of his tawdry defection from Joan to the local pool hall is abruptly derailed by his bawdy recollections of an earlier sexual escapade, including a naked escape through a bathroom window and a subsequent intended reprimand by a visiting priest who turns out to be none other than Neal's godfather, John Harley Schmitt, who has not seen him for years. Schmitt is clearly so joyful to see Neal again that it entirely abolishes the admonitory point of his visit.

The narrative content of the fragment is not only rather slight but suspect as well, having the ring of *The Amorous Adventures of Moll Flanders* or some other picaresque seventeenth-century novel packed with bawdy incidents and frankly improbable familial coincidences. "But it really happened," Carolyn Cassady insists, even though the event took place before she ever met Neal. We are entitled to remain skeptical, so closely does this anecdote resemble some of Neal's earlier embellished or untrue anecdotes that conclude with a major coincidence. However, in this case the force of Neal's letter lay not in its literal content but rather in the energy and imaginative dislocation of its style. Here is personal adventure recounted in vital, associative prose that creates the written equivalent of Neal telling the story in person. At the same time it has a literary quality—a shape and a tone—that while not perhaps that of traditional narrative, nonetheless conveys a sense of having been structured for artistic effect. Even the best of Neal's previous letters had been disorganized if vibrant lists of incidents, celebrations, thoughts, ambitions, and complaints, but this one found—and founded—a new style of writing. That is what galvanized Kerouac and laid the foundation for him to create *On the Road*.

The surviving fragment begins with a reminiscence of youthful Neal's hospital visit to Joan, the young woman who aborted his child and whom he subsequently avoided.

> To have seen a specter isn't everything, and there are deathmasks piled, one atop the other, clear to heaven. Commoner still are the wan visages of those returning from the shadow of the valley. This means little to those who have not lifted the veil.
>
> The ward nurse cautioned me not to excite her (how can one prevent that?) and I was allowed only a few minutes. The head nurse also stopped me to say I was permitted to see her just because she always called my name and I must cheer her. She had had a very near brush and was not rallying properly, actually was in marked decline, and still much in danger. Quite impressed to my duties, I entered and gazed down on her slender form resting so quietly on the high white bed. Her pale face was whiter; like chalk. It was pathetically clear how utterly weak she was, there seemed absolutely no blood left in her body. I stared and stared, she didn't breathe, didn't move; I would never have recognized her, she was a waxed mummy. White is the absence of color, she was white; all white, unless beneath the covers, whose top caressed her breasts, was still hidden a speck of pink. The thin ivory arms tapered inward until they reached the slight outward bulge of narrow palms, and the hands in turn bent inward with a more sharp taper only to quickly end in long fingers curled to a point. These things, and her head, with its completely matted hair so black

> and contrasting with all the whiteness, were the only parts of her visible. Quite normal, I know, but I just couldn't get over how awfully dead she looked. I had so arranged my head above hers that when her eyes opened, after about ten minutes, they were in direct line with mine; they showed no surprise, nor changed their position in the slightest. The faintest of smiles, the merest of voices, "hello." I placed my hand on her arm, it was all I could do to restrain myself from jumping on the bed to hold her. I saw she was too weak to talk and told her not to, I, however, rambled on at a great rate.

Just one year had passed since Neal had set out on his quixotic bid to give the Hinkles a honeymoon. In that time he had driven innumerable miles, ridden many hundreds more on the SPRR, "divorced" Carolyn (though this was never actually finalized), reprised his affair with LuAnne, married Diana, moved back in with Carolyn, and written another dense batch of letters—one of which would change the history of twentieth-century American literature.

Christmas was, at last, a happy one for Carolyn, with Neal back in the fold, a Christmas Eve celebration with the Hinkles (who were leaving for Denver immediately afterward), and even a touch of schadenfreude-laden pleasure that the advent of the holiday season seemed to help Diana accept Neal's defection from her life. "Not much to say," Diana wrote on December 20. "I suppose sooner or later we'd better do something legal about dissolving marriage."

When in a more positive mood Diana had sometime earlier contacted Neal's father with news of her son's birth, addressing her letter "c/o Zaza's Barbershop, Larimer Street, Denver" and supplying Neal's address on the return section of the envelope. This in turn resulted in a letter from Neal's father in the dying days of 1950.

Neal Sr.'s first communication with his son for some years, full of misspellings and vague goodwill, ended with the forlorn words: "Awful sorry

I didn't have any money but will send you the first I get. Am in the Co jail lieu a $3 hundred fine. Will be out 15 Feb. Excuse pencil."

Neal immediately sprang into action, formulating another of his elaborate itineraries, this time planning to leave San Francisco at the beginning of January in order to boom (a "boomer" was an experienced railroad worker who moved from railroad to railroad in search of temporary employment) in either "Tucson, El Paso or Tucumcari," then on to "N. Orleans, Montgomery, Atlanta, Washington, and New Y," returning the same way with a possible detour to see Neal Sr. in Denver and arrange for him to come and live at Russell Street. The Kerouacs, too, Neal now envisioned as close neighbors living in the shadow of Telegraph Hill. All this he told to Jack in a letter dated December 30 along with a complex scheme involving transferred passes that would allow Jack and Joan to travel to Texas or San Francisco. In fact Neal's plan was not only complicated, it was also premature. There was no work for boomers in January on the route he proposed, and instead he found work in Oakland, postponing his trip east until the end of the month. Then a lull in work made him bring it forward again, leaving San Francisco on January 10. When he reached New York he saw Diana and his son Curtis with a view to making plans about the future they would not now be sharing. Jack Kerouac described Neal's short visit to New York thus, with Neal as Dean, Diana as Inez, Carolyn as Camille, Cathy as Amy, and Jami as Joanie: "[Dean] stayed in New York three days and hastily made preparations to get back on the train with his railroad passes and again recross the continent, five days and five nights in dusty coaches and hardbench crummies, and of course we had no money for a truck and couldn't go back with him. With Inez he spent one night explaining and sweating and fighting, and she threw him out. A letter came for him, care of me. I saw it. It was from Camille. 'My heart broke when I saw you go across the tracks with your bag. I pray and pray you get back safe . . . I do want Sal [Jack] and his friend [wife Joan] to come and live on the same street . . . I know you'll make it but I can't help worrying—now that we've decided everything. . . . Dear Dean, it's the end of the first half of the century. Welcome with love and kisses to spend the other half with us. We all wait for you. [Signed] Camille, Amy, and little Joanie.'"

Before Neal even got back to San Francisco in his dusty cars and hardbench crummies, Carolyn confirmed what she had now suspected for some weeks: she was once again pregnant. She was unsure how Neal would take this news. Ever unpredictable, he replied that he was "pleased, happy, amazed, proud, overjoyed."

19

AT THE START of 1951 the Korean War was still in its early stages. The conflict between Communist and non-Communist forces on the Korean Peninsula had escalated in June 1950 when the northern Communist forces finally invaded the South. President Truman committed American troops to lead the United Nations combat forces without the approval of Congress; the ensuing conflict would continue until an Armistice agreement was signed in July 1953.

Neal Cassady had briefly addressed the prosecution of this war in a letter to Jack Kerouac in the fall of 1950. The terms he used demonstrated his tendency to treat almost all external events—that is, those that did not concern his own immediate personal circumstances—as fodder for his playful, allusive style of writing. He wrote on October 22, 1950: "The importance of the recent Truearthur meeting in the Pacific led to renewed speculation by usually reliable sources in this city of rumors that to balance the effects and offset the advantage gained by Dugout Doug [Douglas MacArthur] and Tess Trueheart's [comic strip hero Dick Tracy's girlfriend] erstwhile sugar daddy Harry, Big Dick Cass and slept with the best of 'em, semi longish John would meet in the east just north of Horseshit Harry's Hideaway."

On the domestic front, at the start of 1951 there were optimistic signs that Neal's relationship with Carolyn was about to enter a comparatively stable phase. He was just twenty-five. He had been married three times, he had two children with Carolyn, and now a third was on the way, about which he seemed genuinely excited. The SPRR continued to offer him a reliable and flexible form of employment that suited him well. San Francisco and the rail routes and postings he drew allowed him to combine the illusion of being domestically committed while giving him the mobility and opportunity for the mischief he craved. (Neal's psyche, which would be analyzed by mental health professionals in later years, was already defined by one central characteristic that would never change: for him freedom was always equated with travel and he never felt freer than when he was on his way somewhere.)

In January 1951, however, the (largely false) signs were that Neal had come to a genuine accommodation with his many conflicting impulses. His letter of reassurance to Carolyn when she had told him of her new pregnancy did seem to reflect a degree of commitment over and above the instant response of being "pleased, happy, amazed, proud, overjoyed." It continued: "The wonderful and absolute joy I know and feel at thoughts of next quarter century with you . . . I've learned how to treat possessions. . . . WORRY ABOUT NOTHING—including the third child . . . you come first, first, first in everything—kids next—perfect just to watch you, work for you, and I'm not hung on lazy kicks any more!!"

But by February 13 he was already feeling sorry for himself. In a letter, he appealed to Jack, in mock cowboy lingo, to "'Come Save the Westerners' you must get on your hihorse and gallop o'er hill and vale to the secluded nook with a 41 Packard at its door (with initial C, in gold, for knocker) and be treated with infamous hospitality."

Neal was now sending Diana and her son money each month, although supplementary payments in the form of collect telephone calls seem to have prompted some domestic discord at Russell Street.

"I can only send you $50.00 believe me," Neal wrote Diana on February 27. "Your previous call (2 months or so) was paid for by me, which deducted from your $50 leaves $43.37 since it was cheap, only $6.63. This is serious only because C. & I have fought bitter battles over this damn $6.63. But, naturally, I won't—too low a trick—deduct it, although she thinks I will.

"I can cover up $6.63 but your last phone call would be impossible to hide, so, if fucking phone Co. tried to collect I must deduct it from next 50, which, incidently [*sic*] you will receive the 1st of every month."

Also troubling him was his continuing inability to make much progress with *The First Third*, which he revealingly starts referring to as "a novel" in a letter to Allen Ginsberg dated April 1, 1951. This date was also Neal and Carolyn's third wedding anniversary, which Neal celebrated with an affectionate and mildly lubricious anniversary poem that ended with the coy pretense of an obscenity cut short by a lack of writing paper:

> For conscience never has been forgot
> The pacts made three years ago this day
> When each to the other did say
> Those eternal vows that cost ten bucks
> To get from you my legal—shucks. No paper

It is worth noting that Ginsberg, not Kerouac, was the chosen sounding board for Neal's worries about his writing skills. Jack had already published a novel, and it looked as if he'd be publishing quite a few more, and so by example perhaps he made Neal more keenly aware of the gap between his own literary aspirations and achievements. Ginsberg, on the other hand, was all poems, mystical fragments, and spiritual explorations, and so perhaps represented less of a direct rival to Neal (who of course favored long, breathless linear narratives). Whatever the reason, it was Ginsberg who received one of Neal's most lucid and detailed letters, setting out the difficulties he experienced when writing as well as his musings on the distinction between writing letters and writing a "novel" (which is what, in his mind, his "family history" now seemed to have become). Interestingly, in a letter to Carolyn Cassady dated October 21, 1962, Kerouac would make tantalizing reference to what seems to be a much longer version of *The First Third* in which he says "the final divine chapters about switches and rails in San Jose" were written around 1953 and 1954 when Neal was living with Carolyn. No such chapters have survived, and all published versions of the *The First Third* end with Neal still a child.

"In my first 25 years I've written only a rambling prologue, an even weaker first 20 pages and pitifully few letters," Neal declared to Ginsberg, selling himself short on at least two counts. The prologue to *The First Third* (omitted from its initial publication in 1971) is actually quite well structured. Although its long, rather old-fashioned sentences do seem overly influenced by William Faulkner and Thomas Wolfe, and although it is so factually unreliable as to be almost entirely fictitious, it is hardly rambling. And "pitifully few letters" is a major understatement. *Neal Cassady Collected Letters, 1944–1967* (Penguin Books 2004) contains well over a hundred of Neal's letters written and sent in the six years prior to 1951 alone; many of them are of epic length. How many more from that period were omitted, lost, or forgotten is anyone's guess.

"At best I write only from sentence to sentence and can't construct beyond this," Neal confessed to Allen. "After the first statement is out, and often before, I get hopelessly involved in words to contain the increasing number of ideas . . . I am soon so overextended—stretched grammatically and logically to the point where any semblance of clarity is lost—that I am forced to stop."

Neal's perception of his problem is particularly interesting in view of the fact that the same challenge seems to have had the reverse effect on Jack Kerouac. As Neal was writing to Allen on May 15, 1951, Jack had just completed the marathon three-week burst of creativity during which he wrote the bulk of *On the Road* by just such a process of tension between a runaway torrent of ideas and the slower process of expressing them in typewritten words. Kerouac would improve his odds of success by "speeding up" the typing process, using a homemade scroll of paper that allowed him to keep pecking away at top speed without even having to stop to insert individual sheets of paper. Neal's solution had been to "slow down" his thoughts by recording them onto magnetic audiotape and replaying them to set them down later. Yet Neal's Ekotape trial had not so far been successful.

"The experiment has proved somewhat disappointing," he wrote Ginsberg, "so was abandoned in its infancy a few months ago, but when I again get 10 bucks to get it out of the repair shop (magnetized by sitting next to a radio in long disusement) I will begin a new attempt with it."

Neal also explained his differing methods of composition for letters and fiction. "Now if I'm on a novel I write longhand and type it up with a bit of changing as I go along; if I'm writing a letter I just type word for word as I think of them, unless I get particularly involved, then I write that sentence or two in longhand before typing."

It now seems curious that Neal's doubts about his own writing attempts coincided so closely with Kerouac's creative blitz on his novel. At the time there was no way of knowing that Kerouac's novel, which remained in manuscript form until 1957, would even find a publisher, let alone become a significant book. Nor could Neal Cassady have guessed quite how important his own contribution (both literal and inspirational) to Kerouac's seminal work would turn out to have been.

Literally speaking, *On the Road* contained some almost verbatim passages from Cassady's letters to Kerouac; stylistically speaking, Cassady's Joan Anderson letter had provided Kerouac with the perfect paradigm of a hyperactive first-person narrative written as though it were a long letter to a friend. Cassady the legendary hustler had, in a sense, given to Jack, gratis, his own most valuable assets: the vision and the style that, for reasons of temperament, he seemed chronically unable to transform into the books he desperately wanted to write.

Such considerations were far from Neal's mind as he tried to come to terms with the circumstances of his reprised family life. Diana Hansen recruited Allen Ginsberg to help keep her circumstances uppermost in Neal's mind. ("I saw Diana 3 times for lunch," Allen wrote to Neal and Carolyn, "and I think she is quite upset since all is confusion, not so much amatorily [I think she's cured] but financially. . . .")

Neal and Carolyn, fearing that the patterns of the past might be repeated, turned to psychological therapy at San Francisco's Langley Porter Clinic. The idea seems to have been Carolyn's but with Neal an apparently willing and almost eager conscript.

Carolyn's recollections of how they fared there suggest unstructured sessions with a procession of different therapists who were not up to the challenge posed by two lively and unconventional minds, at least one of which was usually under the influence of marijuana."They treated [Neal] with hauteur and hostility," recalled Carolyn, "unable to conceal their disapproval."

Although the psychotherapy failed, it did prefigure a mutual interest in opening up the Cassady marriage to external evaluation, something that would take an unexpected spiritual turn in later years.

In June 1951 Jack and Joan separated. Joan's posthumously published autobiography offered a bleak rationale for the failure of the marriage, suggesting her imposed role was that of housekeeper, muse, and sex slave, not to mention the fact that Jack was in permanent thrall to his demanding mother, Gabrielle. Neal responded at once by sending Jack a message whose uncharacteristic brevity was the result of its being a telegram, not a letter: "Wait. No foolish moves. This serious. Unparalleled opportunity. You come here. Orders. You must obey. We mean it. You need it. Carolyn agrees. Hurry. Letter follows."

The letter that did follow promised work for Jack on the SPRR, but for some reason Kerouac went instead with his mother to visit his sister in North Carolina. From there he responded more positively to Neal's invitation although the next piece of news was that a recurrence of phlebitis had unexpectedly put him into the Veterans Hospital in the Bronx.

So summer ended without the reunion for which both Neal and Carolyn had hoped. Also the June deadline for finalization of Neal and Carolyn's divorce had come and gone with Carolyn making no attempt to chase her lawyer—a telling act of omission. Neal had by now earned sufficient seniority to work passenger trains as well as freight and was enjoying the variety—and uncertainty—of being called for either duty. With a better income he had indulged in two purchases: a station wagon, which was a success, and a saxophone, which was not. The story of the saxophone is diverting in that it shows Neal recounting exactly the same facts twice, presenting them first as an opportunity and then as a drawback. As he had explained to Jack Kerouac when he was thinking of buying this particular instrument from "a fine old conductor I know," its special attraction was that it was a C-Melody saxophone. This, Neal said, meant it was in "the natural key, like a piano," so the music did not need to be transposed. By the summer Neal was the owner of this instrument but was now lamenting, "the C-Melody is so unpopular that I can't find an instruction book, and there is almost no music written for it."

On Saturday, September 8, stopping off in Santa Clara to await the departure of the train he was to take from San Jose to Watsonville, Neal idly picked up a copy of the *Oakland Tribune*. In it he saw a report of William Burroughs's fatal shooting of his common-law wife Joan Vollmer in what is usually referred to as the "William Tell" incident in a Mexico City apartment. Exactly how and why Burroughs came to shoot Joan in the head is unlikely ever to be known, although his intention to hit a tumbler of water balanced on her head is the most popular legend and the reason for referring to the Swiss folk hero who—rather more accurately—shot with a crossbow bolt an apple balanced on his own son's head. Burroughs himself first proposed that version of the incident and then, probably on legal advice, quickly retracted it in favor of saying Joan was shot when he accidentally dropped his newly purchased .38-caliber pistol. (Burroughs soon skipped bail and retreated to Ecuador in search of ever more powerful drugs. He was later tried, found guilty of "negligent homicide," and given a two-year suspended sentence.) Neal's fascination with this sensational news item about his friend saw him hastily collect as many different newspaper versions of the story as possible before traveling on to Watsonville. He finally arrived back in San Francisco at six o'clock the following morning, a Sunday, to find the Hinkles in residence at Russell Street since Carolyn was in the hospital, having just given birth to their first boy, John Allen Cassady.

• • •

On December 17, 1951, Jack Kerouac finally made it to the Cassady household; after working four days as a railroad baggage-handler with Neal, he went south to spend Christmas in San Pedro with Henri Cru, then returned on December 26. It was a good-natured reunion, and he offered his hosts his version of the split with Joan, which he suggested, perhaps not altogether plausibly, was really due to Joan's upbringing by man-hating women who had plotted to make him the fall guy for their lifelong loathing. He also claimed that he had caught Joan with a Puerto Rican he suspected of being the father of the child she was now carrying. "She says it's my child," Carolyn reported him saying. "Ha—it ain't *my* child." (Janet Michelle Kerouac, as the baby was named, was in fact Jack Kerouac's child. She was born on February 16, 1952, in Albany, New York. Jack had nothing to do with her upbringing and continued to dispute his paternity until Jan, as she became known, was ten years old and Joan Haverty successfully took him to court where he agreed to pay fifty two dollars a month for child support.)

Jack moved into the attic, which Carolyn had decked out with a very large homemade desk (orange crates supporting a huge sheet of enamel-painted plywood) and a low box spring and mattress covered with a paisley spread. The only internal access was through the Cassadys' bedroom, a fact which seemed to discomfit Jack, but he settled in, his main worry being that he considered himself a burden, especially when he found out that his arrival had coincided with a particularly bad time for getting work as a brakeman. However, Neal got him a job in the baggage room at the depot, which removed some of the pressure.

Less easy was the odd dynamic of this particular domestic arrangement. As Carolyn Cassady has noted, it was not unusual in the 1950s to find multiple tenants in households, but in this instance the history of this trio of adults did give her cause for alarm. It seemed automatically to cast her in the role of drudge while Neal went carousing with his buddy. She tried to contain her worry and later blamed this suppression for causing a sudden attack of Bell's palsy, a temporary condition that causes the facial muscles to weaken or become paralyzed. In Carolyn's case, her mouth drooped on one side, adding to her general sense of inferiority, a condition that was hardly improved by her doctor's odd treatment of hooking a paperclip in the corner of her mouth in order to pull it back into a normal position with the aid of a rubber band.

When, late on February 8—Neal's birthday—Jack and Neal tried to smuggle a young black woman into Jack's attic after fabricating an elaborate lie to excuse going out on the town together, Carolyn's anger finally erupted. This ensured a frosty atmosphere with Jack hiding in his room until he had the tact (or good sense) to append a heartfelt apology to his original inscription in Carolyn's copy of *The Town and the City*. The gesture was appreciated, good relations were restored, Carolyn underwent treatment for the facial paralysis, and a workable domestic routine was re-established. Jack started writing some additional passages for "Visions of Neal," some of which would later metamorphose into *Visions of Cody*.

Neal's confidence in his own writing took another knock when he finally responded to requests from Carl Solomon in New York (to whom Kerouac had warmly recommended Neal's writing), and sent him some of *The First Third*. Solomon was the nephew of Aaron A. Wyn, the publisher of Ace paperback books and a man for whom Solomon worked intermittently. Ginsberg tried to use the connection to get several of his friends published, and Ace did eventually publish William Burroughs's first novel, *Junkie*, as half of a pulp thriller titled *Two Books in One*. But when Neal submitted some of *The First Third* to Solomon, the response was discouraging. Solomon saw Neal as a natural storyteller who had not yet learned the rudiments of writing. Solomon described *The First Third*'s prologue merely as "too self-conscious . . . an old amateur's device to provide an excuse for writing at all. So you were born, so you had ancestors, so you have a reason for writing a book."

He also advised him to "read Mickey Spillane," a highly successful pulp fiction writer of the 1940s and '50s whose books were liberally spiced with violence, sex, and sadism. Neal, in the thrall of Thomas Wolfe and Marcel Proust, most likely considered Spillane beneath him. Solomon concluded, "I feel you would profit greatly from taking and then transcending a creative writing course given by any reputable institution in the evening."

When Neal suddenly drew a two-week stint in San Luis Obispo he abruptly removed the buffer between Carolyn and Jack, both of whom were nervous at the prospect of living together without Neal for two weeks. Neal's joshing and insensitive farewell ("You know what they say—my best pal and my best gal!") did nothing to improve things. What sounded to Carolyn like a crass suggestion (or an even crasser invitation) simply piled on more inhibitions so that by the time Neal returned, his best pal and his best gal had spent two weeks neurotically trying to avoid being alone together. Knowing full well that in her position Neal would have had no inhibitions about being unfaithful, Carolyn was particularly annoyed when, on his return, Neal seemed to assume that intimacy had taken place. Quietly, she resolved to profit from his lack of trust. The next time Neal was away overnight, she set the candlelight scene and duly seduced Jack . . . or at least created the conditions in which their mutual attraction would inevitably be parlayed into action.

Jack proved to be an attentive lover—a pleasant change after Neal's always aggressive sexual style—and this sudden shift in the dynamic of the household greatly improved Carolyn's standing and self-confidence.

"Now I was part of all they did," she wrote. "I felt like the sun of their solar system, all revolved around me."

• • •

In keeping with her new role, Carolyn attended a few bohemian get-togethers, including a solemn gathering convened to try peyote, the much-vaunted hallucinogenic cactus that was at the time an unknown quantity to many San Franciscan drug experimenters. It seemed to have little effect. No one could report any significant responses after taking it. Some peyote remained in the Cassady refrigerator for a time before finally being thrown out after it was officially declared illegal; of course illegality was no obstacle when it came to marijuana, but to Neal Cassady peyote, unlike marijuana, seemed to confer criminal status without delivering any obvious benefits. Carolyn still used marijuana on and off but never shared Neal's obsessive enthusiasm for it.

She tried more adventurous employment too, but her bid to become a camera girl (someone who took pictures of nightclub patrons for tips) at some of San Francisco's more exotic clubs also foundered, although it did give her an enjoyable glimpse of a side of the city she had not previously known.

Though Carolyn craved a conventional family life, her affair with Jack (which continued discreetly through the first four months of 1952) had, oddly, been a stabilizing influence on her relationship with Neal.

Jack, to Carolyn, was as much a comforting presence for her as he was a partner in mischief for Neal. Things were soon to change. Jack was becoming troubled by the ongoing dispute with his ex-wife, and he now had very little money, since the baggage job did not pay anywhere near as much as the brakeman's job that had never materialized. Jack began seriously to consider a move to Mexico. Carolyn meanwhile felt it was high time to take her children to meet her parents for the first time at their farm in Nashville. A now-familiar Cassady road itinerary took shape, acquiring potential offshoots and diversions at every turn. Neal would now at last get to see the Tennessee property . . . but he also saw the trip as a chance to look up his father in Denver. For his part, Jack could be driven to the border town of Nogales, south of Tucson. California stopovers with various of Neal's half-sisters and brothers were incorporated into the trip with an informality that struck Carolyn as intrusive but was the natural order of things for Neal and his extended family. The overriding atmosphere of this road trip, with its three adults and three children, was circumspect—with the sense of a fling terminated (or at least suspended). Jack and Carolyn, occasionally sitting together in the back, sometimes separated by the driving duties, knew that this was a bittersweet goodbye that could not be openly indulged. Neal was clearly complaisant about the affair, but there was no question of open discussion. On the outskirts of Nogales, they parked the car at a wire fence at an unmanned border, which they crossed on foot for a farewell drink in a rundown café. It was a muted and awkward parting that disappointed Jack, who later wrote them "you could have come through with the car that morning . . . and seen a fiesta in the afternoon in the gay little city of Nogales. You have no idea what is ten feet beyond that wire fence."

Neal, at least, had a perfectly good idea of what went on beyond the wire fence ("Everything fine. Is not hard to enjoin yourself in Mehico"), and Carolyn felt that he was regretful not so much because Jack was going but because he himself *wasn't.*

On the family visit to the farm owned by Carolyn's parents, Neal was charm personified, although his legendary "cowboy" image was quickly revealed to be strictly figurative.

"A cowboy he wasn't," noted Carolyn dryly, "and I couldn't get him on a horse."

On the return trip the Cassady clan visited Neal's brother Jim in Kansas City. Neal apparently bore Jim no grudge for his childhood torments.

In Denver they briefly visited Neal Sr., by now in mental decline but seemingly content enough and being attended by "a wonderful floozy of a woman" (Carolyn's words).

They returned to Russell Street to find letters from Allen Ginsberg, one extending a cautious gesture of friendship to Carolyn, so ending a five-year frostiness that she had never fully understood, another addressed to Neal, dealing with Jack and his current writings. Soon Jack would make Allen his agent for *On the Road*, and he seemed so optimistic about its success that he had already written a third of his next project *Dr. Sax* in Mexico "in case I catch on like wildfire in New York."

In fact the shifting dynamics of the group—Allen, Jack, Neal, and Carolyn—were still unsettled at this point, and geographical distance always posed its own problems. Everyone's most elementary understanding of what might be happening to the others was habitually distorted by the vagaries of the mail, including out-of-sequence deliveries or the complete disappearance of certain correspondence altogether.

Allen, Jack's newly appointed agent, wrote the Cassadys that "On the Road" (he was referring to what would later be published as *Visions of Cody*), although brilliant, was "a holy mess." Jack for his part seemed to have had some undefined altercation with a publisher or publishers, and wrote, "I'm very unlucky and doomed to be robbed by all the cheap litterateurs [*sic*] of my time." His disaffection was reflected in a sudden declared intention to go and live in isolation in an adobe hut in some valley where he would not write "for a long time."

Carolyn, ever practical, worried about her marriage, pondered the value of more psychological therapy, and explored the idea of a move to the country for the Cassady family, something she thought would benefit them all, especially the children.

Neal, now deeply discouraged about *The First Third* and his own literary potential—and perhaps still envying Jack's rootless life—was restless and clearly depressed by a shortage of marijuana and adventure.

In August 1952, the Cassadys moved to a huge rented house in a valley on the outskirts of San Jose (nicknamed "Nowheresville"), the town where Neal's passenger runs currently started and ended and where the Hinkles also lived. Carolyn saw it as an exciting family move to a lovely area, and she harbored ambitions for the family to fit in with the couple who would be their nearest new neighbors, the refreshingly square Dick and Marie Woods and their children Chris and Cindy. Neal, on the other hand, saw it as an ideal place to grow marijuana (now increasingly difficult and expensive to acquire) and to act as a rallying point for the old gang. In fact the move was tentative in nature; the Cassadys planned to explore the vast surrounding valley from their newly rented house, and Neal would discover how the new location fit in with his work.

Neal also immediately tried to arrange a secret meeting with Diana, and his letter of August 21 to her indicates considerable pent-up frustration. "For no good reason at all, absolutely no reason at all, I left you," he wrote. "You had done nothing wrong, you had always been loving & wonderful to me, your body was always mine whenever I wanted it . . . what to do? Carolyn confessed she destroyed your turn-of-the-year letters. Jack was here screwing her & everybody was happy. She wanted no interruptions."

The letter included a proposal that they resume their relationship that winter—and several warnings not to tell Carolyn of the offer. If Diana ever replied to this, her letter no longer seems to exist.

"Damn you for being in Mexico without me," Neal then wrote to Jack. "Why in hell not give up the Indians to come back and tell me about them and still earn about 2000 bucks on RR before year's out? You can easily live in our big 9 room house here in sunny San Jose and ride about in my new station wagon." This reference to Neal's new Nash Rambler was hardly tactful since he still owed money to Jack from the last Mexican trip.

Jack, who had in the meantime run out of money himself and gone to stay with his mother at his sister's North Carolina home, accepted

Neal's invitation, notionally spurred by the urgency of a new SPRR ruling that no new men over the age of thirty would be hired (Jack had just turned thirty but Neal knew a way to get around the ruling if he came immediately). Another factor in Jack's decision may have been that his enjoyable affair with Carolyn had obviously been suspended rather than broken off. When he returned, the relationship resumed almost at once, aided by Neal's work hours, enlivened by the setting of the new, generously sized house, tactfully indulged with concern for the children, and harmonious insofar as Jack's shyness and Carolyn's decorousness complemented each other perfectly.

The ménage à trois was entering phase two . . . in sunny San Jose.

20

FROM THE START the domestic arrangements at the San Jose house revolved around the rail schedules. Some nights Jack and Carolyn would be alone, and Carolyn's recollections of these occasions are unashamedly romantic.

"We sat dreamily sipping our wine in the flickering patterns of the candlelight, absorbing the music of blues and ballad," she wrote. "Jack's voice broke the stillness like a great mellow gong, vibrating clear through me and reverberating in the air: 'God . . . I love you.'"

Jack certainly much better fitted Carolyn's image of a dreamy lover than Neal ever could. They also enjoyed evenings when the three of them meshed most naturally. One such occasion was captured by the Ekotape and, unusually, this recording survived, so that it is still possible to hear Neal Cassady reading Proust out loud (Jack later overdubbed corrections to Neal's pronunciation of French names—*Gilberte* posed particular difficulty), eventually giving way to Jack who reads from *Dr. Sax*, eliciting in the process one of Neal's protracted signature yells of approval: "Yeaaaah!"

Carolyn was now the emotional focus of the house, and there is some evidence that Jack was on the brink of becoming drawn into a deeper relationship with her. He got on well with Jami and Cathy, taking them on daily walks and therefore to some extent usurping Neal's role as father. Neal's gradual disaffection with this new arrangement was apparent, although it is an open question as to which troubled him more, Jack's close relations with his wife and children, or Jack's apparent abdication from the role of his good-time buddy.

To ease the growing pressure, in mid-October 1952 Jack moved to San Francisco, staying at the Cameo Hotel at Harrison and Third, at that time the city's skid row. There he wrote about his railroad experiences in a piece that would eventually be known as *October in the Railroad Earth.* Neal was initially pleased by Jack's moving out, but when one day he came upon him asleep on a derelict couch at the side of the rail tracks, he took pity and invited him back to the San Jose house. It made little difference, because by December SPRR started laying off men on a "last in, first out" basis. Jack was naturally among the first to go, but this sudden change of circumstance seemed to energize him and give him a new sense of purpose. He was unsuited to his brakeman's job anyway. He lacked Neal's fast reflexes and physical dynamism, preferring to explore the romantic aspects of a brakeman's life in prose rather than grapple with the awkward reality of actually living it. With new enthusiasm, Jack announced his plans to go to Mexico, suggesting that Carolyn should award herself a hard-earned vacation by accompanying him. After an odd domestic "deal" brokered by Neal (he would drive Jack to Mexico and return with marijuana, at which point Carolyn would be free to go to Jack for her "vacation"), Neal and Jack departed in the Rambler, heading for William Burroughs's Mexico City home. From there Neal wrote Carolyn assuring her that "I have not, and will not, touched any kind of ole female; I am with B.B. [Burroughs] & [Bill] Garver and Jack, talking only." (Garver, Burroughs's friend who had been the supplier of saleable overcoats back in New York, was a morphine addict who now also lived in Mexico City.)

The second part of the "deal" never came about. Carolyn started to have second thoughts, Neal seemed jealous and possessive again, and Jack, after writing to Carolyn with a seductive reinforcement of his invitation ("my little pad is all ready . . . all the fresh air of the Indian plateau blows into it . . . Come on and get your vacation with me! We'll have wine, tea, oysters at midnight . . . "), abruptly canceled the arrangement altogether by announcing that he was going home for Christmas.

The 1952 holiday season at the Cassadys proved to be an enjoyable one. Carolyn wondered if Neal's sunny disposition might owe something to a clandestine affair in San Francisco—there was no evidence of this, but she had by now learned not to take Neal at face value even when she was tempted to do so.

The New Year then brought further changes of fortune. There was now no railroad work in the SPRR's coastal division so Neal was obliged to travel five hundred miles to the city of Indio in south-central California, seeking freelance employment. Back east, Jack's uneasy relationship with his mother resumed, and he moved to Long Island with her. Allen Ginsberg, the Cassadys' steady source of news from New York City, reported: "Jack is back here. Have not seen him much though. He's at mother's house hiding out . . . came in time for New Years, cried drunk & high in cab at dawn. . . . "

Allen thought that Jack, despite constant avowals about wanting to see his New York friends, could never really give them his full attention when in their company: "he always hung up on noise, noise, music bands, tea, excitement, organizing—have feeling he doesn't respect individual he's with (me) and is creating artificial excitement."

All the evidence was that Kerouac had lost his sense of direction. Mood swings, shifting objectives, and a preoccupation with the fortunes of others all seemed to conspire to keep him adrift and unfocused. His recent fantasy that the ideal life lay south of the border in the land of soft warm evenings, cheap food, and plentiful marijuana was now supplanted by a declared love of "New York . . . winter weather, storms, snow, long walks in overshoes." A few weeks after writing warmly to Allen and saying that "*Go* is alright when you see it between book covers, it's sincere, each page . . . so Holmes is better than they say," he wrote to Neal and Carolyn, saying, "Allen is getting fat-faced and ugly . . . Holmes (made $20,000 on *Go*) (will inherit $80,000 from family) eats in expensive restaurants and spends all his time chasing and hailing cabs with his coat flapping anxiously."

When Jack and Neal had been together as occasional road buddies, it was hard to separate them in their shared enthusiasm. Now, as they approached thirty-one and twenty-seven respectively, the thin end of the wedge that would increasingly separate them became apparent. Kerouac seemed ever more locked in the detached role of the observer; Cassady, meanwhile, was still the doer, the self-appointed prime mover of whatever the action might be. However, at the start of 1953, each was at the mercy of outside events that were shaping the dynamic linking Neal, Jack, and Carolyn; she was now the recipient of fond letters from Neal, still exiled in Indio ("I need you and how hopeless I am without you"), and mercurial Jack in New York whose letters lamented their interrupted affair ("I loved you one day last fall so genuinely, you'll never know").

Although originally intending to be gone for only two weeks, Neal decided to profit from the offer of more work and wrote Carolyn to break the news that he would be away until the end of February. His letters to her were now beginning with ever more playfully affectionate salutations: "Dear Heavenly Lifesaver Wife Carolyn Queen," "Dear Sweetie Pie Deluxe Darlingbug," and "Dear Babydoll."

Neal returned to San Jose on March 10 where he was able to resume his regular brakeman's job on SPRR's coastal division.

Exactly one month later on April 10, Neal Cassady—he of the fast reflexes and lightning coordination—finally fell victim to a work accident. He was on top of a boxcar when it hit a safety bumper on a siding, pitching him off. His foot was almost severed when it was forced backward, on impact with the ground. He was taken by ambulance to the Southern Pacific Hospital in San Francisco with the prospect of five weeks of recovery after surgeons had set numerous bones in his foot and ankle, patched it all together again, and sent him home.

As Neal recuperated in San Jose, he and Carolyn received a letter from Allen, who was now apparently in the thrall of oriental philosophy, something that had attracted him when he began studying Chinese art. The New Jersey poet chose to convey his new enthusiasm with one of his less felicitous lines: "you begin to see the vastitude and intelligence of the yellow men."

Just as Carolyn and Neal were absorbing the contents of this letter over a cup of coffee, Jack arrived at their door unannounced. He had been recalled by SPRR.

He stayed with the Cassadys only for the weekend before moving on to San Francisco and then relocating to San Luis Obispo for a two-week work stretch. A letter Jack wrote to Gabrielle indicated that he was considering moving her to California to live with him: "In 2 months, San Luis Obispo will have 2 television stations," he wrote persuasively. "In the paper . . . they advertise lowprice trailers—also houses but they're all in the thousands of dollars. The best idea I think will be for us to start in a trailer . . . til we get a start."

Jack went on to sing the praises of the California climate and lifestyle. "Coming to California has brought me back to life again. I realize now I shouldn't have left last year. I only went to N.Y. to see you. Boy do I hate N.Y. Never again."

A month later a bored Jack left the railroad and impulsively shipped out, through the Seamen's International Union, on the *S.S. William Carruth.* The ship was bound for Alabama, New York, and Korea, but Jack, who had been hired as steward, jumped ship in New Orleans to rejoin Gabrielle in New York.

In San Jose the Cassadys were now cautiously looking forward to a substantial payoff from SPRR. Estimates varied, but they expected a sizable settlement—eventually. Neal, with an unassimilated bone chip in his foot requiring another operation, was restless at home and still worrying about the glacial progress of *The First Third.* He discussed his frustration in a June 1 letter to Allen in which he also invited the "Oriental Ogler" to come visit. Allen had just sent him a fragmentary letter consisting of New York gossip, a translation of a Chinese poem from A.D. 846, a complaint that all of his friends—Neal included—falsely accused him of betraying their infidelities to one another, and, significantly, news that he had telegraphed (at a personal cost of two dollars) President Eisenhower protesting the execution of the Rosenbergs.

Ethel and Julius Rosenberg were the only two American civilians to be executed for conspiracy to commit espionage during the Cold War. The judge who imposed the death penalty maintained that they were responsible not only for espionage but also for loss of life in the Korean War. Ginsberg wrote to Eisenhower (and copied Neal Cassady) thus: "Rosenbergs are pathetic, government Will sordid, execution obscene America caught in crucifixion machine only barbarians want them burned I say stop it before we fill our souls with death-house horror."

As Carolyn noted later, "This marked the first time we heard of Allen doing anything outright about his political complaints, and to us it was a drastic measure. We could not have imagined what it was to lead to."

• • •

Neal was bored. The action man was not going anywhere for a while. He grew a goatee and shaved his head. He read Céline and Dostoyevsky. He listened to ball games on the radio and he went with Carolyn to drive-in movies. The railroad offered only $1,800 as compensation for his accident, which prompted the Cassadys to hire a lawyer. This brought with it the expectation of drawn-out legal proceedings. Languishing at home in San Jose, Neal also tried to track down his old friend Hal Chase, the man who had first introduced him to Ginsberg, Kerouac, and the rest, by writing to Hal's parents.

Allen did not reply until September 4 to Neal's invitation to come and stay: "The thing is there is such a kind of confusion and hesitancy about life-moves in me that I kept putting off . . . I jess don't want to pull up stakes & move my ass yet I guess. Not that I'm doing myself so much good here."

Allen's note also gave early notice of one of American letters' more intriguing alliances: the meeting of Gore Vidal and Jack Kerouac.

"Jack got drunk and boastfully queerlike—and went home with him & couldn't get a hardon & fell asleep in his bathtub." (Vidal later put his spin on this incident in *Two Sisters*, while Kerouac told it his way in *The Subterraneans*.)

That summer Neal's marijuana crop, planted on an adjacent lot and almost ready for harvest, suffered a narrow escape when the San Jose fire department suddenly came to burn a strategic strip of vegetation in order to create a fire break. The Cassadys sprang into action (reduced action on Neal's part since his cast had only just been removed), rescuing the "weeds" that their neighbors had failed to recognize for what they were and hanging them in a closet behind their winter clothes. This frantic harvest of the illegal crop at first invigorated and enlivened Neal, but perhaps it also reminded him that his present housebound life, although harmonious, was low on excitement of any sort. Soon afterward he became listless. Carolyn wrote that "he withdrew into himself and rarely participated in family life, smoked tea constantly and, mesmerized, lay for hours listening to the radio, especially to ball games. He moved his seat of operations to our bedroom, read less, slept more, masturbated frequently, and spoke hardly a word to anyone except the children, with whom he always put on a show of normalcy."

But by the fall, Neal's injury had healed well enough for him to take a job in a local parking lot, a job he hoped to be able to hand over to Allen or Jack when he himself resumed work on the railroad later in the new year. He wrote to them outlining this plan. Jack's reply expressed an interest in taking the job until spring, then working on the railroad for the summer before wintering in Mexico. Allen could take over the parking lot job when Jack left. Already the year of 1954 was being most coherently planned. What had not been factored was a new spiritual dimension that would shape the rest of the life of lapsed Catholic Neal Cassady.

• • •

Until the mid-1950s, twentieth-century psychological thinking was dominated by two schools: behaviorism and psychoanalysis. Behaviorists believed that people are conditioned to act in a certain manner by a system of rewards and punishments. Psychoanalysts simply sought to understand the unconscious motivations and internal instincts that produced patterns of behavior. Although both approaches contributed to a better understanding of human beings, neither attempted to take a holistic view of the individual. It was not until 1954 that humanistic psychology emerged, complementing behaviorism and psychoanalysis with a new approach that viewed the individual as a whole person. Abraham Maslow's *Motivation and Personality*, written in 1954, codified this new approach, which, although scientific in its method, seemed much more in harmony with the ways artists and poets viewed the human condition. Maslow saw each individual not just at an entity defined by needs and impulses, but as a holistic being with unlimited capacity for growth. His approach therefore had a lot in common with the spiritual explorations of Allen Ginsberg and all the other "subterraneans," who were approaching the "holistic" ideal from various informal vantage points, many of them rooted in Eastern religions.

Carolyn Cassady was no stranger to conventional psychoanalysis. She had studied it in school and at the postgraduate level in the army. "Looking back, I'm surprised that I never viewed Neal's extreme swings in mood and behavior from that standpoint," she wrote later. As Neal now seemed to be slipping away from her again (unexplained trips to San Francisco were becoming more frequent), she began to consider new strategies for saving their relationship from what looked like a recurring pattern of decline. When Jack Kerouac recommended to them Wilhelm Reich's *Functions of the Orgasm*, its subject matter held less attraction for Carolyn than for Neal, but it did prompt Carolyn to dig out all her old psychology books. *Motivation and Personality* (which might have struck a resonant chord with both of them) would not be published for a few months yet and, looking for a self-help road map among her existing psychoanalysis books, all Carolyn came up with were traditional labels and diagnoses. Neal, for example, emerged from psychological tests with the label "a sociopathic personality with schizophrenic and manic-depressive tendencies that could develop into psychosis." This depressed him without offering any solution to the problem it had defined.

"I'd been deeply discouraged by having to abandon my hopes for psychology," Carolyn wrote, "though I continued to toy with the idea of returning to psychoanalysis. Each time I thought of it, the expense and the time involved depressed me further, and I couldn't rouse the courage to act. I also felt vaguely that this was not the missing piece of the puzzle. It seemed to me that what Neal and I lacked most was a common belief in a set of absolute values."

Hungry for spiritual guidance, Carolyn found that providence would supply it. By chance, early in 1954, Neal discovered a book on the backseat of one of the cars at the parking lot. *Many Mansions,* by Dr. Gina Cerminara, was an account of the life of Edgar Cayce.

Cayce, born in 1877, near Hopkinsville, Kentucky, was a "spiritual channel" who in 1925 settled in Virginia Beach, Virginia, where he established a hospital and the Association for Research and Enlightenment (ARE) in 1931. Dr. Cerminara's book described how Cayce claimed to see past the barriers of space and time, how he penetrated the past lives of his subjects, and how he performed his fantastic cures and prophecies. Neal was bowled over by the book, which he read at a single sitting. He quickly reassured Carolyn that the owner said he could borrow it for her to read and that he would return it. (One wonders about the truth of this. When interviewed for this book, the poet and proprietor of San Francisco's City Lights Bookstore, Lawrence Ferlinghetti, clearly recalled his initial encounter with Neal Cassady. "I first met him when he came in the bookstore and stole a copy of Edgar Cayce," he said. "He drew up to the curb, left the car running, and left the door open. He knew just where the book was, came in, took it, and just walked out. He tried it on other occasions, but the Edgar Cayce was the only book he ever stole.")

Carolyn read *Many Mansions* and her response matched Neal's. Their mutual conversion to the world according to Cayce was instantaneous. Spiritual discussions extended into the night. Amused skepticism from neighbors Dick and Marie Woods and their old friends the Hinkles puzzled but did not deter them. Cayce, who had died in 1945, exerted a powerful influence on the Cassadys. When Carolyn recently looked back on Cayce's initial impact on their lives, she remembered seeing it as a great panacea.

"It seemed to explain so many things," she said, "like why we were together anyway . . . there was just this tremendous relief . . . we just couldn't stop talking about it, it was so miraculous. The interesting thing to us was that it was written by a Ph.D. psychologist . . . and we had been concerned about psychology for years and years, and it wasn't doing anything. I had written reams and reams of self-analysis . . . but all it told you was your problems, without any solutions. So this book, having been written by a psychologist, was the perfect next step. *Now* it doesn't mean anything to me—I can hardly read it—but it was the exact right timing, and the right approach for where we were."

The intricacies of the Cayce worldview are daunting to anyone who is not predisposed to explore them in detail, but, simply put, Cayce was not a conventional spiritual leader. He was a man who had presented himself as a "channel." His utterances when in a trancelike state assumed in his audience a blind acceptance of the tenets of reincarnation and karmic law: we are imperfect beings inhabiting a continuum of selves, each determined by the individual's actions in a previous life. Cayce—and subsequently his Virginia Beach followers—offered "readings," essentially supernatural peepshows into an individual's previous incarnations that placed the subject on the colorful canvas of human history, often rubbing shoulders with famous historical figures. Subjects could experience the dark thrill of reviewing their past misdeeds and balance this against the inexhaustible opportunity for future redemption. This appealed to Neal Cassady enormously. An impulsive man of the present, he could hardly fail to embrace a spiritual view that in effect proposed a perpetual present tense. Also, unlike Catholicism, reincarnation encouraged Neal to view his own tendencies as part of a morally neutral evolution in which self-condemnation was a sin, not a virtue. For Carolyn it provided a rationale that legitimized her chronically difficult relationship with the man she loved: "All that emphasis on the wrong I had been doing (to say nothing of Neal)—going over and over the negative actions—could only produce more of the same." Reincarnation was why they were together, Neal and Carolyn decided, and they were destined to repeat their previous emotional mistakes until they learned a better way of dealing with their negative impulses. Whether the Woods and the Hinkles saw this as a self-awarded license for Neal to behave self-indulgently without feeling bad about it, or whether they simply felt uneasy about the concept of reincarnation per se can only be guessed.

The Cassadys remained hopeful that Allen and Jack would give them a more sympathetic hearing. This hope, as things turned out, proved unfounded, but before it could be tested Allen sent them a letter from Mérida, Yucatán, Mexico, in early January. His latest trip seemed to have put him in a critical frame of mind. Traveling via "horrid" Havana and "more horrid" Miami Beach, he met one of William Burroughs's boyfriends: "I must say Bill's taste in boys is Macabre . . . he is so starved looking & rickety & pitifully purseymouthed & 'laid'—French for ugly & with disgusting birthmark below left ear." The rest of the letter was a long travelogue, a mixture of tourist tips to do with mosquito nets, local homeopathic remedies, and smoky local cathedrals. It seemed, too, to mark the start of a more communicative Ginsberg who followed up with several more letters as he planned to reenter the Cassadys' lives on his imminent return from Mexico.

Jack had finally made it to San Jose on February 5, 1954—in time for Neal's birthday—and started working alongside Neal at the parking lot, again staying at the Cassady home. Since Jack now had a growing interest in Buddhism he was in no frame of mind to buy into Cayce, and he and

Neal argued long and hard about the comparative merits of their recently acquired belief systems.

The visit was not a success on any level. Jack's lack of natural physical dexterity made him something of a liability at the parking lot, and there was no recall to the railroad in the offing. Divergent opinions about the merits of Cayce further served to isolate Jack from his hosts. On top of that, Neal resented Jack's warmth toward Carolyn, and this animosity was transferred to arguments about the cost of Jack's food and, finally, the division of a pound of marijuana. In April Carolyn drove Jack to his old escape hatch, the Cameo Hotel in San Francisco, and stayed there with him briefly. Kerouac stayed on for a week, writing the poem "San Francisco Blues" before returning to Richmond Hill, New York, from where he sent a curt letter to the Cassadys asking for his mail to be sent on.

In March the trial began to determine the extent of the railroad's liability for Neal's accident; Carolyn was appalled at the theatricality of the proceedings but the verdict was never in serious question even though Neal's recovery had been remarkable and pride prevented him from affecting the limp that his lawyer felt he'd be well advised to display. Allen, meanwhile, seemed to be taking longer than expected to conclude his Mexico trip and make it to San Jose. On April 9, Neal had sent him some money, which had been returned by Western Union. William Burroughs had been bombarding Jack with mail for Allen; Jack in turn wrote to Allen care of the Cassadys, thinking he must have arrived there. May came but still Allen did not appear. Jack suggested in a letter that Allen was already back in New York, hiding out, because "there's no danger in Mexico so much." This warmer letter from Jack to Neal also contained his musings on spirituality, Buddha, *The Brothers Karamazov*, and Cayce (about whom he was still dismissive).

Also in May Neal was finally awarded compensation by SPRR: almost $30,000 minus fees, two years' support, and insurance deductions, leaving him with $16,747. Neal sent Diana and Curtis Hansen $1,000 and, with the zeal of the converted, an earnest recommendation that she should buy *Many Mansions* and some other Cayce-related material.

Neal and Carolyn's enthusiasm for Cayce now led them to attend a series of lectures given by Edgar's son Hugh Lynn Cayce. The couple also began counseling with Hugh Lynn and his associate Elsie Sechrist at one of their annual programs in San Jose, and subsequently by mail. They joined a number of study groups and, according to Carolyn, "worked hard to master the alien activities of prayer and meditation, now revealed to hold a previously unsuspected meaning and power." Neal and Carolyn had previously been intellectually engaged only by the physical sciences and philosophy. The new spiritual possibilities promised by Cayce demanded careful evaluation by their hitherto exclusively logic-based minds; for as long as they were engaged by Caycean thought they tended to pick and choose, accepting some precepts ("all life is purposeful") and questioning others ("but what is that knowledge for?").

Eventually, in June 1954 Allen arrived at the Cassadys'. Carolyn was initially ill at ease with the man she had not seen for seven years and who had rarely even spelled her name correctly in his letters. Soon, though, his enthusiasm won her over as he produced mementos of the New York crowd plus trophies from his travels in Mexico.

With Neal now back at work on the railroad, Allen and Carolyn spent a lot of time together, and she wondered on what her resistance to him had been based. He was stimulating company, and even if he too was not persuaded by Cayce, he was at least uncritical of their enthusiasm. He would read his poetry aloud and record it on the Ekotape machine. He would also record himself as percussionist, having acquired some small drums on his recent trip. Not averse to shedding all his clothes when there were no strangers present, Allen was a most circumspect guest when the Woods or the Hinkles came around. For the six weeks or so that he stayed at the house he was welcomed by Carolyn and happy to accompany Neal on the occasional trip to San Francisco; he also did all of the cooking, at which he was most adept.

The idyll came to an abrupt end when Carolyn walked into Allen's room one afternoon to find him giving Neal a blow job. Haring believed Allen's avowal that his sexual attraction to Neal was long over, she was confronted not only by graphic evidence to the contrary but also by her own conflicting responses—she had always championed homosexuals, but this was different!—Carolyn was crushed. Allen's rapid departure was inevitable. She drove him to San Francisco to look up old friends and find a place to stay. Neal was contrite and even Jack, to whom Carolyn poured out her heart in a letter, was gracious. "Poor Neal needs love more than anybody else," he wrote. "Try to give it to him. Don't worry about Allen—Allen and Neal are old buddies and hit the road together and seen visions together; don't be harsh with our prophets, Miss Virago."

21

FOR ONCE the Cassadys had money. True, it was Neal's money, strictly speaking, but relations were good enough for both him and Carolyn to consider their $16,000-plus payout as "family" money. After the $1,000 donation to Diana Hansen and a few other purchases, they invested $5,000 and used the bulk of the remainder to put a down payment on a house in Los Gatos, a picturesque town adjacent to the Santa Cruz mountains and some ten miles southwest of San Jose, which was still Neal's railroad jumping-off point. Carolyn wrote to Jack about this new development, probably to reinforce the notion that an implicit invitation to visit was still extended, despite the spats and fallings-out.

Jack replied enthusiastically that Los Gatos was well known in New York among his Columbia friends. "I'm sure Katherine Windsor had an estate at Los Gatos," he wrote. "Strangely in my novel of last summer about the colored girl, I used Los Gatos as the place where we weekended."

Kerouac was misspelling and referring to Kathleen Winsor, an American writer who had achieved notoriety with her 1944 novel *Forever Amber*, the story of a promiscuous young woman in Restoration England. *Forever Amber* caused a scandal, sold 100,000 copies its first week, and paved the way for the subsequent "bodice-ripper" genre of fiction. Kerouac's "novel of last summer" was *The Subterraneans* and in it "the colored girl" was named Mardou Fox, a pseudonym for Alene Lee who had been Kerouac's girlfriend in 1953.

Kerouac might also have added that violin prodigy Yehudi Menuhin had spent some of his formative years in Los Gatos, as had the actress Olivia de Havilland (who attended the local high school). John Steinbeck had lived nearby in the late 1930s.

At last the Cassadys could afford a TV and were happy to join the nation's more conventional couples sitting on the family sofa (or in the Cassadys' case, the bed) watching cozy popular sitcoms. Neal, the intellectual magpie, found everything on TV of interest, especially the appearances of Oral Roberts, who was among the first evangelists to recognize the vast potential of using TV as a pulpit.

Carolyn began to get the occasional commission to paint portraits of neighbors and their families. She also became involved with creating costumes for the local ballet school that her daughters Cathy and Jami attended. The signs were that Neal and Carolyn's married life in Los Gatos might take on even more conventional characteristics . . . always depending, of course, on Neal's capacity for settling down.

But Neal was not so much adapting as compartmentalizing his life. Now with sufficient seniority to hold down a regular passenger run between San Jose and San Francisco, he was able to spend his free days in San Francisco before the evening run home. By day he could hang out with one circle of friends, but in the evening he could still come home to Carolyn and play with the children for his shift as "family man."

In San Francisco Ginsberg had started building a new life for himself and was introducing Neal to new members of his circle. One was Robert LaVigne, a San Francisco painter who lived with his model and companion Peter Orlovsky. One of LaVigne's paintings, a mural, featured a nude redheaded woman; the model was Natalie Jackson, who was part of the North Beach set to which Allen now belonged and whose main notoriety stemmed from her proficiency at oral sex. In October 1954 Natalie and Neal met . . . with predictable results. Afterward LaVigne would sometimes display a photograph of Neal embracing Natalie with one hand and reaching beneath her dress with another. Years later Allen's notes for an art exhibition further revealed the exceptional sexual intimacy of the group: "Robert LaVigne was so to speak the 'Court Painter' for the large group of poets gathered in mid Fifties during 'San Francisco Poetry Renaissance' beat period," Allen wrote. "His work—large oils & drawings of Peter Orlovsky & John Wieners—occupies an honored corner of the Whitney Exhibition 'Beat Culture & the New America 1950–1965.' . . . LaVigne was painter among poets, and made sketches of Neal Cassady & his lady Natalie Jackson . . . his orgy drawings of myself, Natalie J. & Peter Orlovsky can be found in my *Collected & Selected Poems* under the appropriate texts."

"The San Francisco Poetry Renaissance" cited by Ginsberg began as a fragmentary and strictly local affair and might have remained so had it not been for the focusing influence of the poet Lawrence Ferlinghetti, who, along with Peter Martin, founded City Lights in June 1953. The bookstore had pragmatic beginnings, being established primarily to pay the rent for the second floor editorial offices of *City Lights,* a film magazine Martin edited, which ran for only five issues. City Lights sold new, quality paperbacks—there were no other paperback-only stores at the time—and early alternative newspapers and magazines. Outside there were used books sold in lockable display boxes based on the *bouquinistes* of Paris, a city where Ferlinghetti had studied. With its European overtones and its distinctive triangular premises, City Lights soon became a trendy meeting place for artists and writers—and a commercial success.

When the magazine closed and Peter Martin left for New York in 1954, Shigeyoshi Murao was hired as manager and eventually became a co-owner with Ferlinghetti. The following year a publishing house, City Lights Books, was launched by Ferlinghetti to help support the bookstore that itself had been started to help support a magazine. Publishing enterprise and store would act as mutual supports over the years, depending on their respective fortunes. The first book in City Lights Books' Pocket Poets series was Ferlinghetti's own *Pictures of the Gone World,* published in 1955. The second was Kenneth Rexroth's translation, *Thirty Spanish Poems of Love and Exile.* The third was Kenneth Patchen's *Poems of Humor and Protest.* The fourth would cause a seismic upheaval.

Poet, bookstore proprietor, and publisher, Lawrence Ferlinghetti was a Columbia graduate and the possessor of a doctorate from the Sorbonne. He moved to San Francisco because of the city's literary activity, and it was there his spiritual and ecological interests led him to become friends with Buddhist converts Allen Ginsberg and Gary Snyder; Ferlinghetti would later call Snyder "the Thoreau of the Beat Generation."

Like Ferlinghetti and Snyder, poet Michael McLure was fascinated with wildlife and nature and once wrote, "When a man does not admit that he is an animal, he is less than an animal. Not more but less." After arriving in San Francisco from Seattle, McLure participated in a poetry workshop and was soon drawn into the City Lights milieu.

It was, however, Kenneth Rexroth who was widely credited with starting the San Francisco Poetry Renaissance since he was already an established poet with a considerable reputation. Writer, translator, essayist, and philosopher, he had been a founding member of the San Francisco Poetry Center, receiving the California Literature Silver Medal Award in 1941 for his book *In What Hour.* Also it was Rexroth who, upon meeting Ferlinghetti in Paris, had persuaded him that San Francisco was the place for a poet to be in the mid-1950s. Rexroth explored Japanese poetry with a scholar's eye and a poet's passion, at one point writing from the perspective of a Japanese woman.

Philip Lamantia was another leading figure on the San Francisco poetry scene. Born in the city, he was introduced to surrealism by the Miro and Dalí retrospectives at the San Francisco Museum of Art when he was sixteen. He said he immediately recognized an affinity for Surrealism in his own temperament. Lamantia began to write surrealist poetry, crossed the country to join the Surrealists in New York, and was acclaimed by André Breton as "a voice that rises once a hundred years." His first book, *Erotic Poems,* was published in Berkeley in 1946.

Philip Whalen from Portland, Oregon, was a roommate of Gary Snyder during college and became another of the driving forces behind the San Francisco Poetry Renaissance. In retrospect his nonpolitical approach and self-deprecating sense of humor would seem to have put him at odds with the rest of a movement hardly noted for either of these qualities. In later years Whalen too would embrace Buddhism.

For these men and other writers, City Lights Bookshop was a social and cultural touchstone. Despite the variety of their personalities and preoccupations, they had certain sensibilities in common. For them the very existence of City Lights symbolized their unifying sympathies toward Eastern mysticism, the back-to-nature-legacy of Thoreau's *Walden,* and opposition to what they saw as unethical government. These were sympathies that, in tandem with the New York–based instincts of *The Subterraneans,* would soon inform the birth of a new social movement.

After Carolyn had thrown Allen out in August 1954 he quite soon—and somewhat surprisingly—found a market research job in San Francisco with Towne-Oller Associates. Even more surprisingly he found himself a girlfriend, Sheila Williams Boucher, with whom he soon went to live in a Pine Street apartment on prestigious Nob Hill. Williams was a copywriter for a San Francisco department store by day and a jazz singer by night. This period seemed to mark an abrupt attempt on Allen's part to go straight in every sense. He was earning $250 a month. He was short-haired, tweed-jacketed, and aiming to become heterosexual.

"It was the first time I'd had a balanced heterosexual life," he later recalled, "to the point where I really wanted to get married and have kids and settle down to a life in advertising." The possibility of Burroughs coming to San Francisco was mooted, and Allen was deeply alarmed by the possibility of attendant drug busts and the impact of Burroughs's enduring infatuation with him. Neal, now feeling free of the emotional pressure brought on by Allen's obsession, would occasionally visit the unlikely couple, usually to bring or borrow marijuana. On one occasion he brought a pusher with him. Ginsberg wrote nothing during this period, and gradually his relationship with Sheila began to deteriorate. Allen began to see her as "prey to girlish psychological semi-dramatizations" and said she saw him as "a stuffy old nag." When he finally told her of his homosexuality and history with Neal, she was revolted and no longer wanted to sleep with him. Then in December 1954 he flew to New York to attend the wedding of his brother Eugene. On the trip he also visited his ailing mother, now in sad decline in a mental institution and ravaged by the effects of electroshock treatment and a lobotomy.

Upheaval awaited Ginsberg on his return. He found Neal living with Natalie in LaVigne's Gough Street apartment. Sheila had started sleeping with Al Hinkle, and now Ginsberg was suddenly invited to go and live with LaVigne and Orlovsky. He accepted, and his affair with Orlovsky began at that point, filling him with wild elation ("I'm happy, Kerouac, your madman Allen's finally made it: discovered a new young cat, and my imagination of an eternal boy walks on the streets of San Francisco, handsome, and meets me in cafeterias and loves me"). Neal and Natalie were in the full throes of their affair, now mainly conducted in her room at the back of the house; Allen and Peter moved into Peter's room in the middle of the house; and a large communal kitchen served as a meeting place for all tenants. The entire arrangement reminded Allen of the heyday of Joan Vollmer's 115th Street apartment.

In May 1955 Allen lost his job when Towne-Oller closed its San Francisco office. Supported by unemployment payments, he started to write again and catch up on his reading—he was currently enamored of Catullus and modern Spanish and French poetry. He also enrolled at the University of California at Berkeley with an eye toward completing his masters in English. In August 1955, taking to heart criticism from Rexroth that his poems were too formal and traditional, he decided to write something looser and more personal, "something I wouldn't be able to show anybody, writ for my own soul's ear and a few other golden ears." The result was *Howl*, which would become that fourth, notorious publication from City Lights. Ferlinghetti had already rejected *Empty Mirror*, Ginsberg's book of Whitmanesque poems. *Howl* he accepted readily, agreeing to publish it alone in a booklet. When Allen sent it to Jack, the response was one of only qualified praise; Jack assumed the numerous erasures and alterations were evidence of later editing, which flew in the face of his own much-vaunted spontaneity. In reality, the erasures were part of the original draft.

Neal's affair with Natalie, facilitated by his convenient railroad schedule, continued. Allen had once shown Carolyn, on a trip to San Francisco, LaVigne's mural featuring the naked Natalie, without mentioning its personal significance. Carolyn had not found out about the affair until the spring of 1955, when she discovered graphic correspondence between Natalie and Neal in the pocket of a pair of Neal's jeans. "Dear N. 11.10 PM—We're stimulated by pleasurable unexpected surprises," began Natalie's note, unpromisingly enough for Carolyn. "I know every inch, mole, blemish, hair, scar, pore . . . the different tastes of different parts of your body," and so on.

"I believe it quite possible, but rare, to feel a perfect lover, one with whom you are one because each match, as radio stations attuned perhaps," Neal had begun in his incriminating, unfinished reply.

Carolyn, defeated again, immediately sought advice from her spiritual guide Elsie Sechrist, whose counsel was to avoid any rash reaction, to trust that God would make any necessary separation, and to keep praying. She also came up with some recommended reading: *Release* by Starr Daily.

Neal was still vacillating between San Francisco and family life in Los Gatos. He seemed prepared at least to go through the motions of working toward reconciliation with Carolyn.

Together they read *Release*, Daily's dramatic account of his misspent youth, brutal incarceration, and subsequent religious conversion. The metaphor of prison bars defeated by faith ran throughout Daily's religious writings (*Love Can Open Prison Doors* was another of his works), and this was supposed to stimulate faith in readers by showing them a life so depraved and societal retribution so harsh that all readers would feel that they had never sinned as egregiously as Daily. If salvation was granted to *him*, surely they, too, must stand a chance.

"[Neal] was particularly impressed," reported Carolyn, "because Starr had been far more depraved in his youth than Neal had, and far more cruel."

Personal consultations with Hugh Lynn Cayce and Elsie Sechrist took place that spring, but their persistent advocacy of taking no action ("Keep still" was the mantra) served Carolyn poorly. "I'd bite my tongue and try," she said, "[but] I never was successful for more than twenty minutes at a time."

Jack's letters to Carolyn that April seemed to hint that he knew his relationship with Neal—and perhaps with her too—had moved into a new phase and that things were somehow different. "Apparently something has changed," he wrote, "we've become cautious, you, I, Neal, Allen, afraid to say something for fear it'll be taken wrong, changing what we meant to say, do, revising our ways to the grave of old age and suspicion."

Since April 1954 Jack had been living in Richmond Hill, New York. Then in April 1955 he moved again to his sister's in Rocky Mount, North Carolina, from where he sent the above letter and became progressively more bored and unproductive. He made a listless return to writing a previously abandoned science fiction story—"cityCityCITY"—and became even more depressed when no one would publish a Buddhist handbook he had written called *Buddha Tells Us* (also known as *Wake Up*). He had not corresponded with Neal Cassady for almost a year, and although he finally wrote him a sentimentally affable letter while suffering from a hangover after a trip to New York, the overall tone is one of trying to wind up a friendship in a benign spirit. Jack's next two letters to Carolyn also suggested that his close relationship with Neal was over: "he apparently is so far gone he doesnt [*sic*] write anymore [here Kerouac is referring to *The First Third*]. Apparently something has happened and everybody has changed."

In May 1955 Neal effectively moved out of the Los Gatos home altogether, although he would still drop in on his family from time to time for odd reasons. He was staying at home when he wrote Carolyn his only surviving letter of 1955: "DEAR MA; I hate myself & you know it, but, I looked long and hard at my son last night & I fully realize my responsibilities, plus, I am in full fear of my feeling that once a man starts down he never comes back—never. N."

In the summer of 1955 Jack Kerouac, now in receipt of a $200 stipend from the National Academy of Arts and Letters, had gone to Mexico City, where in addition to the usual attractions he hoped to acquire cheap penicillin treatment for his recurring phlebitis. He stayed in a rooftop apartment in the house where Burroughs's acquaintance Bill Garver lived, and he remained in Mexico until mid-September. Then in late September he finally moved to California, this time staying at a cottage in Berkeley that Allen Ginsberg, now a student once more, had been loaned and from which he was making periodic forays into San Francisco, where he sometimes met with Neal and Natalie.

Natalie remained something of a mystery, not just to Carolyn but even to people who had met her. Neal had taken her to the Hinkles' home on one occasion, and Helen reported that Natalie had seemed weirdly inanimate, almost "catatonic."

When it became clear that Kerouac was back in California and staying with Ginsberg, there were separate and combined attempts from Carolyn and Neal to meet with him, but he visited rarely, although on one occasion he did so—and quite memorably. Carolyn Cassady invited a member of the Liberal Catholic Church, a young Swiss, Bishop Romano, to visit the Los Gatos home one evening. Allen and Jack were also in attendance. The bishop came accompanied by his mother and his aunt. Romano's sect accepted reincarnation, but faced with Neal's bid to bring in Caycean theory at the first opportunity—and Allen in a decidedly mischievous mood—the bishop sensed that he was up against it. When Allen jovially addressed the mother and aunt with a hearty "Now then—what about sex?" the evening was effectively over. The company dissolved, Neal going back to San Francisco and Natalie, leaving Jack and Carolyn alone with the unexpected gift of a night together.

"Jack and I had not anticipated being alone together," Carolyn wrote. "We fairly smothered each other with released longing, grasping and clutching and hanging on for dear life, pouring into each other our pent-up affection and sorrow."

Jack repaired to a sleeping bag outside in the early morning so that the children should not find him in Carolyn's bed.

This evening of low humor was to prove so memorable that Jack Kerouac would include it in his little-known 1957 play *The Beat Generation.* A year later it would be immortalized in a thirty-minute movie called *Pull My Daisy,* based on the play's third act. With saxophonist and painter Larry Rivers playing Neal, and French actress Beltiane, aka Delphine Seyrig (soon to become famous as the female lead in Alain Resnais's impenetrable art house classic *L'Annèe Dernière Marienbad*) making her screen debut as Carolyn, *Pull My Daisy* was directed by Robert Frank and Alfred Leslie. It also featured Allen Ginsberg, David Amram, Gregory Corso, and Peter Orlovsky playing themselves. Jack narrated.

By the fall of 1955 Allen was sequestered in Berkeley, his joyous affair with Orlovsky continuing fitfully. Jack, after a year of isolation from his friends, was coming to stay with him. Neal was still working on the railroad, living with Natalie in San Francisco, and intermittently visiting his wife and children in Los Gatos. Ginsberg was the sole point of contact with the San Francisco Poetry Renaissance, which was about to get a major shot in the arm.

Ginsberg already knew Ferlinghetti, Rexroth, and McClure, and when the latter was asked to organize a poetry reading, he turned to Ginsberg. Rexroth recommended adding Gary Snyder to the list of readers. Allen was much impressed with this graduate student of Chinese and Japanese who, it transpired, kept his poems in identical binders to those Allen used and, like Allen, admired William Carlos Williams. It was at this point that Kerouac appeared at Ginsberg's cottage, and Allen recommended him to Snyder. Snyder in turn nominated Philip Whalen for inclusion in the reading. A new alliance of cultural compadres was forming, and the imminent poetry reading would turn out to be an epochal San Francisco event.

On October 7 Neal and Natalie were in the audience attending the Six Gallery poetry reading, the event at which Allen Ginsberg famously stole the show with his first reading of "Howl." The Six Gallery occupied a former auto repair shop near the intersection of Union and Fillmore, and it was there that an audience of about 150 convened to hear a number of new poets, not all of whom were known to one other, read their own work.

Jack Kerouac also attended but did not read, contenting himself with bringing in and distributing jugs of red wine with great bravado. Philip Lamantia read a series of poems by his late friend John Hoffman, who had just died of a peyote overdose. Michael McClure read "Point Lobos: Animism" and "For the Death of 100 Whales." Philip Whalen read "Plus Ça Change." Then the penultimate reader, a drunk Allen Ginsberg, delivered "Howl" (still incomplete) in a quasi-biblical declamatory style. It was a roof-raising performance that started nervously and ended triumphantly. Ginsberg had arrived, in the American West at least. Finally Gary Snyder let the crowd quiet down before reading his poem "A Berry Feast." Afterward all agreed the evening had been a great success, but it was also to stand as a famous turning point where poetry rediscovered its oral tradition and pushed the confessional boundaries further than they had been pushed before.

"In all our memories no one had been so outspoken in poetry before," Michael McClure would later recall of the evening in general and "Howl" in particular. "We had gone beyond a point of no return—and we were ready for it, for a point of no return. None of us wanted to go back to the gray, chill, militaristic silence, to the intellectual void—to the land without poetry—to the spiritual drabness. We wanted to make it new and we wanted to invent it and the process of it. We wanted voice and we wanted vision."

Neal did not participate, and few accounts even mention his presence at the reading, although Kerouac did draw a pen portrait of Neal and Natalie in *Dharma Bums*: "Among the people standing in the audience was Rosie Buchanan [Natalie] a girl with short haircut, red-haired, bony, handsome, a real gone chick and friend of everybody of any consequence on the beach, who'd been a painter's model and a writer herself and was bubbling with excitement at that time because she was in love with my old buddy Cody [Neal]. 'Great, hey Rosie?' I yelled, and she took a big slug from my jug and shined eyes at me. Cody just stood behind her with both arms around her waist."

If Carolyn, back in Los Gatos, thought that the worst Neal was up to was enjoying the San Francisco poetry scene with lover Natalie on his arm, she had underestimated him once again. Neal had also started gambling on the horses and, lacking stake money, had persuaded Natalie to impersonate Carolyn in order to help him fraudulently withdraw $2,500 from his and Carolyn's joint investment fund. True, he had first tried to interest Carolyn in bankrolling his patently stupid betting "system" ("always bet on the third-choice horse on the grounds that the odds are better and the first two choices are often overrated"), but when fair means failed he turned to fraud. Carolyn was alerted to the scam by a banker in Cupertino, but—whether as a result of Hugh Lynn Cayce's advocacy of passivity, her own innate generosity of spirit, or simple exhaustion—she chose to ignore the banker's professional advice to take out a warrant for Natalie's arrest.

As things turned out, it was perhaps just as well. Carolyn suppressed her resentment, limited herself to writing a rather sarcastic but philosophical note to Neal about this new foray into financial double dealing, and confirmed that she would not be pressing charges against Natalie. Originally it had been Neal's money anyway, although since there had been both a personal and legal decision to invest the money jointly, Carolyn could have taken a hard line had she chosen to. If she had, Natalie's subsequent fate might have weighed on Carolyn's conscience. As it was, the deadly events of November 30, 1955, could be attributed to a number of causes, all unconnected with Carolyn but some most certainly implicating Neal.

Overwhelmed by guilt at the fraud she had perpetrated, the already imbalanced Natalie first attempted suicide by trying to cut her wrists with a dull knife. She failed and a few days later, in the Franklin Street apartment she and Neal shared, she exhibited such signs of neurosis that Neal recruited Jack, who was in town, to "mind" her while he went out. Later the same day after Jack had departed but while Neal was asleep, Natalie, twenty-four years old and obviously dangerously unstable, ventured out onto the roof of the building where she eventually cut her throat, probably with a shard of glass from the broken skylight. Even as a policeman attempted to grab her she jumped or fell, and Officer O'Rourke (as the newspaper reports identified him) was left impotently holding her empty robe as she plunged naked to her death in the street below. Neal left the building by the back way and immediately called Carolyn, who asked if he would like to come home. Yes, he would. Neal seemed stunned, guilty, and deeply affected by Natalie's death when he got home that evening and, for at least a short time, practical Carolyn seemed to have the upper hand. She briskly persuaded him that perhaps Natalie's death had been a blessing, a way out for a hopelessly troubled young woman; this reading of the tragedy made Neal brighten a little. Apparently without any discussion, Neal moved his things back home the next morning.

• • •

Jack stopped off again at the Cassady house in mid-December 1955 on his way to North Carolina, where he planned to spend Christmas. Carolyn remembers that at this time Jack seemed to feel he was an outsider in their home. He cut a rather lonesome figure, sleeping on the sofa (there was no spare room at the Los Gatos house) and often talking about his rootlessness. He duly departed and reported on the trip in a letter, dated December 30 and addressed to Carolyn: "Hopped a Zipper [The Zephyr, the nightly freight train from San Francisco] to LA tho I had to sneak off at each stop to hide in bushes from prying cops with flashlites looking for bums who break open trucks in cold . . . met truckdriver & had big night and so it was all the way from sultry Mexican bars to Christmas farmlands of Ohio, one ride, and I came home."

While there, Jack wrote *Visions of Gerard* in two Benzedrine-fueled weeks. Unpublished until 1965, the novel was about the textures and sensations of Jack's childhood in Lowell, Massachusetts, and the short, bittersweet life of his brother Gerard. It is hard not to be struck by the contrast between Kerouac's breakneck writing speed and that of Neal Cassady, whose own memoirs at this time seemed indefinitely stalled, as did his normally prolific letter writing.

• • •

The time between New Year's 1956 and April 1958 was a period of general uncertainty and renewed spiritual doubt for Neal Cassady. He remained haunted by Natalie's death. In a penitent 1958 letter to Father Harley Schmitt, Neal would write: "I became involved with a younger most sensitive girl who, when the money was gone and apparently despairing because of disappointment in me, committed suicide by leaping off the roof while I slept on in lazy indifference below."

Suicide was an egregious sin in the eyes of Cayce's followers, and Caycean thought was still a potent force in the Cassady household even though Neal and Carolyn's adherence to it marked them as eccentrics to many friends and acquaintances. Then suddenly in 1956 it seemed that, for once, Neal and Carolyn were not as alone in their belief as they thought. A much wider interest in reincarnation was stimulated by the publication, in January of that year, of *The Search for Bridey Murphy*. This bestselling "faction" book by hypnotist Morey Bernstein focused on Colorado housewife Virginia Tighe and her apparent hypnotic regression into a past life as a nineteenth-century Irishwoman. The same year a movie of the book cast Teresa Wright as Virginia Tighe (renamed Ruth Simmons in the screenplay) and even depicted Edgar Cayce, whose own posthumous fortunes were considerably revived by the *Bridey Murphy* craze (despite subsequent suspicions that Virginia Tighe had simply—if imaginatively—recycled colorful tales gleaned from an elderly Irish neighbor). Even Jack Kerouac bought into the *Bridey* phenomenon and for a time seemed prepared to give Cayce the benefit of the doubt. "[S]udden realization that Cayce must be right," he wrote to the Cassadys, "and Bridey Murphy excitement, which has carried over to my sister, and she and I want you to send us Cayce's literature address at Atlantic Beach so we can send for literature, my sister especially het up now on Astrology."

Jack had even started to take Oral Roberts seriously. From the start, Roberts's reputation as a miraculous healer had been offset by his equally convincing reputation as a charlatan. In his later years, when completion of his extravagant project the City of Faith Hospital complex was threatened because of lack of funds, Roberts claimed to have been visited by a 900-foot Jesus. Roberts had "only seen Jesus once before," but "there I was, face to face with Jesus Christ, the Son of the Living God. He reached down, put his Hands under the City of Faith, lifted it, and said to me, 'See how easy it is for Me to lift it!'"

Jack's leap of faith was facilitated by his discovery that "Oral Roberts is a Cherokee Indian. A real old-fashioned witchdoctor's what he is . . . he has great compassionate heart. I don't disbelieve him." Carolyn insists that this last sentence was a joke for Neal's benefit.

In any event, the Cassadys continued to pursue the Cayce doctrine, and at the 1956 Cayce spring conference the featured speaker was none other than Starr Daily, author of *Release.* Neal immediately turned to him for answers. Ex-con Daily certainly looked like Cassady's sort of man, a bullish and rugged religious convert who would surely give appropriate advice. But this was not the case. With some degree of irony for Catholic-raised Cassady, Caycean Starr Daily seemed more like the kind of tough Irish priest that featured regularly in the gangster movies of the 1930s—morally inflexible but still capable of slugging a sinner if the need arose. His advice to Neal amounted to little more than "pray like the devil and discipline yourself," whereas what Neal was probably hoping for was an epiphany followed by a fast-track route to enlightenment and salvation.

Carolyn put it differently, saying that Neal simply could not accept that divinity lay in him and that he ought to celebrate the God within: "Neal could not surrender his feelings of guilt and unworthiness; his prayers were the apologies and supplications not of a God-filled vessel affirming his divinity, but of a miserable worm."

Meanwhile Jack was making unexpected literary progress. In mid-March he had written Carolyn excitedly to say that he had made arrangements with Viking Press to finish modifying *On the Road* at Stanford University with respected Viking editor Malcolm Cowley. This would bring him back west again. At Cowley's suggestion, Kerouac would edit the manuscript to make it more acceptable to the publishers. The length was reduced, everyone was given pseudonyms, and a passage reflecting Neal Cassady's interest in an underage girl was excised.

Then he wrote to her even more enthusiastically saying that he had secured a job in the Pacific Northwest as a ranger in Washington State's Cascade Mountains. This prompted the daydream: "It will be my life work, in my hut there, and city apartment in Mex. City, and in transit twice a year I can knock on yore door and pester you for a meal, a few weeks at a crack with my charming tired presence and roaring fires and priceless comments at television and if you want a camping trip to the Sierra with the kids we can do it whenever you're ready. Know just the place, just the trail, just the beautiful lake."

After a brief stopover in California, Jack went north to his mountains for the summer of 1956, staying at the fire watchers' station at Desolation Peak where he stopped writing letters and started writing a journal about his experiences there. These would eventually form the basis of his book *Desolation Angels*, a novel whose mystical and romantic tone did not really reflect his personal reaction to the mountain wilderness, which in truth left him feeling bored and lonely. He was back in the San Francisco area by September, and he never returned to the ranger job.

Also in San Francisco at this time was another recently published young poet basking in the afterglow of the poetry boom that had been kick-started by the famous Six Gallery poetry reading of the previous year. Gregory Corso, born in 1930 in New York City, had a lawless childhood and adolescence; he had begun to read literature and write poetry in prison. After his release, he met Allen Ginsberg in a Greenwich Village bar in 1950. Allen subsequently showed Corso's prison poems to Mark Van Doren, a Columbia English professor and distinguished poet, in an effort to encourage Corso.

Corso had also provided Jack Kerouac with a plotline for *The Subterraneans* when he seduced Jack's girlfriend Alene Lee (Mardou in the novel) in the summer of 1953. Now Corso was in San Francisco, but Jack's attempts to induce a friendship between Neal and Corso did not work out. A disagreement at the racetrack was followed by a weekend at the Cassadys' home that similarly failed to impress Corso. Neal did not live up to his legendary reputation as a charismatic life force, especially when he insisted they watch Oral Roberts on TV. Later Corso softened, and that same summer he wrote to Neal from Amsterdam to apologize for his surliness when they met. "As I write this letter I am happy to remember that you were kind to me and liked me . . . I love you—Gregory."

In the late fall of 1956 Allen Ginsberg, Peter Orlovsky, and Gregory Corso were passing through Los Angeles on their way to Mexico City where they planned to meet Jack to plan a European trip. Carolyn wrote to Allen in Los Angeles on November 1 to tell him that Neal had just suffered another railroad accident, this time cutting his other foot badly on a trackside metal marker as his train sped past. It was a simple accident that Neal persisted in viewing as a karmic demonstration of some sort (there had been recent semi-serious speculation from Neal about staging another accident to earn another big payoff). Since this accident was for real and he could not collect a cent in compensation (technically he was off duty when it happened), he was happy to see his misadventure as part of some divine scheme.

The accident put him in plaster again and meant more time laid off from work. Also—although no one was aware of it at the time—it effectively marked the beginning of the end for Jack, Allen, and Neal as a close trio. They would all meet again over the next ten years, but Neal's latest plaster cast seemed like an emblem of the newly static nature of both his life and his literary ambitions.

In contrast Jack Kerouac would become an overnight sensation when *On the Road* was finally published in September 1957. Neal Cassady, whose *The First Third* was now looking like a rudderless enterprise, inhabited Kerouac's celebrated novel, in spirit, deed, and literal word.

Allen Ginsberg had also found fame and notoriety following the fall trial of the City Lights for the publication of his epic poem "Howl." Full of language likely to be considered obscene, it was printed in the U.K. and made it through U.S. customs without incident. Part of a second printing was stopped by U.S. customs on March 25, 1957, after another title issuing from the same British printer had been seized. An obscenity charge was brought against Ferlinghetti, the poem's publisher. Nine literary experts testified on the poem's behalf and, supported by the American Civil Liberties Union, Ferlinghetti won. The court decided that the poem was of "redeeming social importance." It contained the passage:

> N.C., secret hero of these poems, cocksman and Adonis of Denver-joy to the memory of his innumerable lays of girls in empty lots & diner backyards, moviehouses' rickety rows, on mountaintops in caves or with gaunt waitresses in familiar roadside lonely petticoat upliftings & especially secret gas-station solipsisms of johns, & hometown alleys too . . .

Seen in retrospect, Allen's three-pronged dedication of *Howl and Other Poems* to Jack Kerouac, William Burroughs, and Neal Cassady seems to take on a valedictory tinge. In it he cataloged eleven of Jack's books as well as Burroughs's *Naked Lunch*, and he ended his dedication with the words: "Neal Cassady, author of *The First Third*, an autobiography (1949) which enlightened Buddha. All these books are published in Heaven."

Jack and Allen had, each in his own way, captured a little of Neal's lightning in a jar. If they would never completely understand him, they had at least managed to incorporate something of his extraordinary life-affirming presence in their work. It meant that from now on his role in their lives and careers would be subtly changed; he was no longer a complete mystery, but part of a myth.

• • •

Allen was already traveling in Europe with Peter Orlovsky when the *Howl* trial was playing out; Neal and Carolyn monitored proceedings on his behalf, keeping newspaper clippings and tracking the absent poet's rise from obscurity to national fame. Jack was living in Tangiers, part of a trip he had envisioned as a kind of cultural grand tour. "[G]oing to Europe with Allen to see ole Bill in Tangiers," he had written to the Cassadys, "and write in sunny Spain, and April in Paris . . . read *FinnegansWake* [*sic*] in Dublin Library and visit Céline (got his address)."

In fact, Jack had gone straight to Tangiers to await the others, and from there he wrote a letter with coy references to Carolyn's assumed sensitivity, about the "lil ole Arab gals with veils, that charge 3 bucks" as well as "a whole culture of t-smokers."

From Tangiers the united party traveled to Paris. Then Jack abruptly returned to the United States only to take off on an ill-judged series of cross-country travels that first saw him relocate with his mother to

Berkeley, California. This made him a potential neighbor of the Cassadys, but without even visiting them in Los Gatos, he abruptly moved his mother and himself back east (Gabrielle, it seemed, had not taken to California), just in time for the publication of *On the Road.* Almost at once the former brakeman and firewatcher was besieged by the press for interviews and approached by Warner Bros. with a movie deal. He appeared in front of forty million TV viewers when he was interviewed on John Wingate's program *Nightbeat.* Jack Kerouac was about to discover that fame, like the past, is another country, where things are done differently.

Neal Cassady too discovered that there was a sting in the tail to Jack's sudden celebrity. Among the hostile reviews of *On the Road, Time* magazine nailed "Dean Moriarty" with an analysis that was much too close to home for Neal's self-image: "Moriarty seems close to a prison psychosis that is a variety of the Ganser Syndrome," the review commented. "Its symptoms, as described by one psychiatrist, sound like a playback from Kerouac's novel: 'The patient exaggerates his mood and feelings; he "lets himself go" and gets himself into highly emotional states. He is uncooperative, refuses to answer questions and obey orders . . . his talk may be disjointed and difficult to follow.'"

Ganser Syndrome had been first described in 1898 by German psychiatrist Sigbert Ganser. A commonly suggested symptom was the urge to avoid an unpleasant situation and its corresponding burden of responsibility. Most sufferers had a personality disorder. Because of the disruption between the usually integrated functions of consciousness, memory, identity, and perception of the environment, the Ganser Syndrome was described as a dissociative disorder.

The same review also unconsciously pointed up a great irony of Neal Cassady's current life. "Excitement and movement mean everything to [the beats]," it claimed. "Steady jobs and homes in the suburbs are for 'squares.'" Neal, who thrived on excitement, movement, and marijuana, was also a suburbanite with a regular job and responsibilities!

The bad reviews disturbed Kerouac too, outweighing the many good ones in his mind. Always happy to discuss and dissect his own personality within the comfort zone of his own peer group, Kerouac was quite unable to weather public attacks such as that mounted by Art Cohn in the *San Francisco Chronicle*. Cohn's bracing assault, entitled "Sick Little Bums," dismissed Kerouac's world, which Cohn characterized as fueled by a "new religion" of ridicule, defilement, and negativity. Cohn ended with the following tacit dismissal: "Amen, you pathetic, self-pitying, degenerate bums, amen!"

The furor surrounding *On the Road* and the gradual crystallization of what would come to be called "the Beat Generation" marked the point at which the private lives of "our prophets" intersected finally and fatally with the mass media. Allen Ginsberg would handle the attention best. Every generation needs a readily recognizable representative, so, in the age of expanding TV and printed media, the beatnik poet might as well be Ginsberg. With his unruly hair, wild eyes, and trademark spectacles he was simply easier to remember than Gary Snyder or Lawrence Ferlinghetti for the people who did not read the poems but read the popular magazines. Jack Kerouac, on the other hand, although blessed with brooding good looks, did not come over well on TV. His discomfort showed, never more so than when he appeared on *The Steve Allen Plymouth Show* reading woodenly from his hit novel while Allen, who created the show and presented it from 1954 to 1957, overlaid jazzy piano riffs, turning *On the Road* into a kind of awful dinner theater entertainment.

Neal Cassady would have no such problems. He was a folk hero in his neck of the woods, but Jack Kerouac's expectation that the press would beat a path to Neal's door to meet Dean Moriarty in person was mistaken, as was his fantasy that Neal might play Dean in the (never to be) Warner Bros. film version of his book. Neal's wider fame would come, but it would be of a different and unique sort.

As another New Year came Neal found himself attracting more unwanted attention, but not in connection with *On the Road* or *Howl*. In

San Francisco, where he had embarked upon a relationship with a young woman named Jacqueline Gibson, he was known not just as a cult figure but also as an informal dealer in marijuana. (Carolyn has always questioned this on the grounds that getting enough marijuana for himself was task enough for Neal, although others stick to the "informal dealer" version.) Calling himself Johnny Potseed, he was allegedly the man to see in North Beach. When he supplied joints to three men who offered him a lift back to his train after a North Beach party in February 1958, he figured out too late that they were narcotics agents. An earlier attempt to entrap him had failed when, smelling a rat, he took the forty dollars and ran, believing his would-be customers to be agents; this time he had not been so smart.

"I was too late to catch a train, see," he explained to journalist Al Aronowitz later. "Ten years and I didn't miss a run, and there were three guys, and I say, 'Hey, I'll give you a couple of joints,' so I gave three joints to the police officers in exchange for a ride downtown to the station—only I didn't know they were police officers. But then I got suspicious, see, because they didn't smoke it, they didn't light up, they just exchanged significant glances. So right away the thought goes through my mind, humm, if they're police officers, I'll try to head them off, I'll try to give them a big story so they won't arrest me right then and there, because, see, they didn't know my name and I thought I would just take off. So I say, real cagey, see, 'Wanta buy another five hundred dollars' worth?' and then I say, 'I don't use the stuff anymore'. So on the one hand I tried to tell them I was quitting and on the other hand I tried to make them think I was a big dealer." The version he told Carolyn at the time was not so explicit.

Nothing happened until April when a dawn visit from two policemen with an arrest warrant confirmed Neal and Carolyn's worst fears. He was taken away in handcuffs, but it turned out that the arrest was really to scare him into informing on other users and, more specifically, on the larger supply chain. He was uncooperative, and with the help of a sympathetic public defender, Robert Nicco, the charge was thrown out of court for lack of evidence, and Neal was freed after a week in the San Francisco City Jail. He thought his troubles were over, but after a brief family celebration, the very next day he was rearrested and bail was set at $12,000. That bail was to be the basis of a serious domestic disagreement and proved a watershed in the Cassady marriage. Neal assumed that Carolyn would post his bail, which she could only do by getting a property bond on the Los Gatos house. After much agonizing she refused to do so, convinced that Neal would skip bail once released, thereby sacrificing the only house they had ever owned or were likely to own.

Neal was transferred to the county facility at San Bruno in a state of shocked disbelief that Carolyn would not get the property bond. From there he wrote, desperately claiming that if he were free he could organize an unbeatable defense that would otherwise be unavailable to him with a now uncongenial public defender, one Mr. McNamara, in his corner. When Neal finally realized that Carolyn would not change her mind, the final paragraph of his letter dated May 24, 1958, descended into incoherent abuse: "since you can't justify your treason . . . I therefore know you're completely NUTS. So, dimwit dope, this dope hopes that years hence, you can dope out some good dope to dope the kids about my absence."

He had now been in custody for forty-seven days and his disillusionment with Carolyn was so complete that he did not even advise her of the date of his trial. It came, and with no help from his ineffectual public defender, he was summarily convicted on the charge of sale of marijuana. Carolyn subsequently went to the sentencing with a forlorn hope of pleading for leniency. Brazenly Neal told the sentencing judge that he did not use marijuana. He repeated this damning answer when asked again. Presiding Judge Carpanetti concluded that Neal must therefore be a pusher, angrily denounced his "double life," bad character, and general refusal to cooperate with the law. Adding that he did not like Neal's attitude, the judge sentenced him to two counts of five years to life, the sentences to run concurrently.

22

THERE EXISTS a faded color snapshot showing Neal Cassady standing next to his three children and the family dog, Cayce. In his brown suit and shoes, white shirt, and blue necktie, Neal looks every inch the respectable all-American 1950s father posing in his neat garden with his well-turned-out kids. The picture was taken by Carolyn on Easter 1957, and one year later Neal suggested that she send this or a similar one along to the court with a plea for leniency prior to his sentencing on the drug charges. She did, but it failed to sway the sentencing judge, Walter Carpanetti, and perhaps even animated the judge's "double life" tirade against Neal. Certainly the unremarkable suburban snapshot made a stark contrast with an unfavorable (and later retracted) *San Jose Mercury* article alleging that, according to the police, Neal was the leader of a gang of marijuana smugglers bringing large quantities of the drug into the United States from Mexico on Southern Pacific trains in "a pretty cozy operation."

Eventually Neal would serve over two years, from April 18, 1958, to June 3, 1960. The experience would see him move through various spiritual and philosophical stages as well as two very different penal institutions.

From the city jail in San Francisco he was transferred to the county jail in San Bruno, a commuter town south of the city. There he began writing letters with all his old vigor, although he was constrained by new privations.

"At first Neal was allowed visits and correspondence only with women," Carolyn noted in her foreword to *Grace Beats Karma: Letters from Prison 1958–60*. Neal's old Denver benefactor, Father Harley Schmitt, a principal character in the famous "Joan Anderson" letter, was excepted from this rule, but Ginsberg, Kerouac, and even Hugh Lynn Cayce were banned. LuAnne and Jacqueline Gibson were permitted.

"Ex-wives and lovers were welcomed as was Helen Hinkle and myself," wrote Carolyn. "Figure that."

Carolyn's outrage at Neal's treatment by the police and courts was complete, although her belief that he was "falsely accused" and "unjustly condemned" seems to depend upon her acceptance that Neal was telling the truth, something that experience had surely taught her he did only when it suited him. It seems likely that part of her outrage stemmed from a belated and bitter realization that the police and the courts were not the blameless institutions her sheltered upbringing and crime-free life had led her to believe. The idea that Neal was roughed up by detectives on his original arrest ("they hit you in the stomach 'cause it doesn't show," Neal reported) appalled her, and she even characterized McNamara, the second public defender, as a "collaborator" appointed to ensure a conviction, when in all likelihood he was probably just feeble. Certainly the abrupt convening of a grand jury suggested that the authorities were this time leaving nothing to chance. Carolyn's response was entirely understandable and to some extent justified, although Neal, known as a supplier of marijuana in North Beach, was probably not as innocent as he made out. He came close to admitting as much in an early prison letter to Father Harley Schmitt. Neal would write, in the course of one convoluted 170-word sentence, "I had drifted into acting in accord with the main . . . responsibility entailed in mastership of 'Beathood,' namely helping the brothers to attain that state . . . by the simple expedient of smoking marijuana."

A year after the event, journalist Alfred Aronowitz interviewed agents in the narcotics squad office for a series of twelve articles about the beats. The following extract comes from one of those articles:

> "Oh there's no question," said Sergeant William Logan, "that (Cassady) was making a buck selling tea. He needed it for the

> horses. Every day, he was down the track—he loved those ponies. And then he had another girlfriend to support, a cute little babe, really a knockout. I think he and another guy were taking turns living with her."
>
> A young detective nodded his head. He wore a zippered jacket and dungarees, the way undercover agents dress on television, the way he dressed, in fact, when they arrested Neal. His name was Charles Wetstein and he was on another case.
>
> "To me, he was just an oddball," Wetstein said. "Playing horses, smoking tea—they tell me he emptied out his bank account playing the horses. In a way I guess he was looking to get busted—I understand he used to drive up from LA at ninety miles an hour with a carload of marijuana.
>
> "He was a better than average narco violator, but he was always talking, often incoherently, changing the subject, never finishing what he said. He was one of the most far-gone as far as smoking is concerned. Most teaheads take it or leave it—he seemed as if he really had to have it. Marijuana is supposed to be non-habit forming, but he seemed as if he was really an addict."

Whatever the rights and wrongs of the case, Neal Cassady's term of imprisonment was now a reality, and it marked a radical change of attitude in him. Whereas at the time of his first, failed arraignment he had, according to Carolyn, been "calm, poised, and assured"—at one point instinctively and successfully breaking up a fight between two highly dangerous cell mates—this time anger and resentment took over. Knowing that to give in to these forces would be self-destructive, Neal would instead attempt various metaphysical exercises to deal with them throughout his term of incarceration.

Following his conviction and sentencing he was moved from San Bruno County Jail to the California Medical Facility at Vacaville in northern Solano County, midway between San Francisco and Sacramento. This institution provided a comparatively gentle introduction to the prison system where a kind of inmate triage enabled the authorities to decide who should be transferred to which prison. Neal was hoping for Soledad, which had a good reputation and, as he put it, "kissing facilities." While he waited he responded well to Vacaville's quite civilized and well-equipped regime. From Vacaville Neal fired off at least a dozen letters, mostly to Carolyn, that were as prodigious as any he had ever written. Fizzing with puns, recklessly long mock-Proustian sentences, and an occasional arch pedantic turn of phrase that recalled his old favorite W. C. Fields, Neal tackled every topic from religion to body-building, de Rougemont's *Love in the Western World* to his own renunciations of future extramarital love affairs in favor of a life of prayer ("As for the Nats & Jacs [a reference to Natalie Jackson and Jacqueline Gibson], I expect to be on my knees too much after my release.")

Religion was the dominant and recurring theme of his letters and his life in prison. Another letter, written to Father Schmitt in August 1958, seemed to reaffirm Neal's devotion to the Catholic faith, or at least selected aspects of it. After reprising a catalog of his sins Neal ended his letter: "Suffice to mention that, besides the rosary & other usual ones, my hour of prayer each AM & PM includes many self-composed petitions. Also, the better to emulate, am memorizing NAMES of all 262 Popes."

This preoccupation with lists and feats of memory had always been a part of Neal's character, along with an interest in the hidden significance of sequences and patterns of numbers. The prodigious memory that enabled him to remember long sequences of digits as a party trick would take on new significance inside an institution where everything from personal identity to days served was codified by numbers. Prayers and patterns, metaphysics and sequences, integers and liturgies—all would combine to measure and punctuate his life in prison, or so he hoped, thereby enabling him to control his anger and guilt.

From Vacaville Neal was sent, not to Soledad as he had hoped, but to a notoriously less amenable facility.

San Quentin was established in July 1852 at Point Quentin in Marin County. The prison quickly acquired a fearsome reputation for violence, having been established as a bullish response to California's growing lawlessness at the end of the nineteenth century. By 1958 it had improved only grudgingly in step with the times. When Neal, dressed in a conspicuous white tunic and restrained by leg irons, was transported there to join some 5,000 inmates, he could not see it as anything but a move in the wrong direction.

From his shared cell (4'6" x 7'6" x 9'6") to his work duties sweeping cotton waste in the thundering prison textile mill, Neal found San Quentin a far more abrasive environment than Vacaville, one that demanded correspondingly more extreme responses from him.

His letters to Carolyn became ever more elaborate in their wordplay, often starting with two dozen or more alliterations ("Dearest Devoted Deeply Disturbed Darling Distaff Driver Distributing Delightful . . . [etc.]"). They were so obscure in their content that only a loving wife familiar with all the oblique references and having time on her hands could hope to get the full effect. His letters to his children were suffused with affection but now also full of verbal acrobatics and dictionary-style explanations or strict injunctions to "look it up." Despite the linguistic contrivances, his love for his children was quite apparent, and his attempts to make them an awkward gift of his self-acquired erudition took on an extra poignancy; he was all too aware that he was in no position to give them anything else. Also Carolyn was now struggling financially, having had her welfare assistance summarily terminated in November 1958. She believed the denial of support was the result of a negative report from a visiting social worker who felt that a family that had a car and a swimming pool couldn't possibly be in need. Neal's impotent alarm at this turn of events was exacerbated by the fact he was about to be hospitalized for hemorrhoid surgery and could not even question welfare representatives himself. (For this surgery and other procedures in prison Neal was denied anesthetic on the grounds of being a drug user; Carolyn insists, perhaps correctly, that this denial was an example of gratuitous punishment rather than pharmaceutical caution.)

All he could manage in a letter of November 30, 1958, was "Chin up, Dear Heart, remember that Jesus' Grace will meet our Karma if we keep striving to surrender properly. Cathy Crosby to star in *Beat Generation* by M.G.M., imagine a 'beat' Crosby, revolting, what?"

The Beat Generation (1959) did indeed feature Cathy Crosby—Bing's niece—as "The Singer" in a sublimely tawdry exploitation movie marketed with the following tag: "The wild, weird, world of the Beatniks! . . . Sullen rebels, defiant chicks . . . searching for a life of their own! The pads . . . the jazz . . . the dives . . . those frantic 'way-out' parties . . . beyond belief!"

Carolyn was left to navigate a welfare system that cut off her money then demanded she work at jobs so mind-numbing she did not want them, or else train for employment as a social worker. When Carolyn revealed that she had once received an award called Aid for Needy Children, her own social worker assumed that this might color her professional judgment, and the plan to help her enter the field was summarily dropped. In the end she found more amenable employment first with a local theater group and later with a drama club at the University of Santa Clara.

Al Aronowitz got around to interviewing Neal in early 1959 at San Quentin for his series of *New York Post* articles. The portrait Aronowitz subsequently painted was of a man much more relaxed than the one who emerges in letters to Carolyn of about the same time. Neal told Aronowitz amiable anecdotes, such as one about the time he was brakeman on President Eisenhower's campaign train and, just after inhaling a big lungful of marijuana, found himself approached by Ike's Secret Service men who were walking behind the train. "One of them says, 'Cold night out here tonight,' and there I am with a lungful of marijuana smoke and I couldn't answer. So I used a railroad man's prerogative and I acted grumpy and I didn't say anything."

He also gave Aronowitz his preferred definition of the word *beat.*

"Beat?" he said, shifting in his chair with his legs angular, shifting sometimes to a different chair, looking always, out the window, at the sunlight, "beat means beatific—short for beatific vision, you know, the highest vision you can get. A shortcut is via marijuana. . . . That's why I'm here, ehhh?"

Unexpectedly he referred to Natalie Jackson as "the great love of my life" and downplayed his friendship with Jack Kerouac. (Carolyn Cassady does not remember ever reading that perfidious line about Natalie in Aronowitz's articles, which were sent to her but were later lost. She was shocked to come upon a variant of the quote in *Holiday* magazine in the early 1960s.)

"Oh, yeah, Jack and I, we've had some excitement, but I've reached an age where I've had all that. Jack and I, we drifted apart over the years. He became a Buddhist and I became a Cayceite."

Neal's comment on the encounter with Aronowitz in a letter to Carolyn was: "Had 3 hour interview with Pagan Reporter, no rapport, everytime I began to grant the spiritual reality he forced return to physical one, ugh, when will they leave us alone?"

Neal's assessment was not entirely fair, as Aronowitz had listened to and included some of Neal's spiritual musings, even though they were unlikely to have much appeal for the *New York Post*'s readers.

"You see, the thing with marijuana is that you don't utilize the opening you get—it's not a permanent thing," Aronowitz reported Neal as saying. "The trouble with most people is, like me, I'm living on the four lower glands—I haven't opened the three upper ones. You see the pituitary and the endocrine glands are the centers of the force. . . . It's all in the book—it's part of the Cayce philosophy.

"In the Third Dimension, see, we're under stress here—we're all being pressured beyond the limit of our endurance. . . . If you surrender your will enough through the thymus—Dutch doctors, see they've shown that the pineal glands in certain heads are fossilized at adolescence. . . .

"But if you can get the top three glands working—they work now, of course, but they work through the self will. Each individual is his own law. If you surrender the law then you can be a channel of service. That's why we're all here—to be of service. Self is the great sin. The thing is to get Kundalini Fire to come up the spine to the pineal."

Jack Kerouac particularly liked that last part when he read it. "[T]he best part was Neal's dialogue about 'pineal fire,' etc. Big Cayce, Aurobindo mysticisms suddenly appearing on the page," he wrote to Carolyn. Jack also produced the money for a typewriter that Neal had pointedly requested from him in the course of the interview.

Aronowitz interviewed Carolyn at Los Gatos as well and although she too felt he was disinclined to pay much attention to the more religious aspects of Neal's life, hence missing "the essence of the spiritual search," she liked him and accepted his invitation to accompany him on a drive to see Henry Miller, who had expressed some sympathy toward Kerouac's work. That year Miller wrote a flattering preface to Kerouac's *The Subterraneans*. However, Miller was cautious in his praise of Kerouac's spontaneous style when Al and Carolyn met him at his home. Even so, Carolyn was thrilled to be treated to an impromptu lecture on the role of spontaneity in literature from the Greeks onward. She later wrote insouciantly that Miller's comments had been particularly rewarding "since I'd never been able to get past page one of anything he'd written."

Back at San Quentin Neal's correspondence became even more febrile. Because envelopes were rationed he tended to restrict his writing to Carolyn and his children whose birthdays, in particular, could be guaranteed to make him further fire up his already overheated style. Religious references now saturated his correspondence and a letter to his children dated March 25, 1959, gives some idea of his tendency to put on a baffling display of linguistic fireworks instead of writing in a way that children aged eight to ten might understand: "Dear Dear Children, Cheerful Cathy, Jestful Jamie & Jolly Johnny; Well, well, sweet offspring, I see by the old calendar another, the 1,926th, joyful jubilee has rolled around.

Yes, I mean that stupendous event which matters more to us than does, even if they were, or could be, all added together, any other of the great happenings humanity has witnessed; it is, of course, the Resserection [*sic*] of Jesus, our Christ."

This letter, which is by no means atypical of his output at this time, went on to gloss for his children the ancient Egyptian origins of the Easter egg, Mary Magdalene's instruction of Tiberius in the egg's Christian significance, and the legend of the Turin shroud. Coming reluctantly down to earth, the letter ends on a note of bathos: "Well, John Boy, can you ride your bike without hands yet?"

Neal's other regular correspondent was Father Schmitt, to whom he usually wrote rather more lucid letters, often on themes of guilt and injustice. If the tone of his first letter to Schmitt after his imprisonment had been one of philosophical acceptance and guarded acknowledgment of his own guilt, halfway through his prison sentence Neal reverted to citing bitterly the three marijuana cigarettes he "gave away" as being the sole reason for his incarceration. Neal also became hypersensitive to signs and symbols, seeing dark ironies in light coincidences, such as the time Jami misspelled "hey" as "hay," thereby, in Neal's mind, "cutting my remorse anew by her unwitting giving such appropriate name to Vile Weed used in that selfish habit of vice putting me here."

Similarly, working with metal type when attending a vocational printing course, he would find the letter *j* always reminded him of his son John.

In July 1959 Carolyn proposed to Neal that she and the Hinkles might relocate to Scotland with a view to Neal using his parole period to decide once and for all what he wanted—a life with them or something else. He responded badly to this news as he did to a visit that failed to take place when Carolyn's car broke down. He mocks the idea of the Scottish move and asks her not to write anymore or visit—a request he rescinds in his next letter.

Leon Tabory had been a psychologist doing research on a program called "Intensive Treatment" at Vacaville. He was granted access to any prisoner he felt might help him with his research into high levels of recidivism. He came to know Neal well at this time, and in fact, after Neal's eventual release, fell afoul of the authorities for maintaining social contact with the Cassady family.

"What he feared before his parole from San Quentin was that without the support of his family he would very quickly be returned to prison," Tabory recalled. "That was because he thought that he wouldn't be able to resist the temptations that would be so easily available to him. Just talking about tripping with his friends would light his face up with ecstatic restless excitement. It was clear to me watching him as it was to himself that that was what he was dying to do.

"He did not want to be returned to San Quentin. He was not afraid of work and he was hoping that his family would help him to present to his parole officer an image of a responsible hard working family man, and to not scrutinize his life too closely. But Carolyn . . . had written to him that she was planning to take the kids to Scotland where she had relatives. The scenario which finds his wife and kids gone when he comes out of prison was a sure invitation to an early parole violation, he felt."

Also in July Neal decided to switch his prison courses, abandoning psychology for music only to be told that from then on he would be doing neither; instead he would be learning the printing trade as preparation for his release. He threw himself into this course with customary enthusiasm for any practical task. The following month he wrote to Carolyn describing how (for the third time) he had also stepped into the breach to address the prison's Comparative Religion and Philosophy class when the official visiting teacher, an eccentric astrologist named Gavin Arthur, failed to show. "[A]gain it was my pleasurable duty to instruct the boys in Caycehood," Neal reported.

Chester Alan Arthur III, known as Gavin, was a San Francisco astrologer and gay-liberation pioneer. He was the grandson and namesake of twenty-first U.S. President Chester Alan Arthur. He had helped Alfred Kinsey with his research into gay sexuality. He was also the author of *Circle of Sex*, a book that cataloged sexual preferences by astrological sign. Neal had been quick to join Arthur's course, a fact confidently predicted by Gary Snyder, who knew Arthur socially and was amused when he learned that he was going to be a religious instructor at San Quentin. Referring to Neal, Snyder told Arthur, "He'll be the first one to sign up for your class—you'll see!"

"There was something about Neal when he wasn't taking dope that was absolutely angelic," recalled Gavin Arthur of their first meeting at San Quentin. "I could easily recognize him out of all of those sixty faces. And sure enough, when the talk was over, he shouldered his way down . . . and said, 'Mr. Arthur, you read my name as Neal Cassady but you might know me better as Dean Moriarty.'"

Neal, who was happy to distance himself from Jack's book when talking to Al Aronowitz, clearly knew when his literary connections might work for him instead of against him.

Gavin Arthur, when he attended at all, would sometimes bring guest speakers to his San Quentin class. Gary Snyder was one of the first. Then Allen Ginsberg was recruited when it was rumored that he would be in the area in October. Arthur arranged it with encouragement from Neal, and that was how the infamous Ginsberg, author of the obscenity-case scandal *Howl*, arrived wearing blue jeans (forbidden to prison visitors) and delivered an obscenity-laden, openly gay address to the assembled company that included all three chaplains—Catholic, Protestant, and Jewish—while wearing a borrowed pair of trousers that were too long for him. It was all a roaring success.

There was an attempt to get Jack Kerouac to do the same and Neal wrote him saying that "the entire building would be overpacked to fire hazard proportions if I dared let out that YOU were coming."

Whether Jack ever really intended to address the Comparative Religion class is unclear, although the night before the due date he did appear at the San Francisco Film Festival for a showing of *Pull My Daisy*, the short film based on events at the Cassady home four years earlier. He fell down drunk twice at the festival and might have been incapable of attending the San Quentin class the following day.

Neal was due to be released on June 3, 1960. The New Year came, and a request by Carolyn for Neal's early parole was turned down. She had seriously considered the move to Scotland, accompanying the Hinkles there, but then she learned that such a move was not a possibility because parole conditions stipulated that the prisoner must have both a job and a home to go to. She abandoned her relocation plans. The Hinkles decided to go anyway, planning to tour but not settle down there.

Before Neal's release Carolyn found him a job at a San Jose tire shop where the proprietor was prepared to take a chance on an ex-con. Then the family dog, Cayce, had to be put down before his absent master could return; Neal wrote Carolyn and the children an affecting note about the loss, ending with speculation about the dog's "mighty, loyal, unshaken submission to your hurting-to-help will as you 'shooshed' him into the car—THERE is love for you!"

Jack, now distanced from the Cassadys by his fame and the start of his slow decline into alcoholism, nonetheless responded warmly to Carolyn's note advising him of the date of Neal's release. In a note, he reflected thoughtfully on their complex three-cornered relationship: "I think Neal loves you very much and always will and I'm glad you're going to stick together—I can't picture anything grayer than the thought of Neal in one part of the world, alone, and you in another, alone, lacking your intimate conversation between each other, which, as you remember from the last visit I made, even Gregory Corso couldn't interrupt. . . . It was nice to hear from you my darling blonde aristocratic Carolyn, and my next great moment will be when once again you and Neal and I sit in front of the fireplace with wine and the Television and laugh."

• • •

The day of Neal's release came. Suddenly freed from his world of devotional and obsessive routine, his reentry to the world he had left two years earlier was something of a worrying anticlimax. *Recidivism* was the unspoken word that hung over Neal Cassady at the start of the decade in which his legend would become complete. Despite all the fine intentions, would he be able to settle down and avoid a return to prison? Fear of a relapse into familiar patterns was really what had prevented Carolyn from bailing him out at the outset; backsliding was now made even more likely by the knowledge that his old, convenient SPRR employment was gone forever. Gavin Arthur's belief that Neal was at his most saintly in San Quentin, where the temptations of the flesh did not distract him from exercising his extraordinary mind, suddenly took on a negative resonance.

Certainly when Carolyn picked him up at the prison gatehouse there was little echo of the high-flown paeans with which he had celebrated and flattered her in his florid and emotional letters. He seemed awkward with her on the drive back, distracted by his sudden freedom and unsure about the protocol of "the new start" they had promised themselves. They went to a North Beach jeweler and bought matching gold rings. They were to have a celebratory lunch with Gavin Arthur, but first Neal insisted on delivering a message to someone on behalf of an inmate. Carolyn waited in the car in Columbus Avenue for nearly an hour and later wondered if this had been an excuse for him to visit a lover. Certainly Neal would briefly reprise his interrupted affair with Jacqueline Gibson before "passing her on" to Jack Kerouac later that summer, but Carolyn never wanted to find out the real reason behind the Columbus Avenue hiatus. And she never did.

The lunch went well; so did Neal's first week at home with his family; and so too did his work on the night shift at the San Jose tire shop. After the initial unease of adjustment he seemed to settle down despite being forbidden to leave the county (which meant no racetracks), and Carolyn was able to take her children on a trip to Michigan to see her parents, siblings, and in-laws without worrying too much about what he would get up to in her absence. Her parents had read about Neal's imprisonment in *Life* magazine and responded icily and uncomprehendingly to what he had done; it was not in their nature to discuss such things openly, but their cold disapproval was palpable. In other respects Carolyn's visit was pleasant enough and rekindled many happy memories of her Michigan childhood.

Back in Los Gatos at the end of July Carolyn received a boisterous evening visit from Jack Kerouac and some of his colorful buddies who were unknown to her. At one point they showed up at a local Italian restaurant that was unprepared for a rowdy party of men variously attired as lumberjacks and beach bums, one of whom was apparently a Barnum & Bailey circus roustabout.

A night visit to the tire shop generated the kind of wonderment in the group that most people felt when they saw Neal gripped by fast, reflexive, hard physical work. The incident was dramatized by Kerouac in *Big Sur* with Neal sporting his "Cody" identity and "Dave Wain" being the alias for poet Lew Welch, a San Francisco–based poet who had recently gained wider notice due to the rise of the beats: "There he is wearing goggles working like Vulcan at his forge, throwing tires all over the place with fantastic strength, the good ones high up on a pile, 'This one's no good' down on another, bing, bang, talking all the time a long fantastic lecture on tire recapping which has Dave Wain marvel with amazement—('My God he can do all that and even explain while he's doing it')—but I just mention in connection with the fact that Dave Wain now realizes why I've always loved Cody—expecting to see a bitter ex-con he sees instead a martyr of the American Night in goggles in some dreary tire shop at 2 AM making fellows laugh with joy with his funny explanations yet at the same time to a T performing every bit of the work he's being paid for—Rushing up and ripping tires off car wheels with a jicklo, clang, throwing it on the machine, starting up big roaring steams but yelling explanations over that, darting, bending, flinging, flaying, till Dave Wain said he thought he was going to die laughing or crying right there on the spot."

Then Jack lured Neal off to Big Sur for a weekend with Carolyn's blessing (no one seemed to remember that this out-of-county trip violated Neal's parole). Afterward Neal dutifully returned to Los Gatos, and over the course of a few days so did various members of the informal community that orbited around the Big Sur cabin.

One night at home in Los Gatos Carolyn finally met Jacqueline Gibson. She was reluctantly produced by Jack, who was concerned that Neal would disapprove of Carolyn getting to meet her, even though Jacqueline now appeared to have been "transferred" from Neal to him. Jacqueline had a small child in tow and Jack had intended to leave her outside in the car on a cold night rather than risk a confrontation. There was no confrontation since Carolyn's first instinct was always to be friendly to Neal's other women; only Diana Hansen had tested her consideration beyond endurance.

Laid off from the San Jose tire shop because the owner was having financial difficulties, Neal asked Jack, now a relatively wealthy man, for a loan, which Jack was pleased to give him. The money was hand delivered to him by a posse comprising Jack and his friends who this time included Victor Wong, the artist son of a wealthy San Francisco Chinese family, poet Philip Whalen, and Lawrence Ferlinghetti, publisher, poet, famous victor in the *Howl* obscenity trial, and now the owner of a cabin he had built himself in Big Sur.

Neal need not have worried about the money because almost at once a local firm, the Los Gatos Tire Company, agreed to hire him on the recommendation of a friend. With day-shift hours and now working close to home, Neal seemed to be firmly back on track. His driver's license was restored, so the Cassadys traded in the ailing Nash Rambler and bought a jeep. One weekend the whole family traveled in it to Ferlinghetti's Big Sur cabin where, among the other guests, were the poet Michael McClure and his wife Joanna. The Cassadys spent a lazy and disjointed weekend at Big Sur, a couple of days that, like so many other fragments of their lives, would soon resurface in one of Jack's books. In this case it would be the eponymous *Big Sur* (1962), which contains Jack's assessment of the newly released Neal: "I expect him to be all bitter and out of his head because of this but strangely and magnificently he's become quieter, more radiant, more patient, manly, more friendly even—and tho the wild frenzies of his old road days with me have banked down he still has the same taut eager face and supple muscles and looks like he's ready to go anytime—But actually loves his home, loves his wife in a way tho they fight some, loves his kids."

After the weekend at the cabin they all drifted apart again. That summer marked the end of any possibility of Carolyn's reprising her muted romance with the now celebrated author of *On the Road.* In fact, although they would keep in touch by phone and letter, it was the last time Carolyn would ever see him.

• • •

By 1961 there were signs that the routine of life on parole in Los Gatos was getting Neal Cassady down. He would work at the tire shop and live with his family all week, and then take off for San Francisco and wild times on the weekends. The old pattern was being reestablished, though Neal had lost none of his fascination with the Caycean brand of Christianity. With two years left to run on his parole he was now regularly leaving his county of residence and sometimes openly smoking marijuana. But he also acquired another nickname—"The Preacher"—for the enthusiasm with which he would quote Cayce to anyone who would listen . . . and some who would not. It seemed that the exaltation of spiritual commitment had joined Neal's other obsessions for the long haul. In a sense it was a contradiction, this preoccupation with spirituality in a man driven by thrill-seeking and pleasures of the flesh. Looked at another way it was not. Neal Cassady did nothing by halves. He brought extreme vigor to physical work; he developed extreme skills to underpin his frighteningly fast driving; he declared extreme love for his children and his wife; he demonstrated extreme passion in his writing; and he attributed extreme importance to the religious principles he had adopted. Neal's overriding appetite was really for none of these things, but for extremism itself. His almost preternatural talent for transfixing everyone who ever met him really derived from the spectacle of larger-than-life human desires and aspirations being exuberantly embraced and expressed. Needless to say, none of Neal's appetites was greater than his extreme hunger for sexual adventure. To rail against Neal's sexual promiscuity was, as Carolyn found out too late, futile. It was an indivisible part of the man and it was impervious to reform. If no single sexual relationship in itself ever really changed Neal's life, one or two did coincide with the start of a new phase or direction—as happened in February of 1961. That was when, at a bohemian San Francisco get-together one Saturday afternoon, in a crowded kitchen, Neal met the woman who was to be some sort of regular girlfriend for the next five or six years.

23

ANNE MARIE MAXWELL was born in May 1933 in Oakland, California. A high school aptitude for theater and the arts was matched by sufficient academic ability for her to be accepted by City College of San Francisco (CCSF) in 1950. While auditioning for a college production of *Othello* Anne met her future husband, Mervyn Joseph Murphy, Jr. The couple left school after Anne's second semester. They both took jobs, she in a credit office and he at the SPRR yards. They married in 1951 and she immediately became pregnant. When Mervyn began to suffer from depression the couple uneasily made the decision to have the child, a daughter, adopted. Deciding to complete their education, they both graduated from CCSF, after which Anne majored in art at the University of California at Berkeley. Following a brief foray to New York City (where Anne harbored a revealing ambition to become a Rockette at Radio City Music Hall), the couple returned to Northern California, took and failed at teaching jobs in rural communities for a while, and then in 1959 had another child, this time a son they named Grant.

The subsequent breakup of their troubled marriage was triggered by Anne's affair with another man, an old boyfriend named Burt.

Anne Murphy described what happened next in an interview for this book. "I had left my husband for Burt. He had been the first great love of my life and his wife was my best friend," she said. "When I left my husband, I didn't leave him just like that, he knew there was something wrong—he asked me and I told him. I moved out and Burt moved out, it was very painful, horrible and shattering. . . . Burt and I found an apartment on North Beach and he gave me his car—my first big old Buick—and then he went back to his family! And so that was that. I lived in this lovely apartment in North Beach and Burt continued to pay the rent."

Anne next tried to resume her painting career and while she was preparing for an exhibition, a friend brought over a visitor, a "black guy called David," Anne continued. "I guess he had no place to stay, and he just stayed with me, and pretty soon we were having an affair."

She became pregnant again, this time by David, resulting in an illegal abortion carried out in Montreal (David was from Canada). Afterward the couple moved to New York at his suggestion, but Anne soon returned to San Francisco, half hoping for reconciliation with Burt. It never happened, and then David left her and went back to Canada. With her son, Anne moved into the basement of the Bernal Heights home of a San Francisco poet, Robert Stock, and his wife Harriet. Their house was a well-known rallying point for writers and artists, and there were regular get-togethers marked by lively political and artistic discussions.

"I had been shooting methamphetamine—I mean, I never said no to anything," recalled Anne. "I had to be a hip chick or something . . . anyway, when somebody handed me a needle they had just used, I got hepatitis."

It was in this exhausted state that she first encountered Neal Cassady.

In her erratic magazine memoir entitled "Traveling with the Tripmaster," Anne Murphy wrote "The first time I saw Neal was across the crowded Stock kitchen one Saturday afternoon . . . in 1961. He was on his weekly, weekend City quest from his Los Gatos home for drugs, kicks and women.

"In that intellectual, bohemian gathering Neal stood out like a 500 watt light bulb; so magnetic, clean cut, classically handsome, muscularly lean, clearly intelligent and sexy, with wavy blond hair, fair skin, blazing blue eyes and a full sensuous mouth, modestly clad in the clean white 'T' shirt and 501's that were to become his archetypical uniform, Neal Cassady was, in short, a hunk!" (One of Carolyn's perennial gripes is that for some reason Neal Cassady is frequently misremembered—and in movies usually miscast—as having blond hair.)

Anne and Neal began a five-year affair that would owe a lot to her willingness to be dominated by an assertive and sometimes openly sadistic sexual partner.

With his life split between domestic Los Gatos and the San Francisco drugs-and-sex scene, Neal was in a state of uneasy equilibrium during most of 1961. He carried on working, although his pay at the tire shop was far lower than what he had been used to getting on the SPRR. He spent more and more time betting at the track, driven by an illogical belief that the track "owed" him money for past losses.

Homebound Carolyn was diverted by designing and sewing costumes for the ballet school and the occasional university play, but at heart she felt like an abandoned wife who was still troubled by her own variable responses to the emotional and spiritual challenges posed by her husband.

In June Neal's father sent another of the clumsy letters that always made Neal wince and then fondly laugh at their mix of syntactical errors, inept spellings, and muddled declarations of affection. This time Neal Sr. reported that he had suffered some minor strokes and the loss of his sister Emma. "[S]he was the only mother I even [*sic*] had & my 3 brothers died so that out of 7 of us there is only 1 left the one that fixed us fried chicken for us."

In response Neal went on a two-week vacation to Denver to see his father in August 1961, taking along a notebook with a view to expanding some of the elements of *The First Third*'s prologue with new impressions. Unfortunately, we have no details about this trip.

Then in October, rather unexpectedly, the media took renewed interest in Neal Cassady. This time it was TV. Although Neal's normal response to his unsought notoriety as a character in Kerouac's novels was one of annoyance, he went along with a request to appear in an episode of the Westinghouse TV series *PM West* dedicated to "The Beatnik Poets" and hosted by Terrence O'Flaherty (the episode does not survive). (The word *beatnik* had been coined by Herb Caen, a disapproving *San Francisco Chronicle* journalist, as an echo of the newsworthy Russian "sputnik" satellite, launched on October 4, 1957.) Also appearing on the *PM West* program were Pierre DeLattre, Shigeyoshi Murao (who had been arrested for selling *Howl* when he was the manager of City Lights), and Eileen Kauffman. Neal was paid twenty-four dollars for his appearance.

At around the same time Neal was introduced by some Stanford University students to Perry Lane, a bohemian district of the town adjacent to the campus, Palo Alto. Neal's initial connection with Palo Alto had been through a friend named Bradley Hodgman, a young Stanford tennis scholarship student who lived there and had been known to procure coeds for Neal. Neal and Anne would use Bradley's apartment when he was out of town and often ferry him and his girlfriend back and forth to San Francisco when he was not on tour. On such occasions Anne recalled that they would all wondrously watch Neal "roll a perfect joint with one blunt-fingered hand while the other one steered, shifted, kept the beat to the radio's rhythm 'n' blues and gestured to his non-stop monologue."

In retrospect it is clear that this was the start of the period when Neal Cassady was leaving behind the beat culture of the 1950s and about to become part of the very different counterculture of the 1960s. Nothing marks that shift more clearly than the music he listened to. Bop and jazz provided the soundtrack to his glory days with Kerouac. Now it was rock 'n' roll, rhythm 'n' blues, and soul. In one of Anne Murphy's several lapses into explicit nostalgia that borders on pornography, she wrote of a sex session with Neal in which "Neal fucked to the beat" of a Little Stevie Wonder song on the bedroom radio. Somehow it seems like a strange mood shift from the Neal that John Clellon Holmes wrote about nodding furiously and shouting "Go, go, go!" to a bebop recording in jazz-mad New York City. But Neal, it would seem, was not a dedicated fan of any one genre of music, he simply gravitated toward the prevailing sounds of dissent. From Charlie Parker and Slim Gaillard to Jerry Lee Lewis and the Grateful Dead, Neal would always like the music that sounded to him like a one-finger salute to popular mainstream tastes. Anne particularly remembered a cross-country road trip that took them within range of Wolfman Jack's legendary broadcasts out of Mexico, and how Neal especially loved Lewis, Chuck Berry, and Little Richard. "Remember 'Old Mother Lender' (who was a solid sender)?" Murphy wrote, only approximating the actual lyric ("Oh Malinda") to Neal's favorite Little Richard number, "Slippin' and Slidin'."

Gradually, during the course of late 1961 and early 1962, a new center of operations emerged for Neal. Palo Alto not only had nubile coeds, it had Bradley's apartment, which was very convenient for trysts. Neal now had ambitions to relocate Anne and her son permanently to a room in that apartment. It finally happened, but not before the endgame of his marriage to Carolyn had played out. And before that happened, Palo Alto acquired yet another attraction, a charismatic man whose reputation, like Neal's, preceded him but who, unlike Neal, had already published a novel.

• • •

Ken Kesey, the younger of two sons, was born on September 17, 1935, in La Junta, Colorado. Nine years younger than Neal Cassady, his background and upbringing could hardly have been more different from Cassady's violent and lawless childhood in the slums of Denver. In 1946 Kesey's parents moved to a farm near Springfield in the Willamette Valley, Oregon, there establishing a stable, religious household in which eleven-year-old Ken seemed happy and destined for a settled life in the Pacific Northwest. A youthful obsession with superhero comic books—*Superman* and *The Eternity Kid* were favorites—complemented his fascination with Christian allegories, perhaps giving early notice of a creative mentality. Meanwhile, his high school and college progress established him as a steady, diligent achiever. The well-built young man became a champion wrestler, a good student, and a lover of the theater while being almost routinely voted most likely to succeed. And succeed he would, although when it came, Kesey's success was hardly the kind that Eisenhower's America might easily embrace.

An early hint of rebellion surfaced when he eloped with his high school sweetheart, Faye Haxby, with whom he would subsequently have three children. However, he dutifully attended the University of Oregon, where he took a degree in speech and communications, subsequently receiving a Woodrow Wilson Fellowship to enroll in the creative writing program at Stanford University (motto: "The Wind of Freedom Blows").

The late 1950s and early '60s was a vibrant time for Stanford when, under the presidency of J. E. Wallace Sterling, a Cold War–inspired surge in federal support for research was helping to promote the university from regional to national prominence. Stanford attracted and maintained groups of outstanding researchers who in turn attracted first-rate students. Later in the 1960s, political activism would divide the campus as the wind of freedom blew more gustily than perhaps originally intended by the institution's founders, but in Kesey's early days there, the driving spirit was still one of confident new expansion and well-funded research programs.

In 1959, to earn extra money, Kesey took part in government-funded "psychotomimetic" drug experiments at the local VA hospital in Menlo Park, another town adjacent to Stanford. Participants met one evening a week and were paid twenty dollars a session. "They gave me something," Kesey recalled. "They didn't tell me what. And they tested my reflexes and they tested my blood and how I was breathing . . . just whether I could do motor skills. Then they left me in this little room with only one window."

The chemicals, it turned out, included psilocybin, mescaline, and lysergic acid diethylamide (LSD); Kesey's exposure to them ran parallel with the development of his Stanford writing project and immediately preceded his employment as a night orderly in the psychiatric ward of the Menlo Park VA hospital. At the time he and his family were already living the proto-hippie life in the Perry Lane neighborhood. Its old housing was left over from World War I when Stanford Farm had been taken over for military training and shotgun shacks hastily erected. Those shacks had later grown into a Bohemian village occupied by artists, writers, and others trying to live cheaply for whatever reason. Later still, as Stanford expanded, more students moved in. Among them were the Keseys.

In February 1962 Ken Kesey's university writing project, now a novel titled *One Flew Over the Cuckoo's Nest*, was published to national acclaim. It rapidly established him as a hip new writer whose signature work would later be converted into a hit play with Kirk Douglas and then later still into a hit film starring Jack Nicholson in the central role of Randle Patrick McMurphy. The novel deals with the patients and workers in a mental institution. Through the eyes of a native American narrator is told the story of individualist McMurphy, a man who has sought institutionalization as a means of escaping the rigors of a prison work farm only to become locked in a doomed conflict with the authorities. Ultimately, McMurphy becomes the martyred rebel who inspires an unquenchable appetite for liberty in others.

In a nice example of art imitating an unknown reality, Kesey's invention, the life-affirming character of McMurphy (whose R.P.M. initials were interpreted by some, in those early days of vinyl records and easy symbolism, as code for the drug speed), eerily echoed Cassady's powerful personality with its magnetic charm, its laid-back disdain for authority, and its visceral belief in personal freedom. Kesey and Cassady had never met, but each had heard of the other. When Kesey returned from a trip to Oregon in the spring of 1962, a pivotal meeting would take place at Perry Lane. Neal went to introduce himself to the fêted author of *One Flew Over the Cuckoo's Nest.*

He did it with typical panache, as Kesey was to recall in an interview for this book not long before his death: "Everybody already knew Cassady before they ever met him. A lot of people were there in that area

[Stanford] because of him. I had read *On the Road.* I'd also read *Visions of Cody* [a portion of which had been published by New Directions in 1960]. All of the action was swirling around Cassady. The writers all wrote about him, the hangers-on all hung around with him. His presence was known to me soon after we moved to the San Francisco area and started Stanford. He came swirling into my yard there at Perry Lane driving a jeep. It just fell apart right in my yard and he was out of the thing, working on it, giving orders, telling people what he needed and where to stand—he just took over that whole neighborhood."

Before too long their lives—the driver and the driven, the life-force and the compulsive arch-prankster—would become even more closely intertwined in one of the most famous and ambitious happenings of the 1960s counterculture.

• • •

Intentionally or otherwise Neal was in the process of precipitating the final confrontation in his long marriage of attrition with stoical Carolyn. It was not that he was suddenly doing anything uncharacteristic—quite the opposite in fact, and therein lay the problem. Carolyn, who was now approaching forty and—despite having devised many ingenious psychological and spiritual tricks for surviving a fifteen-year marital roller-coaster ride—was now, at last, considering a divorce to be followed by marriage to the kind of man her family thought she ought to have been with in the first place.

There was of course a final straw in her deteriorating relationship with Neal, who was now eighteen months out of San Quentin and into his three-year parole. Like most final straws it was in itself a comparatively trivial incident that became the flashpoint for an insupportable accumulation of grievances.

Early in the fall of 1962, with Neal's active encouragement, Carolyn had taken the children to a weeklong Cayce conference in the California resort of Pacific Grove. There she attended Elsie Sechrist's meditation classes while the children went swimming or beachcombing. Refreshed spiritually and physically, mother and children returned home to find what Carolyn later characterized with mordant wit as "a macabre version of Goldilocks and the Three Bears."

In the family's absence Neal had put little Grant in his own son's room to play while he took Anne Murphy into the Cassady bedroom where, according to Anne, he instructed her in the correct techniques for stimulating his penis with her hand, for performing fellatio, and, less successfully, for participating in cunnilingus, something she did not want to do because she was menstruating. In the end, running out of time after their exertions, they had to make a very hasty departure from the family home before the family returned.

This was why Carolyn and the children got back to find unwashed, bloodstained bed sheets stuffed in the washing machine, and son Johnny's race car set, a much-prized gift from Neal, trashed and scattered around. In a sudden redundant but painful insight, Carolyn recalled once being mistaken by a man in the Los Gatos tire shop for another woman who had a young son. "This woman and her son must have been Neal's weekend guests," she now surmised, grimly and correctly.

When Neal returned, Carolyn simply announced it was time for a divorce and indicated that she was considering marrying the owner of a local music store but would, of course, wait until the deadline for Neal's parole arrived before filing. For once—and at last—she followed through. Neal appeared to accept her decision as inevitable. He continued to live at the Los Gatos home and work at the Los Gatos Tire Service; he also finally moved Anne and Grant Murphy into Brad Hodgman's apartment in East Palo Alto.

Four days before the end of Neal's parole, Carolyn filed for the divorce that would become final a year later in 1964; and then came the end of the parole itself, the conditional release the conditions of which Neal had repeatedly violated without penalty. He decided to celebrate with a road trip. His father fell seriously ill and so Neal decided to take a vacation from work and travel to see him as the first leg of a longer trip. Accompanying him would be Bradley Hodgman and Anne Murphy. In fact, they set off too late, as a letter Neal wrote to Carolyn from Denver on July 21 was to reveal: "Well, my father died the same afternoon I left to go and see him, but the trip was necessary—to get him buried et al. He left no money, so I had to sign papers & all to get him buried in the Holy Catholic Church. The priest will say a mass for his soul on Tues. I'm driving east to take Brad to NY. Will write soon."

The trio pressed on from Denver to Lansing, Michigan, and from there to see Jack Kerouac in Northport, Long Island, where Neal borrowed ten dollars and his friends were rather coolly received. Carolyn got to hear about this in a letter from Kerouac who wrote that Neal, despite bringing along some unwelcome, "boorish" hangers-on, "was as sweet and gentle and polite and intelligent and interesting as he ever was with me or anyone else he's ever liked." The rest of Kerouac's letter sounded world-weary, suggesting that he probably already suspected he was a spent force.

Meanwhile Neal Cassady's power to charm and inspire seemed intact and was now beginning to look as if it might actually be indestructible. Now it was he, not Kerouac, who had the entourage of admiring fans, and it was clear that he was once again ready and willing to perform his amazing one-man consciousness-raising show for any and all who came within his orbit. Cassady now had less than five years to live, and although given to occasional morbid utterances like "You know I'm not going to be here very long" when seeking sympathy, at the age of thirty-seven he might reasonably have expected to survive long enough to enjoy at least some of the Last Third. In any event, with Kerouac in apparent decline, "the real Dean Moriarty" was about to reinvent himself as a cultural guru one last, dazzling time.

In August 1963 Neal and Anne moved into a bohemian house on Gough Street, San Francisco, an address where he had once lived with Natalie and just around the corner from the Franklin Street building where she had died. Neal found work at yet another tire shop job, this time on the city's Van Ness Avenue. He would occasionally mail money to Carolyn, whose replies to him were unfailingly pleasant and courteous; her only perceptible lingering interest in him seemed to be that he should share more experiences with his children. She particularly wanted him to hear a tape recording of a reading for his daughter Jami by a Dr. Neva Dell Hunter, a Caycean "channel" for a seventh-plane teacher. Neal himself had been subjected to Caycean readings prior to moving out that summer but had been much disturbed by the lurid drama and ongoing resonance of his supposed past lives. He had been, he was told, a Bedouin prince bent on revenge who was fatally stabbed by his own son; in another life he had been castrated for rape, and had then assumed an alias and gone on to amass a fortune; in Babylon he apparently orchestrated evil on an almost industrial scale; in China he became a drug-crazed masochist who eventually killed his own brother while under the influence of opium; and in yet another troubled incarnation he had been instrumental in his own son's death after attaching knives to his chariot wheels.

In his present life Neal Cassady demonstrated that he was willing to indulge Anne Murphy, who seemed resentful about not being a part of his Caycean world. Accordingly he took her for a reading of her own to a psychiatrist and a "channel associate" in Los Angeles where the spiritually impressionable woman, who was already inclined to define people primarily in astrological terms, remained unimpressed. "It seemed to me that my own subconscious was dictating the words to [the channel] and I was disappointed that it wasn't Cayce's venerable Akashic Records she was consulting," she wrote of the visit.

At the Gough Street house, already populated with a number of transients and artistic types, Neal and Anne were joined by Allen Ginsberg and Peter Orlovsky toward the end of 1963. Returning to San Francisco after a tour of Asia, Allen and Peter had first been staying with Lawrence Ferlinghetti, and after they transferred to Gough Street Allen sometimes helped Neal with money for Carolyn. At this time Anne was typing sections of *The First Third* while Neal dictated. Despite the years and effort spent on it, Neal's autobiography would in the end never amount to more than about 138 printed pages, and early versions of it were much shorter. His hopes for it, however, were once again robust.

In January of 1964 Neal met a literary editor, John Bryan, whose magazine *Notes from Underground* (a reference to Dostoyevsky's diary-like novel of introspective self-hatred) would publish the surviving portion of Neal's "Joan Anderson" letter. The circumstances surrounding loss of that letter's greater portion are still unknown, but it had already been depleted by 1964 when Neal helped Bryan run off copies of the magazine that contained the shortened version. At last Neal Cassady was a published writer.

• • •

By the summer of 1964 Ken and Fay Kesey had moved to a cabin on a sprawling estate at La Honda, overlooking Palo Alto. It was a move made possible by the commercial success of *One Flew Over the Cuckoo's Nest.* Some Perry Lane cohorts and assorted outsiders moved in as well, or at least became loosely attached to the new informal community. They became known as the Merry Pranksters and the settlement began to rival—and then eclipse—Perry Lane's reputation for all manner of happenings, drug parties, and experimental activities. There Kesey began throwing parties where guests would ingest LSD, sometimes without their knowledge, while the encircling woods were daubed with luminous paint and dissonant music blasted from several hidden outdoor speakers. Kesey constantly pushed the limits with his experiments and would eventually move the "acid tests," as he called the drug parties, to public venues up and down the West Coast.

In the midst of this—and in what must have been a heroic exercise in concentration—Kesey had already succeeded in writing a second novel, *Sometimes a Great Notion*, which was soon to be published. Neal was a frequent visitor to La Honda and therefore was among the first to hear about an ambitious new project Kesey was planning: a trip to coincide with his second book's publication.

Kesey got it into his head to put together a group road trip to visit the 1964 World's Fair in Flushing, New York. This ambition may or may not have been prompted by the theme of his new novel, which pitted the individualism of the West Coast against the intellectualism of the East Coast, but somehow an epic cross-country drive, linking the two coasts if not the two concepts, became an irresistible communal ambition. Kenneth Babbs, who would have been Kesey's first lieutenant in the Merry Pranksters if such a title existed, was another enthusiastic promoter of the trip.

George Walker, another of the coalescing group of Merry Pranksters, recalled that "Kesey continued to promote the idea of a trip to the World's Fair, and quite a number of his friends were interested. Too many, it turned out, for any one vehicle available. We talked about my station wagon and Ken Babbs's Volkswagen van/pickup, and maybe even a third car to accommodate everyone. Then Kesey and I took a trip to Eugene/Springfield to visit our families, where we found our inspiration. The city of Eugene had quit the transit business. There were no more city buses. Instead, a private company had bought up several small used school buses, with seating capacities of fifteen to twenty people, painted them emerald green (for the Emerald Empire, as the area is known), and taken over the bus routes. It was a great success; people loved the little buses. They caught our attention too. If we had one of those little buses, I told Kesey, we could all go to New York in one vehicle. That would be a lot more fun. 'Great idea,' Kesey said. 'Find one and I'll buy it.'"

He did buy one—for $1,500—using some of the proceeds from his first novel. The original yellow vehicle had already been partly converted for communal living, but further modifications by the Merry Pranksters transferred something of the trappings of the La Honda settlement to a 1939 International Harvester school bus. Part transportation and part cultural battering ram, the bus soon acquired a luminous psychedelic paint job incorporating various whirling ritualistic designs to grab the attention. It was fitted with external speakers to broadcast whatever sounds seemed appropriate at the time, a rough observation/performance platform on the roof from which to play instruments and otherwise incite passersby, external microphones to capture the sounds of the outraged citizenry, and a movie camera and sound recorders to preserve the event. Finally, serendipitously employing alternative spelling to echo the alternative nature of the enterprise, the destination panel was inscribed "Furthur."

This psychically disturbed vehicle would need a driver. It was the role for which Neal Cassady was both practically and spiritually predestined. He could drive anything. His entire adult life resembled a sustained piece of performance art that had never needed stage props. Equipped only with good looks, a brilliant mind, and a fluent tongue, he could work a room of total strangers and become their leader in minutes through sheer charisma. Just think what he could achieve behind the wheel of a bus that looked like it was moving even when it was stationary! He would be the pilot of a mobile home full of spaced-out followers tracing a jagged trajectory across the strait-laced Lyndon Johnson–led USA. It was Kesey's idea but it was Cassady who would be in the driver's seat—in every sense. Ken Babbs would later say, "Cassady was the real link. Kesey and I fell into the crack between the beats and the psychedelic generation."

24

THE NOTORIOUS cross-country bus trip has always resisted clear analysis. If Tom Wolfe's *The Electric Kool-Aid Acid Test* is the most famous prose account, it is not the only one. In a way, there were almost as many trips as Pranksters, since they would all put a personal spin on the journey for years after. Not everyone's memory was good, and some people, in the end, were so impaired by drug abuse that they could barely remember their own names. None of this diminishes the potency of their impressions, some of which offered truly vivid glimpses of Neal Cassady in action. Even so, it is worth pointing out that as far as Cassady was concerned, the legendary cross-country bus trip lasted barely eleven days; he bailed out in New York and returned to California by car. His part of the whole adventure had always been intended to fit into a two-week vacation from work; he missed his deadline by two days only because on the return trip he made a diversion to see Anne Murphy in Oregon.

Ken Babbs (nickname: Intrepid Traveler) wrote a semifictional account of Cassady arriving in La Honda to take up his driving duties for the trip. After a caveat in the form of a William Faulkner quote, "Truth is more than a mere recounting of the facts," Babbs said that he used tape recordings to get Cassady's speech right:

> An unhesitant swerve and the car went across the bridge heading toward the frightened knot of people who scurried for safety behind the bus. They screamed as they ran:
>
> "No, no you can't fit through there!"
>
> "There's two cars in the way!"
>
> "He's trying to jockey through that enormously tiny space!"
>
> "Damn, right between them!"

> "The best driver I've ever seen," George [Walker] begrudgingly conceded. "He can really handle a car."
>
> Dust settled on the driveway. The radio blared: "I've got a little bottle of . . . love potion number nine . . ."
>
> "It was eight to five your getting through there," Kesey said, saluting him with the fire extinguisher; a couple of squirts for decoration.
>
> "Pshaw, nothing to it," Cassady snorted. Smoke blew out his nose. He ground the Camel butt under his heel . . .
>
> . . . He chucked his canvas bag into the bus and walked toward the tires, hammer in hand, checking the rubber and poundage . . . he stopped short, shocked. "What's this? Oh, good gawd, no! Don't paint the tires! Even that piece of glitter there." He scraped it off with his fingernail. "Someone trying to undermine us," he muttered . . . Cassady jumped aboard and hit the starter. The engine roared to life . . . The engine stalled . . . Cassady ground . . . The motor coughed. Then it caught.
>
> "Board," Cassady yelled. "All aboard!"

Jane Burton (nickname: Generally Famished) offered some more prosaic impressions of the trip: "Everything was always screwed up. The bus didn't run very well and we got lost all the time and the equipment always broke down. We kept the money in a plastic sack and it was always getting lost. We had all the acid in the orange juice and somebody guzzled half of it at once. Then we brought along all those movie cameras. We got some good pictures of Neal. He was a good driver but bad on routes. No one paid much attention to how to get from one place to another. Then we got stuck in the mud in Arizona, which was fairly typical, not that we got stuck in the mud a lot, but we were having those kinds of problems. Neal loved every minute of it."

The trip began on June 14, 1964, with the following assumed objectives: to visit the World's Fair in Flushing Meadows, New York;

to get to Manhattan to help promote Kesey's new novel; and to visit Timothy Leary who was currently sequestered in a large house in upstate New York. The itinerary, if it could be said to exist in any formal sense, was encapsulated by Kesey when he was asked, en route, where they were going. "La Honda," he replied. Where did they start from? Same answer. "La Honda."

In fact from La Honda they traveled via Arizona and Texas, calling on Kesey's friend, author Larry McMurtry, in Houston, Texas. (McMurtry was rather nonplussed by the arrival of the troupe, especially Prankster Katrina Daniels [nickname: Stark Naked] who justified her alias by emerging nude from the bus and clasping one of the McMurtry children to her bosom under the hallucinogenic impression that he was one of her own. "Ma'am! Ma'am! Just a minute ma'am!" remonstrated the author of *Lonesome Dove* and *The Last Picture Show.*)

By June 21 they were in New Orleans (where they got into a near-violent confrontation with some black swimmers at Lake Pontchartrain by stumbling, spaced-out and unaware, into a segregated swimming area), finally arriving in New York City on June 25.

Throughout, the main agenda was determined by the Pranksters' desire to go out and make a noise and to challenge straight America on the streets simply by their behavior—"tootling," they called it, a kind of playful goading by outrageous example. In one instance they filmed their vehicle's progress through Phoenix, Arizona, the hometown of Barry Goldwater, who was campaigning at the time. Neal drove the bus in reverse down the town's main drag with "A Vote for Barry Is a Vote for Fun" painted on the bus's side.

On the trip the company would provide itself with a famous metaphor. As Tom Wolfe recountes, you were either "on the bus or off the bus." Although at first this phrase was quite literally applied to waverers who might become uncertain as to whether their minds and metabolisms could survive the entire round trip, it soon took on a broader meaning: are you part of our counterculture or not? Are you with us or against us? The bus supplied a neat physical symbol for making a decision. There was no in-between. You were either on the bus or off it . . . especially when Cassady was driving in his characteristic hell-on-wheels style. To amphetamine-fueled Cassady, sleeping seemed like a luxury to be indulged in only occasionally. His nickname was Sir Speed Limit.

"I'm responsible for nothing past seventeen inches to the right of the driver's seat," he once announced to a group of inquisitive bystanders. "I never use the right-hand rearview mirror anyway. I have nothing to do with that door." Above another door was a rubric that read "The Cogs of Infinity," reflecting the fact that this bus was offering a more metaphysical kind of ride than the kind that simply advises "Watch Your Step."

"You should have seen me when we started," said Cassady later. "I never used earphones before. Roland Kirk blasting away on those tapes and me jumping up and down with the music, driving the bus!"

Kesey was The Chief, but Cassady was The Star. His reputation preceded him, but for added street-theater effect Neal had developed the knack of juggling with a four-pound half jackhammer, the hefty tool he used to test tire pressures ("jackhammer" normally connotes an impact tool with a chisel point so this may be a regional name for what Tom Wolfe identified as a Williams Lok-Hed sledge hammer but what everyone else in Cassady's circle invariably referred to as a jackhammer). Still lean and muscular and with no body fat, Neal was several times photographed during the trip stripped to the waist, spinning that hammer in the air and catching it, usually with at least one adoring young woman looking on. But by now he was juggling with more than hardware—he was gambling with his own physical assets. Ironically those monochrome photographs, unlike the largely unwatchable out-of-focus color movie footage shot on the trip, missed the thrill of the moment when Cassady's fast-talking, reflexive movement and sheer dynamic presence distracted everyone from the one thing that the still camera would freeze: his face. It was now showing signs of the mileage its owner had put in. At thirty-eight, Neal Cassady's features made him look many years older, despite the fact that his physique was still taut and muscular. (Tom Wolfe characterized this duality of appearance in terms of drug usage: "there are two Cassadys. One minute Cassady looks 58 and crazy—speed!—and the next, 28 and peaceful—acid—and Sandy [Lehman-Haupt, nickname Dismount] can tell the peaceful Cassady in an instant, because his nose becomes . . . long and smooth and patrician, whereas the wild Cassady looks beat-up.")

When not under the influence of acid, in real hyperactive life Cassady was rarely still long enough for anyone to dwell on his face in repose, and so his youthful vitality appeared to be undiminished, his encyclopedic knowledge of facts greater than ever, his machine-gun rap unstoppable, his brain still firing on all cylinders. He was definitely on the bus.

If many of the details are forever blurred, the trip did have two quasi-historic moments on which most people agree. Both were anticlimaxes and therefore provide a salutary reminder that historic occasions and memorable ones are not necessarily the same things.

In terms of Cassady's pivotal role, there was a portentous meeting in Manhattan that should have been one for the popular culture history books. Upon Furthur's arrival in New York, Neal Cassady, Jack Kerouac, Allen Ginsberg, and Ken Kesey all met at a party in a borrowed apartment at Madison and 90th. Author and screenwriter Terry Southern was there too . . . or so it appeared until he turned out to be an amiable imposter. What a tableau! Here was Cassady—the dynamo, the catalyst, the inspiration—standing with yesterday's beat icon on one side of him and the emergent primordial hippie on the other. Ginsberg, the independent high-priest poet, seeker of truth, and all-round mystic, was on hand to complete the picture. But individually the potency of these men lay in the eyes of their followers, and together they were a mismatch. This awkward mingling of counterculture party guests probably differed little from innumerable other uncomfortable social occasions where people whom others imagine will find one another fascinating simply do not.

The second almost-historic meeting took place soon afterward when, promotional duties done in the city, the bus struck out up the Hudson Valley toward Millbrook, New York, an hour and a half drive from Manhattan.

Millbrook, in Dutchess County, was home to the Castalia Foundation, the creation of Timothy Leary, who had succeeded in persuading a wealthy and sympathetic New York family to turn over their rambling Victorian house and estate to him and his organization. According to Tom Wolfe, upon their arrival there, the Pranksters received a decidedly cool reception from Leary's people and so they responded by going California crazy, with Ken Babbs conducting an impromptu mock tour of the main house, a Gothic structure, which he had, of course, never even seen before. Leary himself, the heavyweight spiritual detective, declined to appear at all; it was alleged that he was in the middle of a very serious, three-day experiment upstairs. Thirty years later, however, Leary implied he had merely been delayed by illness in New York City, returned to Millbrook after the Pranksters' arrival, and socialized with them there after resting. Allen Ginsberg also identified a picture of Cassady and Leary on the bus as dating from the Millbrook trip.

At any rate, Leary's philosophy of nonconfrontational withdrawal from society was intrinsically at odds with Kesey's preferred strategy of acting out dissent in the most theatrical way possible, so there was to be no future alliance between the Castalia Foundation and the Pranksters.

At this point Neal left the trip in the company of Prankster Ron Bevirt (nickname: The Equipment Hassler), a photographer who was about to become part-owner of a bookstore in Santa Cruz. Neal picked up his own car which had been brought along by Brad Hodgman, and, after a detour to the Oregon coast to meet with Anne Murphy, returned to San Francisco. He was two days late getting back, and he was fired from the tire shop. However, as luck would have it, he was immediately hired by Ron Bevirt to work at the Santa Cruz bookstore.

This biography began with a correction to an apocryphal legend involving a vehicle: Cassady's mythical birth in a makeshift motorized covered wagon in Utah. At this point it may be worth pointing out that his involvement with the great trans-America trip has also been the subject of considerable fable and exaggeration. As ever, the impact of his presence was disproportionately large because of his extraordinary personality, but his one-way stint on the bus did little to suggest that he was particularly in tune with the underlying spirit of the immediate proceedings. By now Cassady had enjoyed a lifetime of creative unruliness, and therefore, superficially at least, he seemed to fit into the mobile mayhem perfectly. "What we didn't know," reflected Kenneth Babbs later, "was that the thing we were just barely starting to explore—coming on in a dramatic, meaningful way—was the thing Cassady had been doing for years."

Yet Cassady's natural terrain was the more ordered event—the party, the get-together, the one-on-one—where he could take charge simply by the power of his presence, through his hypnotic raps and on waves of sexual charisma. On the chaotic trip to New York there was no shortage of big egos and personality disorders, all exaggerated by drug use, but there was also no convention against which to rail, no time to draw breath, and no blank canvas on which Cassady might inscribe the mesmerizing signs and symbols of his own worldview. His most memorable moment on the trip came in Virginia when, stoned and at the wheel of the bus, he decided to freewheel his human cargo down a steep and potentially lethal serpentine road from the top of the Blue Ridge Mountains, sans brakes. Kesey, like a spaced-out tank commander, protruded from the top of the swerving bus, allegedly unfazed by the spectacular risk Cassady was taking with everyone's lives. Tom Wolfe, who was not there, described the incident as one in which no one panicked because they feared their terror might prove infectious for Cassady, who might then also panic and lose his miraculously intuitive death-defying skills.

"[Kesey] had total faith in Cassady, but it was more than faith," Wolfe wrote. "It was as if Cassady, at the wheel, was in a state of satori, as totally into this very moment, Now, as a being can get, and for that moment they all shared it."

In fact Wolfe's mystical overlay to a typical Cassady hell-on-wheels druggy drive now sounds a little overly intellectualized, and perhaps a more revealing insight into the on-the-road relationship between Kesey and Cassady is suggested by a reminiscence from Larry "Ramrod" Shurtliff, later a Grateful Dead roadie who would be part of several Merry Prankster trips in Mexico around 1966. He recalled that on one occasion Kesey admonished Cassady, who was driving the bus in a series of fast swerves intended to miss the worst ruts and bumps on a rural road leading out of Mexico City, "Quit trying to miss those bumps!"

Cassady had ignored him at first and then, when the road was perfectly straight and even, simply slowed down and deliberately ran the bus into a ditch where it came to a halt at a steep angle. It would take half a day and many extra hands to get it back on the road. There seemed to be no explanation until Cassady, who had gone to sleep without comment immediately after marooning the bus, pointedly handed Kesey a book to read. It was a collection of Robert Frost's poems, and Kesey's attention was directed to one called "The Code." This discursive poem contains an anecdote about a skilled farmhand who so resents being told how to do his work by the boss that he buries him under a heavy heap of hay. "The hand that knows his business won't be told/To do work better or faster."

Like this one, many of the most insightful Cassady/Prankster bus anecdotes belong to the episodic trips of later years, not the famous La Honda–New York epic. For example, Jerry Garcia would recall a spaced-out Cassady trying to direct an overdosed George Walker to reverse-park the bus one Sunday morning after a drug-laced happening in Watts, Los Angeles, the night before.

"Neal directed him right into a stop sign and the bus knocked it over and shaved it clean off," Garcia said. "Neal immediately picked it up and tried to stick it back in the hole. And down the street here come two little old ladies on their way to church. Neal's meanwhile walking away from the sign real fast and it hung for a minute and started to topple and just before it fell and hit the ground he caught it and put it back up. Then the ladies see him: is it a disreputable drunk or what? He isn't talking but he decides to clean up his act and what he tries to do is hide the stop sign behind him until the ladies pass by. It was like an elegant Buster Keaton ballet. There was no point to it and it wasn't a verbal experience. It just ended. It represents the way he moved through space. Effortless and perfect. And not divorced from the old ladies either. He took them into account."

Meanwhile back in the summer of 1964 the Cassady-less return journey for the Pranksters' bus involved a detour through Canada and was again fueled by sex, drugs, music, civic provocation, and the recurring litmus test of commitment to the cause: are you on the bus or off the bus?

Because Neal Cassady was now physically off the bus, other hands took over the wheel, but such had been his charisma on the outbound trip, that he had been the star of the show simply by being there and therefore was assumed to be about as "on the bus" as it was possible to get. During his extended association with the Pranksters, Cassady came to be a paradigm of almost superhuman reflexes. Kesey, whose own considerable mind had already produced one distinguished American novel, was to get less brilliant as his often drug-addled life progressed, but even in his prime the ex-wrestler golden boy could never match Cassady for sheer speed of thought, speech, and action. What is more, Kesey never seemed to mind because *no one* could match Cassady in those departments. When Kesey turned his pseudo-academic inquiries to the concept of delay—particularly with regard to how fast the human brain could turn a thought into physical action—he found that one-thirtieth of a second was the limit. Human biology being what it was, no one could do it faster, and most people were quite a bit slower. But in La Honda experiments it was Cassady who routinely hit the one-thirtieth of a second speed barrier.

The Pranksters, and Kesey in particular, insisted on seeing Neal as a kindred spirit, a fellow outlaw, part of their alternative take on the world. Neal, on the other hand, who had spent a busy lifetime demonstrating his sociopathic tendencies to straight society, could sometimes be counted upon to disrupt even the unstructured fabric of Kesey's commune. Writer Ed McClanahan (who named himself "Captain Kentucky") tells of a night when the Pranksters staged an open-house event at La Honda, trying to conduct some kind of thought-transference experiment of which the main requirement was intense group concentration. When Neal burst in unannounced, he was already in the middle of delivering what McClanahan variously referred to as one of his "guerilla-theater dramatic monologues" or "a kind of atonal scat-singing" rooted "not in mere subjects but in themes, leitmotifs."

An unstoppable stream-of-consciousness force, Neal ranted on about racing driver Juan-Manuel Fangio, Pliny the Elder, the Modern Jazz Quartet, and Elizabeth Barrett Browning while hitting riffs that prefigured modern rap in their persuasive trade-offs between sense and percussive rhythm: "there we were coastin' through Houston, or roastin' in Austin if you will, but Proustian-wise, all the authorities *agree*. . . ."

In the end on this particular occasion Kesey, Babbs, and Walker picked him up bodily and carried him out of the room, gently setting him down in the yard . . . from where, like a persistent pet, he immediately followed them back into the room where the thought-transference experiment was at last ruefully abandoned in favor of a joint-rolling competition.

Politically Cassady was a law unto himself. He was reluctant to take responsibility for his own actions unless forced to do so, and he did not care about the opinions of other people. As such, he was an unlikely candidate to fret about the way society in general was going or what might be done about it. The assassination of President Kennedy in November 1963 would, according to Anne Murphy, cast a pall on the liberal Gough Street household, as it would all across the United States and beyond, but if this epochal event had any major personal impact on Neal Cassady, he never seemed to have committed his reactions to paper either in letters or prose, or to have talked about it much. The Pranksters, by contrast, although often guilty of every kind of self-indulgence and self-delusion, did seem to entertain some sort of social conscience and political purpose, however inchoate; Kesey himself was still engaged by issues of social injustice and meaningful protest.

In the period immediately after the bus trip, Anne Murphy, feeling rejected (only selected wives and girlfriends had been invited and she was not among them), took up residence in the seedy Hotel Wentley on San Francisco's Polk Street, where she claimed, probably accurately, that she was its only heterosexual single resident. Foster's, the cafeteria on the hotel's ground floor, was a Mecca for drag queens, pushers, bohemians, painters, and poets who met planning to rent rooms, shoot up, and have sex in the hotel. Anne, who had in the past shown suicidal tendencies, realized that Neal would never stay with her despite his numerous strategic declarations of love and on one occasion an unexpected proposal of marriage. Her bitter response was to slip into an ambient state of drugs and sexual promiscuity while still seeing Neal from time to time. He called her Superslut. "I kind of liked that, I recall," she later admitted.

Neal was now spending a lot of time at La Honda while maintaining a changeable circle of girlfriends at different locations. He also kept getting charged with driving offenses for which he could not pay the fines. On March 24, 1965, he wrote to Carolyn from a jail in Pleasanton, California, to tell her he might be doing more time as a result of these cumulative misdemeanors.

"I'll get out of here Saturday PM unless there's a hold on me from Santa Cruz for doing 60mph in a 50 mph & a #12,50, which is simply not having a valid driver's license in possession," he wrote, insouciantly revealing his intimacy with police terminology. In a P.S. he added that he was making the final version of a record featuring himself rapping while sitting at the wheel of a stationary Buick at Ken Kesey's place. It was a Pranksters' project, and there were plans to add a backing track. The record was not released at the time, but it has resurfaced in various versions during the ensuing years.

Carolyn, meanwhile, was having her habitual money problems as well as difficulties with her son John Allen, who was now fourteen. Despite his exceptionally high intelligence, he was not doing well in school. Carolyn believed that Neal's example—a great intellect, an irresponsible thrill-seeking lifestyle—was hardly sending the right signals to their son.

• • •

Federal agents had started watching the La Honda settlement in late 1964, a process that prompted much joshing of the watchers by the watched in the form of jokey signs personally addressed to individual narcotics agents and miscellaneous banter broadcast over the outdoor sound systems. Neal was now living on the grounds in a white Plymouth, the car packed with his belongings and some of his recent writings, probably including notebooks from his recent Denver trip. In an ironic twist that was not lost on the man who claimed to have stolen more than 500 automobiles by the age that most young men are learning to drive one, Neal's car and its contents were stolen from La Honda. Neal bemoaned only the loss of his writing. Then in April 1965 federal agents finally mounted a raid, charging Kesey and thirteen others, including Neal Cassady, with marijuana possession—LSD not yet being illegal. All were bailed out and later the charges against everyone but Kesey and Prankster Page Browning (nickname: Zelot) were dropped.

Kesey exploited his long bail period by using the press as a pulpit for his ideas, one of which was that his own very successful *Cuckoo* had already paled into insignificance for him because it was just a novel, not real experience.

"I saw that Cassady did everything that a novel does," he announced, "except that he did it better because he was living it, not writing about it."

Anne Murphy started spending more time with Neal at La Honda while he was openly having relationships with at least two other women well known to her: "a gorgeous blonde Aries named June . . . [and] a white-skinned, long-legged, full-bosomed, perfumed red-headed Taurus named Sharon," she later wrote. Murphy characterized herself unflatteringly as "a flat-chested, ill-tempered, much older crazy woman." With her voracious appetite for sex laced with masochism, she could hardly have been more different from Neal's ex-wife Carolyn in temperament, but she was still intermittently harboring doomed ambitions about one day becoming Mrs. Cassady herself in a fantasy setting of calm domesticity and fidelity. Later in 1965 she would write to the absent Neal, "I've been hurt too much right now to have faith that we will be married, which is my dearest wish in the whole world, but married or not, I need to be with you. I love you, and your love is the nourishment of my life. Oh, won't we be happy when we're together?"

In the meantime life at La Honda was getting more outrageous by the day, and the settlement was about to be further enlivened by some equally shocking visitors.

Hunter S. Thompson called La Honda "the world capital of madness," and it was he who introduced the Hell's Angels (about whom he was writing a book) to the community. They arrived, en masse, on Saturday August 7, 1965. The Pranksters introduced them to LSD and the Hell's Angels in turn gave a demonstration of their proficiency at gang-banging. With a few exceptions, the Angels' extended visit turned out to be a surprisingly harmonious occasion. These two tribes of outsiders—freaks and Angels—despite being utterly dissimilar in their motivating forces and lifestyles, seemed quite unable to fall out with each other. If Cassady felt sidelined when Anne Murphy was "joyously" (her word) gang-banged by leather-clad bikers as he watched, it amounted to little more than pique. And although other members of his harem disappeared into the La Honda woods with the leather-clad visitors, Neal consoled himself with one of his more peripheral girlfriends (identified by Anne Murphy only as Rose), who performed fellatio on him as dusk fell and he shouted obscenities at the surrounding police vehicles whose occupants were still diligently keeping watch. The following evening Neal abruptly took off from the settlement with Don Snyder (nickname: Gypsy) on yet another trip east.

On his way to New York, Neal seemed suddenly to rediscover his talent for letter writing. He penned a twenty-two-page letter to Ken Kesey from Wakeman, Ohio, incorporating into it a brief section directed to Anne Murphy.

"Perhaps a rundown on the trip is first in order—Never have I seen one of such disorder!" it began, soon lapsing into a full page of technical minutiae about the vehicle he was currently driving, a 1947 pickup truck. He moves on to describe sex with an Iowa college girl, "truly sweet, small, dark-haired 19 yr. old Grinnell," who was replaced in the same bed by "a tall white-skinned Red-head with green eyes from Big Sur Country now working in an aged Rest Home after flipping." After a rundown of chaotic visits to friends and a chronicle of the protracted checking out of potential automobiles for the trip, Neal describes being taken to see a rock 'n' roll group with a lead singer who was known to the Pranksters. "Signe & The HiWires or the Sextones or the Jefferson Hi Bandits, our pals, ya know; and they sounded great, esp. on one about a Hi Flyin' Bird." (This group was an early incarnation of the Jefferson Airplane, caught soon after the moment of its inception. Lead singer Signe Toly was replaced by Grace Slick the following year.) Neal then bumps into Allen Ginsberg and parties with him and his friends. Next day Neal, Gypsy, and Gypsy's girlfriend Jenny set off for New York in a 1951 Chevrolet that first suffers a flat and then stops dead thirty-nine miles southwest of Cleveland. Eventually trading the useless car for a dying Studebaker, they get to Virginia City, after which the trip becomes so complex—at least in Neal's recounting of it—as to be hard to follow. At one point he slows down to reflect on his family and to consider the possibility of taking up a job offer in Chicago. "I've been offered a hundred and a quarter a week truckdriving job there . . . and ya know damn well how much back child support I owe—almost $1,600 now—incidentally my oldest girl is 17 on Sept 7th & the youngest boy is 14 on September 9th.—so I figure to work a couple of months—sending my ex-wife $100 a week."

When he arrived in New York Neal again embraced his mythic role in Kerouac's work by inscribing messages to 8th Street Bookshop owner Ted Wilentz in copies of *Desolation Angels* and *On the Road.* Wilentz gave Neal a copy of *Desolation Angels,* which he had not yet read. In Wilentz's copy of *On the Road* Neal wrote, "For Ted—Who led me to believe that all bookmen don't resent giving themselves away in their entirety, nay, in their heart, aye!

With love,
NEAL CASSADY,
(Himself, I think)
DEAN MORIARTY"

• • •

Soon after the Hell's Angels incursion, Kesey had caused a major stir by speaking at an anti-Vietnam War rally and march in Berkeley where, introduced as a key speaker, he proceeded to question the value of such rallies and marches, limiting his positive contribution to playing a few bars of "Home on the Range" on a harmonica. Just as Kesey had been disappointed by Timothy Leary ("Don't drop out," Kesey riposted to Leary's "Turn On, Tune In, and Drop Out" dictum, "Drop in on our alter reality"), the antiwar left was now feeling let down by Kesey's obvious lack of support for their methods.

Also at this time the Merry Pranksters decided to parlay their drug parties into what became known as the Kool-Aid Acid Tests: a traveling road show to be staged at a variety of venues up and down the coast—

private residences, industrial buildings, and dance halls in locations that included Portland, Los Angeles, San Francisco, San Jose, Palo Alto, and Santa Cruz.

Kool-Aid, a proprietary soft drink that the Pranksters spiked with LSD, was given out, not necessarily with the recipient's knowledge of its effect. "Can you pass the Acid Test?" became a rhetorical catchphrase, an indicator of hipness. The events varied in composition: there were light shows, live music, movies, and performance art all combined with extemporized discussions and general mayhem. Key participants included a group called the Warlocks (an early incarnation of the Grateful Dead already led by Jerry Garcia); Wavy Gravy (aka Hugh Romney, who would soon achieve folkloric fame as a leading light at the Woodstock Festival of 1969); Kesey's right-hand man, Ken Babbs; and of course, on his return from New York, Neal Cassady. The first such event took place at Ken Babbs's ranch at Soquel, near Santa Cruz, in November 1965.

Over a dozen Acid Tests were held during 1965 and 1966, each event bristling with the latest mid-1960s audiovisual gadgetry and always driven by Kesey's dictum that participants should not come as they were but as who they would like to be. Neal's contribution was only rarely made at the microphone, where he could and sometimes did broadcast his raps to the assembled company; instead he preferred to use his party technique of taking up a position on the perimeter of the gathering, gradually building an audience with one of his magnetic routines, sometimes rapping, sometimes half-seriously analyzing litter on the floor—cigarette butts, torn tickets, and discarded packaging—for runic properties. Jerry Garcia likened Neal's preferred role to "the guy who was out picking pockets while the man on the platform was selling snake oil."

The Acid Test period was another of Neal's golden eras, albeit a brief and patchy one. If he was not always simpatico with the hippie ethos, the Acid Tests, at least, seemed to have been tailor-made for him in that he was required to do nothing but turn up and be himself. Again his reputation preceded him, and the nature of these events meant that he was presented with an uninhibited and receptive audience, many of whom were young women fully aware of the fringe benefits of having sex with the mythic Cassady; in fact, some made the journey to an Acid Test with no other objective in mind.

"They flew up from San Diego and drove down from Oregon," wrote Anne Murphy, who could hardly have been overjoyed at Neal's priapic magnetism. "It was like Disneyland." The Acid Tests had their own logic, but it was not something that could always be easily understood by any but the most committed followers. People expecting some kind of structured event were usually disappointed since the Acid Tests were really designed to do no more than defeat such expectations, opening up participants to a hallucinogenic "reality" denied to them in their day-to-day existence. There might be music or an extravagant theme or there might be dramatic performances, but these were incidental to the central requirement of passing the Acid Test simply by ingesting lysergic acid diethylamide and seeing what happened. Cassady, on the other hand, was a one-man show with instant appeal, and the whole Kool-Aid thing gave him the perfect arena in which to perform. Travel, movement, talk, sex, and excitement were all part of the show, and Cassady was in his element. Was Cassady himself on LSD? Although it seems unlikely that he never tried it during his association with the Pranksters, there is no direct evidence to suggest that he did. Marijuana was his drug of choice, and his naturally exuberant behavior made him harder to read than most when it came to stimulants. He was certainly prepared to drum up audiences for the Acid Tests and, of course, for himself. In doing so he indulged his dubious talent for identifying at a glance women made vulnerable by circumstance or psychosis.

"I think he could look them in the eye and instantly know they were a little bit demented," said Carolyn Adams, aka Mountain Girl. Adams's soon-to-be lover Jerry Garcia added that "Neal would take his women through a whole lifetime of relationships in about an hour."

• • •

By the start of 1966 this particular California dream showed signs of coming to an end. Kesey's long period of bail expired and he received a light sentence—six months in a work camp and three years' probation—which was quickly augmented when San Francisco police raided an apartment building and found him and Carolyn Adams with 3.54 grams of marijuana. To avoid further penalty Kesey hightailed it for Mexico in January 1966, leaving a not particularly convincing fake suicide tableau to confuse the cops . . . which it failed to do. Ken Babbs tried to keep the Acid Tests going, but gradually much of the company drifted south of the border too; Neal went, as did Carolyn Adams who was now carrying Ken Kesey's baby. Mexico, the traditional last refuge of outlaws, had always had its appeal when the heat was on, and now the depleted company drifted through Puerto Vallarta, Mazatlán, Guadalajara, and Mexico City, still staging Acid Tests here and there. In late September 1966 Kesey tired of life on the run in Mexico and reentered the United States to conduct the last of the Acid Tests and, he hoped, to be a thorn in the side of the establishment. Neal soon returned as well, his correspondence to Carolyn now a pale shadow of what it once had been. Amid the terse two- and three-liners ("Hi Love, here's $30.00 and more, I think, this next week"), he did manage one letter that contained a heartfelt enclosure for daughter Cathy on or about her eighteenth birthday.

September 7, 1966

CATHLEEN JOANNE CASSADY

The only one of our three, 2 girls, who had colic also eczema & mother's milk.

Who used to be wheeled, at 109 Liberty St., into the large park behind Galileo High on Dolores Street. So her 3 week-to-month old being could daily take air & sun; not the baseballs or footballs I still enjoy remembering forestalling by the artful angling of fine, new carriage behind tree.

Who loved to be held & walked, more perhaps than any other of my children; who always, eating, of my children in infancy, least perhaps, certainly least well, at least burped best!!!

Hi sweets!! Do you realize as I just did going on in the drivel on reverse to denote your maturity, that this is the first letter I've written to you separately?

. . . so you got your first traffic ticket last month, heh? Now you know what I've been foolish enuf to go thru for more years than you are old, rite? Heh, heh.

On October 6, 1966, LSD was made illegal in California. On October 20, federal agents picked up Kesey on the Bayshore Freeway south of San Francisco. And this is the point at which Tom Wolfe's nonchronological book *The Electric Kool-Aid Acid Test* begins, with Wolfe interviewing Kesey in the San Mateo County jail in Redwood City, where the Oregon Outlaw announces that it is time to move "beyond acid" and on to something else. Kesey would remain faithful to the hippie ideal even as it was changing, and when finally serving out his deferred six-month sentence at the work camp near La Honda the following summer, he predicted that the optimism of the 1960s counterculture would prove durable. "These kids have a certain upbeat that makes them unlike anyone before them, except Neal Cassady," Kesey proclaimed. "They will be that way forever."

It was an over-optimistic assessment, as Kesey was soon to find out. The final valedictory Acid Test was intended to be held at the Winterland Arena in San Francisco on Halloween 1966. It was going to be billed as the Acid Test Graduation—but rumor had it that this would be the biggest Acid Test of them all—a festival of excess at a venue where the very next night Governor Edmund G. ("Jerry") Brown would be celebrated at a rally organized by the California Democratic Party; Brown was running against Ronald Reagan for governor. A crazed plan was entertained if not actually hatched: The Pranksters would smear a cocktail of lysergic acid diethylamide and dimethyl sulfoxide on every touchable surface, because any dimethyl sulfoxide solution was capable of absorption via human skin in seconds. The prospect of the Democratic Party's grandees zonked out on LSD was a seductive one. Perhaps, another rumor ran, Kesey's declared stance of weaning people off and beyond LSD was simply a cover for a plan to saturate gullible local young people with megadoses of the stuff! The Winterland Arena management was certainly getting jittery, and they did not want to deal with the weirdos directly. Consequently the legendary impresario Bill Graham was recruited as a go-between to make the Acid Test Graduation happen.

Graham—born Wolfgang Grajonca in Berlin—had escaped the Nazis by going to France and then relocating to San Francisco via New York after serving in the Korean War. In San Francisco he gave up a promising business career to manage a local mime troupe. Then he became the most famous rock promoter of his day, championing the Jefferson Airplane, Lawrence Ferlinghetti, the Committee, and the Fugs, as well as Allen Ginsberg and the Grateful Dead. In the eyes of the Pranksters Graham therefore seemed somehow magically to straddle the straight world and the counterculture, a rare feat in the 1960s when most people were firmly on one side or the other. However, a chance encounter between Bill Graham and Neal Cassady on the street did not bode well for the Winterland alliance. Graham assumed that Cassady's trademark twirlings with his hammer were a none-too-subtle threat intended to ensure full cooperation. Cassady meanwhile reported the encounter thus: "I ran into Bill Graham. He was out on the street checking tire treads to see if they'd picked up any nickels . . . he says 'Look, Neal, we're in two different worlds. You're a hippie and I'm a square.'" (In telling the story to Kesey and the rest, Cassady demonstrated Graham's gesture that accompanied the word "square"—an invisible rectangle sketched in the air with two index fingers, a bit of fashionable 1960s whimsy prettily reprised nearly thirty years later by Uma Thurman in Quentin Tarantino's movie *Pulp Fiction.*)

Graham pulled out at the last minute, Winterland was withdrawn, and so were the Grateful Dead and Quicksilver, who had considered joining in graduation day at the cost of reneging on previous engagements. Kesey, always a good man in a crisis, calmly regrouped and declared that the Acid Test Graduation would now take place in the grungy garage/warehouse on Harriet Street that the Pranksters were currently using as headquarters.

And it did take place. The Pranksters threw everything into a last-gasp night of lurid mayhem; they dressed the ramshackle venue with a vast orange-and-white silk parachute arranged like a giant canopy. Beneath it they welcomed participants accoutered in every freakish costume and uniform known to man. They embraced magazine correspondents, minor celebrities, television cameras, wary cops, malevolent-looking Hell's Angels, and precocious kids. At one point in the proceedings, Kesey orchestrated a faux-metaphysical moment, some spiritual line in the sand whereby people who were "with him" must surround him and stay while the others must leave. It was another "on the bus/off the bus" moment. Many left simply baffled by the whole thing. The number of Kesey's followers was now looking pretty small. When they were down to about fifty, a mock graduation took place with Cassady, dressed only in loose khaki pants and a mortarboard, ready to hand out diplomas that signified nothing to people who, in the main, had anyway not turned up to receive them, although a few Pranksters did receive their Acid Test Graduation diplomas from school dropout Cassady. And Cassady was on fire. He jerked, twitched, and rapped while the one band that did show—the Anonymous Artists of America—played music behind him that included Edward Elgar's "Pomp and Circumstance" delivered with suitably ironic rock flourishes. The night was deemed a success. The next day its hastily created decor could be seen lying in a tawdry heap in the unforgiving morning light of Harriet Street.

Strictly speaking, this was not the end of the Acid Tests. The owners of the garage picked up on the idea and a little time later held their own version in the same venue. Neal somehow heard about it and turned up, all wired and weird, noticing too late that this was a sanitized event, mellow, hippie-themed, nicely decorated and with sitar accompaniment. He might have guessed; the uncompromising era of Bob Dylan and Joan Baez had quickly produced Peter, Paul and Mary and Sonny and Cher. To the uninitiated, these acts may have sounded or looked like radical folkies but in fact they merely adopted the mannerisms and fashions in the hope of securing a showbiz career or at least a television special. At the Harriet Street neo–Acid Test, Neal was the only authentic remnant of the original concept in attendance, and he was looked upon pityingly as a harmless eccentric as he lurched around and desperately urged everyone present to "get it started—slide it around!"

That occasion marked the end of Neal Cassady's Indian summer as a counterculture hero, too. From today's vantage point he seems always to have been an improbable hippie, even if he was just an honorary one. Weird-looking counterculture people like Hugh Romney and Allen Ginsberg never seemed out of place whatever their age, but Cassady did not look weird, he looked like a handsome devil going to seed—a man who had seen far too much of life to dream of the world as a perfumed garden. His body may have responded to the spirit of free love and his mind may have been sympathetic to the broad principle of hippiedom's spiritual aspirations, but Cassady was a westerner at heart and therefore unlikely to start dreaming of a global village or treating his leading lady as a precious earth mother.

More seriously, Cassady's body was slowing down, the signs of age were becoming more noticeable, and the drugs were no longer working like they used to. In retrospect, Carolyn Cassady says of this latter-day Neal, "He was dying."

Characteristically Neal chose to ignore the mounting evidence of visible deterioration and decided to keep moving, applying his inexhaustible appetite for self-examination to yet another new phase in his life. In early January 1967, he returned to Mexico.

25

PRANKSTER GEORGE WALKER owned a Lotus Elan. Neal Cassady drove this vehicle to Mexico with him while fellow Prankster Steven Lambrecht (nickname: Zonker), Steven's girlfriend Gloria Quarnstrom, and Anne Murphy accompanied them in another car, a Ford sedan belonging to Lambrecht's parents.

"We were high every mile of the way on acid and grass, with Neal additionally jacked up by speed as usual," recalled Anne Murphy. "I think we spent one night in a hotel, but other than that I don't remember ever being off the road for more than an hour."

They crossed the border at Mexicali, and Neal became animated and happy, perhaps experiencing a sense of homecoming. The barber's boy from Salt Lake City had always been energized by Mexico's multiple blessings: cheap drugs, women, booze, and food, and a famously relaxed implementation of the law.

Anne Murphy recalled his running commentary on the people and places they passed en route to Puerta Vallarta. "See that old American couple in the Chrysler?" he would ask. "See how they still love each other after all these years?" Or, spotting a drunken laborer by the roadside, "He wanted to be an artist, see? But after six children when the ol' lady told him another was on the way, he ran out on 'em and now he just gets drunk every day."

On another occasion Neal pointed out, with all the reverence due a shrine, the exact location where he lost first gear on a previous trip to Mexico City "and had to make it all the way back to El Paso without it."

They arrived in Puerta Vallarta, a resort that Anne Murphy mistakenly claimed had not yet, in 1967, "been blessed by Liz, Dick, and the tourists they attracted." In fact, movie star couple Elizabeth Taylor and Richard

Burton had first brought the world's press there three years earlier when Burton was filming Tennessee Williams's *The Night of the Iguana.* The tourists soon followed. Even so, Anne's recollection of the "sleepy little village" was one of an unspoiled paradise in which the group lazed in the sun, went swimming, and slept in a traditional open-sided house with a thatched roof of dried palm leaves called a palapa. They rented this house for two months until a fateful evening in February when two young American couples joined them for an evening of acid, food, and sexual exploration. The two young women, Kathy and Anne Van Leeuwen, were sisters, postgraduate art students currently living in San Miguel de Allende, and their male escorts proved temporary. Anne Murphy rebelled against Neal's evident interest in one of the sisters, caused a scene, and was firmly but politely told to leave by George Walker. Neal had almost certainly tired of Anne by now, and he most likely prompted Walker, in his role as the trip's banker, to tell her that she was no longer welcome. Next day Walker drove her to the airport, gave her twenty dollars, and put her on a plane to Los Angeles. She was thirty-five years old, and it was effectively the end of her turbulent but oddly steady affair with Neal, a relationship that had now spanned some six years.

Anne retreated to Venice, California, another of those places like Haight-Ashbury that would be transformed when the hippies adopted it, and picked up the final strands of a life of hedonism that she hoped would make her forget about Neal once and for all. Fat chance. She wrote to Carolyn Cassady about her round of "playing the races again (and losing) and going to sex orgies (imagine—thirty people all copulating in plush Hollywood pads) and painting (one painting—all breasts, beads & eyelashes) and water skiing and swimming—and going out with handsome bachelors, movie actors, & a bank robber!" Then the tone changed as she bemoaned what she saw as her change of luck, saying, "I have enough sleeping pills to leave this life. So I'm for accepting a 'no' or a beating & my heart is pure, and the next time you hear of me, let's hope it's my funeral or wedding, and put an end to this disgrace."

Neal turned forty-one during the Puerta Vallarta sojourn, a milestone he noted in a postcard to Carolyn Cassady. In defiance of all reasonable expectation, he now seemed to regard Carolyn as a mix of confidante and wife—someone who might conceivably be prepared to pick up the strands of their former relationship at a future time of his choosing. "Starting my 41st at a place marked X on the reverse," he wrote. "To Guadalajara today. Back here 2 or 3 days. Love, N."

After Anne Murphy's enforced departure, Neal, George, Steven, and Gloria were invited to stay with the Van Leeuwen sisters at their apartment in the Palomar Building in San Miguel de Allende. They all moved in at the end of March. Back in the United States a rash of articles had been published alluding to Neal Cassady's role in "Ken Kesey's LSD-oriented Merry Pranksters," as a reviewer of John Clellon Holmes's collection *Nothing More to Declare* put it. Early segments of what would later become Tom Wolfe's *The Electric Kool-Aid Acid Test* were published in a magazine accompanying January and February issues of New York's *World Journal Tribune.* Gradually the print media were waking up to Cassady's unique cultural influence, turning him into a minor in-name-only celebrity. Today he might have been able to parlay his celebrity into a media product, for which he would have been well paid. As it was, Neal Cassady was rapidly declining into poor health and poverty. He was used to being serially insolvent, but being broke and being poor are two different things, one being a temporary lack of money, the other being an all-pervasive state. Now it seemed that he was consigned to the grind of genuine poverty, resigned to not working, and reduced to sending out begging letters, usually to the ever-dependable Allen Ginsberg but also to anyone else who might send him a few dollars to live. At the same time, he railed against what he saw as a new spirit of restrictive Republicanism back in the United States, prompted by California governor Ronald Reagan's policies on welfare and a general hostility toward high-profile counterculture figures.

Meanwhile, in his correspondence to Carolyn and his children Neal no longer even pretended that he would soon be working and sending money; the best he could offer (in a letter written on the nineteenth anniversary of his marriage to Carolyn) were promises to hitchhike home in time for her forty-fourth birthday on April 28 and the hopeful news "Ginsberg sending another $50–100 at once."

In fact, Neal never did make the hitchhiking trip to California, nor did he make it to Dallas, Texas, where in a letter dated April 12, he had, without a shred of explanation, urged Allen Ginsberg to meet him on May 1 at the book depository on Elm Street, the site of the Kennedy assassination.

George Walker, Steven Lambrecht, and Gloria Quarnstrom returned to the United States, but Neal stayed on in San Miguel de Allende, temporarily moving in with another acquaintance, Diane Sward, who lived with her boyfriend and small child on Murillo Street. His reasons for staying behind remain obscure, and he subsequently wrote to Ginsberg with no more explanation than that he had "decided against Dallas," now urging his friend to come to San Miguel de Allende instead, and furnishing characteristically labyrinthine instructions as to how to get there. Ginsberg, who was on tour, never received either message at the time.

A possible reason for Neal's decision to stay in Mexico was that he had met a twenty-three-year-old American woman, Janice Brown, known as J.B. She worked at the theater in San Miguel's Instituto Allende. It is possible that she represented another possible future for Neal: a young single woman with artistic inclinations who actually lived in Mexico. They moved in together but only for a few weeks. Abruptly Neal decided to return to the United States in early May 1967. His destination was Eugene, Oregon; Ken Kesey had recently purchased a farm there. Was La Honda about to be reborn in a Pacific Northwest location? Perhaps Neal Cassady believed so.

So Neal went to stay with Kesey, and when Allen Ginsberg came to visit, they hit the road in the trusty bus that had made the famous cross-country trip three years earlier. This time they were bound for a writers' conference to be held at Western Washington State College in Bellingham. While they were there, on May 26, Neal and Allen appeared onstage at the Sam Carver Gymnasium, performing alongside Jefferson Airplane, now sporting Grace Slick as Signe Toly's replacement. (The very next month would see the band appearing at the Monterey International Pop Festival, the gig that catapulted them to international fame.) At forty-one, Neal Cassady was hobnobbing with the young psychedelic rock crowd. It was on this trip that he suffered a panic attack and ran out of a party at Kesey's place, so overwhelmed that he left his jacket and even his cigarettes, and started hitchhiking back to Carolyn.

"I simply couldn't stand it another second," he told her when he arrived, so giving her hope, however faint, that he might yet abandon the downward slide.

From San Francisco Neal summoned J.B. to leave San Miguel de Allende and join him as he prepared for yet another road trip. This one would involve Neal and J.B. visiting his old friend Ed White in Denver and also, surprisingly, looking up 8th Street Bookshop owner Ted Wilentz and his wife Joan in New York. The Wilentzes were the most casual of acquaintances, and therefore going to see them represented one of Neal's least plausible reasons for driving across the country. The real purpose of the trip still remains unclear, but there is always the possibility that it was simply another case of Neal feeling at his most comfortable when he was in a car alongside a young woman and accelerating into a promising landscape.

At the end of the trip J.B. returned to Mexico, and Neal decided to stay in the United States for a while. During this period his sporadic encounters with Carolyn alarmed her considerably, as it seemed to her that the drugs were now taking a serious toll. One day she openly expressed her dislike for the influence of Kesey and his followers, asking him why he persisted in hanging out with them.

"That's just it. I can't help it anymore," she reported him as saying. "I don't know where else to go. I'm a danger to everyone—to myself most of all. I keep swearing I'm going to stop making an ass of myself, but then I get in a group and everyone stares at me, waiting for me to perform—and my nerves are so shot, I get high—and there I go again. I don't know what else to do. It's horrible."

At one point there seemed to be a real possibility that Neal might be rehired by SPRR due to a change of administration. Encouraged by Al Hinkle, he even made himself presentable and set off from home to meet the people at the railroad. Impeccably groomed, he said goodbye to his family, promising to come back that evening a rehired railroad man. He never came back at all. A couple of weeks later his children John and Jami, in the company of friends, came upon him at the wheel of Kesey's parked bus in San Francisco, where he casually admitted that he had never even presented himself to SPRR at all. "The cops arrested me," he explained casually. "Just got out." He went on to confuse his daughter Jami with a friend of hers, upsetting her considerably, and further eroding his standing as a responsible parent by offering the young group marijuana.

At other times, Carolyn recalled, Neal would become driven to spells of near madness by the sudden belief that lurid Caycean tableaux from his past were taking over his present life. "Oh My God, I've killed my son, I've killed my son!" he cried one day, horrified by visions of his offspring cut to pieces by chariot wheel knives. Minutes later young John appeared safe and well, oblivious to his father's demons. On another occasion Neal claimed to be on speaking terms with the devil. "He lives in the hills above Redwood City," he explained to Carolyn with utter seriousness. Carolyn suspected that J.B.'s influence was not helping matters. J.B. shared Anne Murphy's obsession with astrology and, in addition, she was frequently prompted by mysterious voices in her head.

Neal's letter writing, his true artistic medium and always the key to his innermost thoughts, seems to have dried up forever at about this time. Certainly all that remains is a handful of very short letters or postcards, usually pragmatic in tone and entirely shorn of the linguistic pyrotechnics, passages of self-doubt, and promises of impossible reform that characterized his most prolific periods of correspondence. His life seemed to be unraveling, and all the time his backlog of traffic tickets and other misdemeanors was mounting, making a period of imprisonment an inevitability rather than a likelihood if he stayed in the United States.

He claimed he wanted to live with Carolyn again, but he probably knew it was an impossibility. Prompted by her insistence that he leave the country, he set off once more for Mexico. It was early September 1967 when he visited his daughter Cathy, who was by then living in San Antonio. He had called Carolyn, as she recalls, when he was traveling north from Mexico, although this does not seem logical; but whatever the twists and turns of this particular itinerary, he learned that Cathy had just given birth to a boy, William, and so Neal Cassady visited the hospital to see and hold his grandson.

• • •

Once back in Mexico he found himself penniless yet again as he waited for J.B., who was still in the United States. At that point, he fired off a note to Lucien Carr, wasting little time on pleasantries:

> Dear Lu;
>
> Hi, you old fuck, how about sending me a few bucks to eat on down here?
>
> How's Mardene & everyone with you? . . . ["Mardene" is a reference to Kerouac's old girlfriend Alene Lee, who was now living with Carr. It is a playful conflation of "Alene" and "Mardou," her name in *The Subterraneans*].

Neal sent another even briefer note to Carolyn, coyly hinting that he would return with marijuana. To his son John he sent notes also suggesting he would be coming home soon "& I mean it!!!"

He did return to the United States from Mexico before the year was out, but he first headed for Kesey's farm in Oregon. He finally turned up in Los Gatos for New Year's Eve. He arranged to see Carolyn, but insisted that their meeting should take place at the house of Leon Tabory and his wife, who were entertaining other guests as well. This resulted in a weirdly constrained dinner party at which Neal seemed distant and even uninterested in Carolyn. For her part, Carolyn still appeared to entertain some sentimental hope that Neal might be salvaged from his downward spiral, that she could interest him once again in her and the children, and that some remnant of the old chemistry could be reenergized.

"Neal was . . . seated in a chair on the other side of the room," she wrote, "and I went to sit on the couch opposite him, flashing my most appealing smile. He greeted me casually, and I peered at him, fearing he hadn't recognized me. He had, but he was certainly little moved. He was listening to the music, gazing into space, and now and then he would make a remark that might have been aimed at anyone or no one. Then he started humming, his glance occasionally falling on me as though I were a passing pedestrian. I made a few efforts at establishing contact and failed. There was nothing to do but sit and wait, and since I wasn't in whatever world they were in, repartee was limited. My romantic expectations were turning into equally romantic feelings of rejection, even though I knew them to be unjustified. Throughout the agonizingly slow dinner, Neal waved his fork to the music, hummed between mouthfuls and continued to gaze over my head. I tried to look at a magazine, but the lighting was too dim. At long last the dishes were collected and the company departed, finally leaving us alone as they'd promised."

As she had been urgently summoned to this odd evening by Neal, Carolyn still still assumed that there must be something on his mind. "After a minute or so I said, 'Well, if this is all you wanted to see me for, I have other things to do at home,'" Carolyn continued. "And I rose from the couch. Neal didn't speak, but got up and gently pulled me back down, then stretched out with his head on my lap. Closing his eyes, he clasped my hand to his chest and said 'Please, please tell me about the children—about yourself—everything you've been doing.' His voice sounded weary.

"I dredged up all the trivia that makes up the daily lives of a growing family. Although his eyes remained closed, he was more responsive now, and if I paused or sounded as though he couldn't possibly care, he'd prod me by repeating my last two words or asking a question. For a time, I felt compensated, but soon I became bored, and I didn't want to comment too deeply on the problems with the children, most of which were a result of my having to cope alone. I tried to shift the talk to him, but he was evasive or answered only in monosyllables."

Carolyn urged him to go back to Mexico since he would otherwise surely be arrested, especially if he went into the city. Wearily he replied that he would have to go into the city to get money. He did not specify how he would do that. He seemed defeated and directionless, and when they finally parted that evening—the literal eve of 1968, a definitive year for the alternative culture that Neal had helped to bring into the world—it was with an overwhelming sense of anticlimax.

"I drove home, thoroughly depleted and feeling as though I'd been pouring energy into a void and receiving nothing in return," Carolyn wrote. "I wondered if now he had given all of himself away and only the broken shell was left."

She did not know it at the time, but that odd, muffled encounter in Leon Tabory's house was really the final scene in their long relationship. She may have sensed that the end was near, but there was something about being married to Neal Cassady that always encouraged a triumph of hope over expectation.

Neal did go to Los Angeles, where he stayed with editor John Bryan, the man who had published him in *Notes from Underground* four years earlier. Neal was now asked to help Bryan with his current magazine, *Open City*, but this turned out to be a short assignment. Carolyn says that she received one last phone call from Neal, who said, "I'm coming home." Distraught at having to reject him, she nonetheless begged him to go to Mexico to get well first. He muttered something about perhaps coming home on his birthday, February 8, just a couple of weeks or so away. Then he hung up abruptly.

Neal Cassady left Los Angeles on January 28, 1968, to return to Mexico. This time he was at first refused entry at the border, only succeeding upon a second attempt when he joined up with an experimental filmmaker from UCLA whose crew was allowed in. Neal eventually arrived at Celaya on February 2, leaving some luggage at the railroad station and taking a taxi to San Miguel de Allende, where J.B. had been impatiently waiting for him. A few days before, in the course of a phone call to Carolyn Cassady to see what was keeping Neal, J.B. had revealed that "my voices tell me he's going to be all right." Carolyn said she hoped so too, but in truth she was not so sure.

There were no more letters and no more phone calls. Neal and J.B. were reunited. J.B. later reported that they fought and argued, although this was in no way out of the ordinary. On February 3 Neal, reportedly high on drugs, set off on foot for the San Miguel train station from where he claimed he was going to follow the tracks to Celaya station in order to collect those belongings he had for some reason left there. Near the San Miguel station he came upon a Mexican wedding where he lingered for a while. He was found lying by the railroad track the next morning and never recovered consciousness. He had walked only about a quarter of a mile before collapsing. He was just four days shy of his forty-second birthday.

• • •

The aftermath of death first demands that practicalities be dealt with. Only later do the implications of this or that specific fatality emerge and coalesce to form the real memorial. Accordingly it was mysterious J.B., one of the more peripheral of Neal's steady girlfriends but someone who spoke Spanish and was close at hand in Mexico, who was charged with arranging Neal's cremation. Carolyn Cassady informed the Hinkles of his death, and then, by telephone, she informed Allen Ginsberg and Jack Kerouac. "Allen was subdued, fatalistic, sad . . . [Jack] said all the beautiful things I wanted to hear about Neal—but he still wouldn't believe Neal was really gone."

Carolyn also sent a note to Anne Murphy and, unexpectedly, one of the craziest of Neal's lovers—even by her own admission—reacted with grace and calm to Neal's death even though she, too, refused to believe he was really gone.

"I'm at my mother's now and wouldn't want to go to any funeral or wake," she wrote back. "Still, if there's anything I can do for *you*, please let me know. He told me to try to be a perfect human being."

Perhaps surprisingly, an excellent eulogy of Neal Cassady appeared in the *Los Gatos Times—Saratoga* of February 6, 1968. Local author William J. Craddock had been a big fan of Neal's, and his impressionistic and touching piece recognized and conveyed something of its subject's unique influence and charisma. This eulogy sat in stark contrast to most of the newspaper reports, which were more or less factual but usually betrayed a sense of uncertainty as to why Cassady was newsworthy at all except for his past association with more famous people. For example, from AP in San Miguel de Allende, February 4, 1968, came this terse announcement: "Neal Cassady, 43, of San Francisco, a former railroad conductor and long associate of prominent members of the beatnik and hippie generations, has died here. Police reports said Cassady was found unconscious but still alive early in the morning along the railroad tracks. Cassady was a friend of novelist Jack Kerouac and the poet, Allen Ginsberg."

• • •

After four months, J.B. arrived in San Jose with a box containing Neal's ashes. Carolyn had never expected to see them—J.B., a wild-looking hippie girl, seemed to be permanently under the influence of astrological or occult forces. Carolyn had great difficulty separating J.B. from the box. Then after almost forcibly taking the woman to San Francisco to get rid of her, Carolyn was deeply alarmed when she returned to the Cassady home a few days later "to see the ashes once more." Firmly repelling J.B. a final time, Carolyn thought she was at last free of morbid claims on Neal's remains. But then Diana Hansen fired the opening shot in a dogged telephone campaign to get a small helping of the ashes. After a protracted long-distance battle Carolyn suddenly and inexplicably lost all animosity to the only one of Neal's women she had never been able to stand. She sent Diana some ashes, with love.

Neal had believed that cremation would assist his soul's quicker passage to release, his fondness for speed seemingly extending even to his plans for the afterlife. Certainly those desiccated ashes had little to do with the flesh-and-blood life force that had been Neal Cassady. His light, like that of a dead star, would continue to shine long after its source had been extinguished, and that would be the only thing he left of himself to the world. Diana got her ashes, but innumerable others—family, friends, and strangers not even born yet—would get much more from the legend of Neal Cassady's extraordinary life.

Epilogue

NEAL CASSADY'S LIFE ENDED as it had begun, surrounded by rumor and uncertainty. Whereas the obligation of the biographer is, as far as possible, to separate truth from fiction when it comes to his or her subject's earthly existence, that duty evaporates when considering the influence the life in question may have upon those left behind and those yet to come. Perhaps it is enough to examine the fables and fantasies not for objective truth, but in order to consider their nature and so gain further insight into what kind of exceptional person might inspire such myths.

First, there are the stories surrounding Neal's death. Chief among them is that it was somehow caused by a fatal mix of pulque (a thick fermented alcoholic beverage made from agave) that he drank at the wedding party in San Miguel de Allende, and the drugs he had taken before he set off. Other versions of this story actually have him washing down Seconals with the muddy brew. There are good reasons to doubt these accounts, the chief one being that Neal Cassady did not like alcohol and always avoided it when he could; another is that he was only too aware of the dangers of mixing drugs and alcohol. Those who knew him allowed that he might take one drink out of politeness at a celebration such as a wedding—it had been known to happen—but that would probably be the extent of it.

Second, there is the somehow more seductive idea, told in several variations, that Neal was counting the railroad ties when he collapsed on his lonely walk. This perhaps rings most true to those who knew about his preoccupation with sequences, patterns, and numbers, a minor obsession that Neal sometimes expressed flippantly through party tricks involving serial numbers on paper money. At other, darker times he clung to sequences more seriously, as when he was in prison and elaborate numerical sequences and patterns provided him with a kind of formal thread to hold onto. Of course, we can never know what Neal was thinking on his last walk, but another, more probable (although equally unprovable) theory is that counting ties could have been nothing more than a simple railroad man's trick for calculating distances along the track. Certainly his proposed trackside walk was a long one—at over fifteen miles, perhaps longer than he knew—and he may have casually mentioned to J.B. his intention to measure the distance from San Miguel de Allende to Celaya by this method. A humdrum detail could then have taken on resonant overtones following his death. Again, we can never know, although one overwrought and apocryphal story even relates Neal Cassady's last gasped words as "Sixty-four thousand nine hundred and twenty-eight." This fable finds its origins in Ken Kesey's "The Day After Superman Died," which seeks to explain the significance of Neal Cassady's life and death in a short story whose central character is redubbed "'Sir Speed' Houlihan."

The Mexican authorities' vague definition of Neal's cause of death—"generalized congestion"—was likely intended only to absolve them from taking action on a drugs-related fatality (the newspapers reported "overexposure" instead). However, this very imprecision added to the mystery of Neal's passing: a gregarious, fast-moving American whom most people remembered as fit, energetic, and obsessed with automobile travel, died of unknown causes after walking alone and lying down by a railroad track on a February night in Mexico. Local cremation by his last and most mysterious girlfriend (albeit at Carolyn Cassady's legitimate request) seemed to add to the unsatisfactory unexpectedness of his death.

Of course, those who knew him well toward the end could see that he was in serious decline. Those who knew him best probably suspected that there was no way back for burned-out Neal Cassady and that it was now only a matter of time before his light was extinguished. When J.B. called Carolyn with the news of his death, Carolyn's first response was

"Thank God. Released at last." Yet everyone who had known him personally at some point in his life seemed somehow shocked by his death. If Sir Speed Limit was dead, then everyone's hold on life was a little more tenuous than before.

Yet, typically, Neal Cassady had one more metaphysical trick up his sleeve. The well-worn gag about showbiz stars upon whom death seems to confer a new marketability ("Good career move, Elvis!") might also apply to Neal Cassady in an oblique way. Without a celebrated novel, play, film, painting, or any other enduring piece of creative work to leave behind, Cassady's pervasive presence would nonetheless endure and expand into new decades and even into a new millennium, surfacing here and there, usually as a peripheral figure, often as a name that few recognize at first, but an entity still, somehow, making things happen.

In death he is more widely famous than he ever was when he was alive, famous not perhaps as a recognizable name or face, but as a recurring presence discovered by successive generations in their reappraisals of the beats, the hippies, and twentieth-century American popular culture in general. His profound influence upon Kerouac has already been explored in this book, and Kerouac's influence on twentieth-century American literature is itself profound. Through Kerouac many fragments of Neal Cassady's pyrotechnic letters live on, transplanted into fiction but little altered, still fizzing and crackling brightly as each new generation picks up and reads *On the Road.* Yet look for Neal Cassady on the library shelves and you will find only *The First Third,* if anything. The book that galvanized his literary aspirations and absorbed so much of his energy and ambition for years is a flawed and minor work, proof only that as a writer Neal was a talented sprinter, not a marathon runner. Admittedly it has sold steadily all over the world since 1971, but perhaps that is due to its iconic status as Cassady's only published work; one suspects that while letters and life suited him as a means of expression, novels and self-conscious art did not. So what exactly is it that makes Cassady a modern folk hero four decades after his death?

Not the movies, certainly. They have served the beats poorly, and if time lends distance, it has certainly not lent quality to Hollywood's periodic attempts to cinematize the lives of Neal and his friends.

The Last Time I Committed Suicide (1997) is a film loosely based on Neal's "Joan Anderson" letter. It features Keanu Reeves and Thomas Jane in a highly forgettable drama sloppily tagged by Hollywood with a T-shirt slogan: "Life is what happens when you're busy making plans."

Heart Beat (1979), based on an early published section of what would become Carolyn Cassady's *Off the Road*, cast Nick Nolte as Neal ("Why do they always choose blonds to play Neal?" Carolyn Cassady would ask once more), John Heard as Jack Kerouac, and Sissy Spacek as Carolyn Cassady. Despite the distinguished cast, the result was not widely admired. For her part Carolyn was infuriated about the project. "What they did is not only to exploit me to get Jack's story but also completely stereotyped our characters," she wrote in an article titled "Heart Break." "They have completely *reversed* OUR psyches and put words in our mouths and actions in our lives that are the *antithesis* of what we were and aspired to be. It's a nightmare: a hideous mockery of our ideals and our struggle to rise above the mediocre mindless herd instincts." Carolyn did, however, praise the actors, particularly Sissy Spacek who "fought valiantly to insert some truth into it." But Carolyn believed that the film "added immensely to the historical confusion already rampant."

Neal himself appeared in archive footage that was used in three films made after his death: *The Beat Generation: An American Dream* (1987), *Timothy Leary's Last Trip* (1997), and *The Source* (1999). Janet Forman's *The Beat Generation* is the best of these, a decent documentary record of the main players of the Beat Generation, although Neal's appearance in it, with Allen Ginsberg, conveys little of his fabled energy and charisma. He is declaiming, as usual, but seems tired, as Allen Ginsberg looks on adoringly.

Strangely, the only Jack Kerouac novel to be filmed to date remains *The Subterraneans* (1960), a chaotic and absurd travesty starring George

Peppard and directed by Ranald McDougall. Mardou Fox, "the colored girl" character to whom Jack referred in his letter about the Cassadys' move to Los Gatos, was played by the very white French actress Leslie Caron. The tagline was: "These are The Subterraneans. Today's Young Rebels—who live and love in a world of their own. This is their story told to the hot rhythms of fabulous jazz!"

Whether the character of Ray Hicks in Karel Reisz's *Who'll Stop the Rain* (aka *Dog Soldiers*, 1978) shares much with Neal is debatable, but again Nick Nolte was cast (he was already researching Neal for the following year's *Heart Beat*). His performance combined with Reisz's creditable direction resulted in a rather distinguished but hardly biographical post-Vietnam movie that also, incidentally, features a speaker-bedecked rural hideout complete with graffiti that seems to be vaguely modeled on Kesey's La Honda settlement.

Apart from *Who'll Stop the Rain* and the curio value of his depiction by painter/actor Larry Rivers in the thirty-minute short *Pull My Daisy* (1958), Neal Cassady has simply not been well represented by the medium that transfixed him as a child in Denver's Zaza movie theater. Plans for a movie of *On the Road*, at one point involving Francis Coppola, rumbled on for years, and at this writing the project is finally slated for a 2007 start with Walter Salles directing.

In literature Neal Cassady is a different matter. Ken Kesey explored Cassady's life directly not only in his short story "The Day After Superman Died," but also in a play, *Over the Border*, a fictionalized account of the retreat the Merry Pranksters took to Mexico in 1966.

Robert Stone based two characters very loosely upon Neal: "Willie Wings" in his short story "Porque No Tiene, Porque La Falta," and "Ray Hicks" in the novel upon which *Who'll Stop the Rain* was based, *Dog Soldiers*. Willie Wings is a man contemptuous of "literary" types and those who do not live "the conscious life." As commentator Gregory Stephenson noted, "For Willie Wings boredom and inertia are far more dangerous than uncertainty and insecurity, and surviving intact, with joy, humor, fantasy, and style, is far more important than merely surviving." As for Ray Hicks, another character in *Dog Soldiers* says of him, "He acted everything out. There was absolutely no difference between thought and action for him. . . . It was exactly the same. An enormous self-respect. Whatever he believed in he had to embody absolutely."

Allen Ginsberg, who through changing times and fortunes never seemed to lose his capacity for being awestruck by Neal, dedicated a group of poems in his collection *The Fall of America* (1972) to his lost friend. This collection includes "The Green Automobile" (quoted in Chapter 18). Here was an extravagant composite portrait of Cassady the intimate friend and Cassady a force for human consciousness.

"If anyone had strength to hear the invisible/and drive thru Maya Wall/you *had* it," wrote Allen. (*Maya* is a Hindu word referring to the transitory, illusory appearance of the physical world that obscures the spiritual reality from which it originates.) Allen concludes that his spiritual affinity with Neal is even greater now that the temptations of the flesh can no longer confuse and bedevil their relationship.

Of course the leading keeper of the Neal Cassady flame has been Carolyn Cassady, who in her eighties has been of invaluable assistance in the writing of this particular book. An accomplished author in her own right, she has spanned the public and private worlds of Neal Cassady for almost forty years following his death, always trying to balance her deeply personal view with a more broadly objective one—and succeeding perhaps as well as that particular balancing act can be done. Except of course that it cannot be done. In 2004 Carolyn herself finally admitted that "I find I am as guilty as anyone else of promoting myths about him."

There were as many Neals as there were people who met him. His relationship with his own children was typically ambivalent. His ecstasy at Cathy's birth and during her infant years was certainly followed by consistent love for his expanding family, yet his children were only part of an unspooling life that was primarily devoted to impetuous self-expression and self-indulgence. They were, therefore, necessarily excluded—and sometimes disadvantaged. Neal's son John Allen Cassady is often invited to speak about his father, and while he will dutifully answer the same questions over and over again (usually the maddeningly vague "What was it like to be Neal Cassady's son?"), he seems most animated and affectionate when unearthing those little anecdotes from his sometimes troubled childhood that seem to show Neal as an honorary child himself.

John told David Sandison of a typical childhood incident involving a go-kart that belonged to another kid named George. The go-kart had to be dragged uphill, as it had brakes but no motor. "I told my dad about it and—I can't believe he did this—he came down kind of just to have a look at it and next thing we know he is on it with his knees sticking out to the side. We 'borrowed' it from George's dad's garage without permission and next thing you know Neal is there, coming down the driveway doing a hairpin turn so he's almost on two wheels."

The rightful owner's returning mother was outraged to find that the ringleader of the go-kart gang was an adult. "She was reading Neal the riot act—how dare you encourage these kids to steal our son's car! And he has his head bowed saying, I'm sorry. But he didn't blame us. He never raised his voice to us or yelled at us. You can't yell at a kid when you are high on pot. It was tough on Carolyn because she had to be the tough guy."

When Ken Babbs put together a collection of other people's impressions of Neal Cassady (issue #6 of *Spit in the Ocean* magazine, 1981), he received a very mixed bag. The most reserved came from the reclusive bestselling author Larry McMurtry, who diligently tried to think of something to say about the man he hardly knew (although he doubtless met Neal when the bus hit his hometown and Stark Naked burst onto his porch). He came up with the following: "I think what I think is that too much has been written about Cassady already. He was obviously a great stimulus to Kerouac and Ginsberg and they responded to the stimulus by making him into a quasi-mythological figure. 'The Green Automobile' and the first *Visions of Cody* are to my mind the important writings about

Cassady. The rest—and there is a lot—is self-repetitious and considerably less inspired.

"To me he seemed like a rather common Western type: The cowboy, roughneck, dozer driver or whatever who is enormously capable physically and has added to that capability random scraps of ill-absorbed education.

"There are hundreds of such people about the west, boomers mostly. They're all a little crazy. They can do anything with a machine or an animal. They accumulate two or three wives and passels of kids and girlfriends. They run all over the place, drinking, fucking, fighting, talking interestingly at times and boringly at other times.

"Most of them don't fall in with the literary crowd at Columbia, of course."

As a companion piece to McMurtry's cool assessment, it is perhaps worth considering Gary Snyder's "western" take on Neal Cassady in Ann Charters's *Kerouac: A Biography* (1973).

"My vision of Cassady is of the 1890s cowboys, the type of person who works the high plains of the 1880s and 1890s . . . he is the Denver grandchild of the 1880s cowboys with no range left to work on. Cassady's type is that frontier type, reduced to pool halls and driving back and forth across the country. . . . Cassady was the energy of the archetypal west, the energy of the frontier, still coming down. Cassady is the cowboy crashing."

As a footnote to these cowboy analogies, it is also worth noting that in 1955, the year of Natalie Jackson's suicide and a period marking one of Neal Cassady's lowest ebbs, pioneer environmentalist Edward Abbey wrote a memorable novel entitled *The Brave Cowboy.* Having nothing to do with Cassady in particular, it had a lot to do with that out-of-time western scenario that Snyder evoked. In 1962 the novel was filmed as *Lonely Are the Brave* with Kirk Douglas (the actor who was also the original stage incarnation of Kesey's R. P. McMurphy). An early scene shows Douglas as cowboy Jack Burns out on the deserted range. The actor and the scenery look much the same as they had in a string of more traditional Douglas westerns that came before—*Man Without a Star, Gunfight at the O.K. Corral,* and *Last Train from Gun Hill.* However, as Burns dismounts his horse and settles down to sleep in the dust beneath a tree, a jarring image suddenly fractures audience expectations. An airplane screams by overhead . . . and two worlds collide. Later, challenged by a cop, this walking anachronism is asked, "Where's your papers? . . . Your I.D.—draft card, social security, driver's license?" His answer: "Don't have none. Don't need none. I already know who I am." One can imagine Cassady delighting in that exchange, endorsing it with a series of furious, approving nods and drawn-out affirmatives.

So why does Cassady the folk hero endure? Surely not for the same reason that so many famous figures who died at a relatively young age do. In his final days, bloated Elvis Presley was an embarrassment he was much easier to market after he was dead. And as a result of an overenthusiastic driving style, James Dean never lived to become a middle-aged has-been; death kept him young and rebellious forever. Che Guevara never had time to sell out or make shady political compromises, so he remained an incorruptible poster icon on a million student bedroom walls. Neal Cassady, though, did not share that kind of fame. His celebrity was of a different sort. Now, with the man himself long dead, his influence seems to persist precisely because we have only the legends and varying memories and impressions of his friends and family. In one sense almost invisible to posterity, Neal Cassady remains a life-affirming muse that every generation seems to need, and one that is perhaps made all the more potent by the blurriness of his outline. Like the Mexican revolutionary Emilio Zapata, the man may be gone but his spirit lives on in the hills.

Ken Kesey gave one of his last ever interviews to David Sandison. In it the author of "The Day After Superman Died" reflected on one of the comic book heroes he had so enjoyed as a youngster in Oregon. "Kid Eternity was one of the comic book characters we had back then," he recalled. "He could contact people from anyplace or anytime in history, people like Davy Crockett—anybody. The comics disappeared but then, many years later . . . in the 1990s I think, they brought *Kid Eternity* back again. Somebody sent me a copy of one issue where Kid Eternity needed somebody to keep him enlightened. He called for Neal who became the main character in that comic book." Kesey laughed at the pleasing irony of it. "In the background were really nice pictures of Ginsberg and Burroughs."

Bibliography

Cassady, Carolyn. *Heart Beat: My Life with Jack and Neal.* Berkeley: Creative Arts, 1976.

———. *Off the Road.* New York: Morrow, 1990.

Cassady, Neal. *Collected Letters, 1944–1967.* New York: Penguin, 2004.

———. *The First Third.* San Francisco: City Lights Books, 1971/1981.

———. *Grace Beats Karma: Letters from Prison, 1958–60.* New York: Blast Books, 1993.

Cassady, Neal, and Allen Ginsberg. *As Ever: The Collected Correspondence of Allen Ginsberg & Neal Cassady.* Berkeley: Creative Arts, 1977.

"The Cassady Issue." *Spit in the Ocean* magazine, 1981.

Christopher, Tom, ed. *Neal Cassady,* volumes 1 and 2. Self-published, 1980s.

Ginsberg, Allen. *Howl & Other Poems.* San Francisco: City Lights, 1956.

Holmes, John Clellon. *Go.* New York: Scribners, 1952.

Kerouac, Jack. *On the Road.* New York: Viking, 1957.

———. *Selected Letters 1940–1956.* New York: Penguin, 1995.

Kesey, Ken. "The Day After Superman Died." *Esquire,* October 1979.

Miles, Barry. *Ginsberg: A Biography.* New York: Simon & Schuster, 1989.

Murphy, Anne. "Traveling with the Tripmaster." *High Times,* 1991.

Plummer, William. *The Holy Goof.* Englewood Cliffs, N.J.: Prentice Hall, 1981.

Stephenson, Gregory. *Friendly and Flowing Savage.* Textile Bridge Press, 1987.

Stone, Robert. *Dog Soldiers.* New York: Houghton-Mifflin, 1974.

Trumbo, Dalton. *Lonely Are the Brave* script. 1962.

Wolfe, Tom. *The Electric Kool-Aid Acid Test.* New York: Farrar, Straus & Giroux, 1968.

Index

O

P